AF477908

PERSPECTIVE IN BRITISH HISTORICAL FICTION TODAY

PERSPECTIVE IN BRITISH HISTORICAL FICTION TODAY

Neil McEwan

Lecturer in English
University of Qatar

LONGWOOD ACADEMIC: WOLFEBORO
NEW HAMPSHIRE

First published in 1987 by Longwood Academic, a division of
Longwood Publishing Group, Inc., 27 South Main Street,
Wolfeboro, New Hampshire 03894–2069.

Printed in Hong Kong

Library of Congress Cataloging-in-Publication Data
McEwan, Neil.
Perspective in British historical fiction today.
Bibliography: p.
Includes index.
1. Historical fiction, English. 2. English
fiction—20th century—History and criticism.
I. Title.
PR888.H5M34   1987   823'.081'09   86–7200
ISBN 0–89341–547–2

To my parents

Contents

1 Introduction

Perspective in historical fiction is taken here to mean a view of the past adjusted to present interests. It is always difficult to be fair to both. Present interests are never quite those of the past and are liable to distort the view. An historical novelist is constantly involved in compromise. One way of looking at the hybrid nature of the genre is to see it as a mixture, of verifiable history, and of fiction – which need be true only to the reader's experience of life; but all other realistic fiction claims to be true at least to the social history of the present or the recent past. My argument is that the best contemporary authors of historical fiction in Britain have been honest and creative in their compromises between the conflicting claims of past and present, achieving a useful perspective on various periods of history. The results are especially heartening because the last thirty years have seen widespread, radical questioning of both narrative history and realistic fiction. Given that this species of literature has always been unsure of itself, even at the time when novelists and historians wrote with greatest confidence, this current vitality is not only pleasing in itself: it is evidence of a division which now exists, at least in Britain, between avant-garde critical theory and the most original creative practice.

My starting point is the conclusion to Avrom Fleishman's *The English Historical Novel: Walter Scott to Virginia Woolf* (1971),[1] a survey which includes some novels of the 1950s but which sees Virginia Woolf as the end of a tradition.

Despite the considerable learning of many recent historical novelists, their lack of methodological self-consciousness leaves them among the conventions of the realist novel, and the critical reader will persist in seeing their best efforts as costume flummery. The historical novel of our time will probably join the experimental movement of the modern novel or retire from the province of serious literature.[2]

Fourteen years later, the situation today seems more complex and interesting than that. Anthony Burgess and Robert Nye display 'methodological self-consciousness'. Burgess's *Nothing Like the Sun* (1964), reissued in 1982, and *Napoleon Symphony* (1974), and Nye's *Falstaff* (1976), are works conspicuously influenced by modern experiment, and so is John Fowles's *The French Lieutenant's Woman* (1969). William Golding, whose *Rites of Passage* (1980) is set in the early nineteenth century, has always merged the traditional and the experimental, in technique and effect. Mary Renault, who completed her trilogy of novels about Alexander the Great (and her eighth historical novel) with *Funeral Games* in 1981, might be thought to have 'left' her work 'among the conventions of the realist novel'; but many readers (including, in 1971, Avrom Fleishman) find her, none the less, to have been far above 'flummery'. Gore Vidal, for example, has claimed (in the publisher's advertisement to the Penguin edition of *Funeral Games*) 'it is plain that her Alexandriad is one of this century's most unexpectedly original works of art'. His tribute is healthy in attitude, at least, because it is free from the now rather old fashioned assumption that originality means Joycean experiment with technique. Joyce represents one line of twentieth-century development; Mary Renault belongs to another. When J. G. Farrell died in 1979 he was midway through *The Hill Station*, an addition to *Troubles* (1970), *The Siege of Krishnapur* (1973) and *The Singapore Grip* (1978). These are not books which fall on one or other side of a line separating experimental from realist fiction. Renault, Burgess, Nye, Farrell, Fowles and Golding are traditional in one essential respect which links them with the best novelists from Scott onwards who are considered in Fleishman's book. They are committed to the permanent problem of perspective, of how to be true to the time in which the story is set and to the time in which they write, of how to see the past fairly from a contemporary vantage-point.

The present period is more sceptical about the possibility of doing so than any earlier generation. There are advantages in scepticism about how well we can know the past, and there are limits to the advantages. J. R. Seeley wrote in *The Expansion of England* (1883) that 'if [facts] lead to no great truths having at the same time scientific generality and momentous practical bearings then history is but an amusement and will scarcely hold its own in the conflict of studies'.[3] The title of his book is one clue to his meaning. Few British historians or novelists would put the alternatives in such extreme terms. Some would say that no historiography is more than an amusement since no truths can be found. But without even wanting the scientific assurance or the momentous bearings of Seeley's condition, we can still hope for more than simple amusement in historical novels. This chapter first considers the background and implications of contemporary scepticism, and then outlines the positions of the novelists, Mary Renault, Anthony Burgess and Robert Nye, and J. G. Farrell, who are studied in the chapters which follow. I propose that there are three kinds of approach among these writers which illustrate the diversity and the basic common purpose of historical novelists today – to be found in others, including Fowles and Golding who are discussed in the last chapter before the 'Conclusion'.

The most obvious advantage for a contemporary writer is freedom from Victorian self-censorship. Here is Thackeray, opening his essay on Steele in *The English Humourists of the Eighteenth Century* (1853):

> We can't tell – you would not bear to be told the whole truth regarding those men and manners. You could no more suffer in a British drawing-room under the reign of Queen Victoria, a fine gentleman or fine lady of Queen Anne's time, or hear what they heard and said, than you would receive an ancient Briton.[4]

Fashions change; the rake and the ancient Briton would be gladly received today; some of our historical fiction might shock them both. In so far as Thackeray was thinking of sexual mores, modern licence has reached a far extreme from his prudishness. The present fascination with sexual behaviour in rakes and savages will probably come to seem as far-fetched as the Victorian's reticence.

Other forms of censorship and prejudice hampered historical imagination in the nineteenth century. British self-confidence made modern attitudes seem natural, and therefore present although submerged in 'ordinary people' of all ages as they struggled against unnatural conditions – slavery, feudalism, medieval Catholicism – in their slow but sure progress towards Victorian England. This is the 'Whig' view of history which makes the past a prologue to the present and distorts it by hindsight. J. W. Burrow's *A Liberal Descent: Victorian Historians and the English Past* (1981) is a recent study of how political opinions shaped the work of historians. Recent studies of historical fiction have been very conscious of the influence of the 'Whig' view (also present in Tories) that the past is no more than its contribution to the present. Andrew Sanders's *The Victorian Historical Novel: 1840–1880* (1978) argues that a simply conceived idea of progress dominates the fiction of his period: 'history offered proof that men were moving inexorably onwards. . .'.[5] The first chapter of Peacock's *Headlong Hall* of 1837 is a reminder that not everyone was convinced; of the three 'philosophers and men of taste' who argue their way to Wales, one is a 'perfectibilian' but another a 'deteriorationist' ('the whole species must at length be exterminated by its own imbecility and vileness') and the third believes, as a 'statu-quo-ite', that all progress entails an equal measure of retrogression. Nostalgia for pre-industrial England could interfere as badly as naive belief in progress with attempts to imagine the past. Thackeray's *Henry Esmond* (1852) mingles self-satisfaction with regret over the century of changes which separated Esmond's lifetime from his own. But Sanders is of course right. There was an overwhelming tendency to see earlier times as unevolved versions of the nineteenth century.

The past is still put entirely at the disposal of present interests in committed literature, but the relatively weak influence of Marxism in the British literary world can be seen in the general rejection of Georg Lukacs's vision of the Waverley novels in *The Historical Novel*, as the first appearance of the 'modern historical consciousness' in so far as 'modern' is synonymous with 'Marxist'. David Brown, for example, follows many nineteenth-century critics in seeing Scott as a Tory.[6] James Anderson wrongly says that history was nothing to Scott but 'a storehouse of material for fiction'.[7] J. H. Raleigh's *Time, Place and Idea* (1968) shows again the originality of Scott's insights into history and his involvement in his era: 'for the first time in literature, Scott had dramatised the basic processes of modern history . . . he also saw the inevitability and necessity of progressing away from it'.[8] From this double-vision, Scott created, in the novels of recent Scottish history, work of a Shakespearean richness. Later nineteenth-century writers were always under his influence but scarcely ever rivalled him.

G. P. R. James and W. Harrison Ainsworth are dull, after Scott, when they try to recreate the past, and even more dull, as contemporaries of Dickens, in what they have to say to their own time. In this they are distinct from many mid-Victorian novelists whose history is strongly affected by current affairs. Because there was a sense that the past was the childhood of the present (a favourite metaphor of Marx), novelists sought analogies. James C. Simmons has studied these in *The Novelist as Historian*; Robert Lee Wolff, reviewing him in the *Times Literary Supplement*, attacked many of Simmons's judgements, deriding him for having said that Newman's *Callista* (1856) 'used' historical fiction to purvey Catholic doctrine; it is hard not to see *Callista* and Kingsley's torrid *Hypatia* of 1853 (which is now unintentionally very funny, in many parts) as works of religious polemic more than imaginative explorations of life in antiquity. Wolff rightly points out that Bulwer Lytton used medieval stories for modern propaganda; *The Last of the Barons* (1843) and *Harold: the Last of the Saxon Kings* (1848) are stories of how medieval affairs foreshadowed political tensions among mercantile, aristocratic, and radical interests of the 1840s; 'to read any of these novels in any other way is to miss their chief interest', Wolff concludes.

> The best Victorian historical novels were not, it is clear, written by Mr Simmons's 'novelist as historian'. The novels that were so written no longer teach history, and seldom retain much interest as fiction.[9]

'Their chief, if not their sole, claim to be read today' is that they treat Victorian issues in the disguise of the past. Wolff's 'seldom' and 'much' allow some room for disagreement. But Scott apart, *Esmond*, and Dickens's two novels set in the recent past, are probably the only works of historical fiction before Kipling which are now willingly read except by specialists in some Victorian field; *Romola* (1863) is read dutifully only by those who enjoy George Eliot's other novels. Even if one takes the more generous view of Avrom Fleishman who finds historical imagination in Kingsley and Charles Reade, it must be admitted that this was a most difficult genre in the great age of the novel, and that the claims of the present most often overcame those of the past.

It would be wrong to claim that any later writers have achieved an objectivity transcending the preoccupations of their culture, and equally wrong to require that novelists try to achieve it. Perspective means that the past is viewed through present consciousness. But when Flaubert said that 'history is only the reflection of the present on the past and that is why it is forever to be rewritten', he implied such an appropriation as can be found in *Salammbó* where conditions in France in 1862 are 'reflected on' ancient Carthage.[10] That is to deny integrity to the past. It can be claimed that a better compromise has been reached today. Just how difficult it is to avoid seeing history as a 'prelude to the present' was recognised by Lord Raglan on the first page of *The Hero* (1936).

> Only the smallest fraction of the human race has ever acquired the habit of taking an objective view of the past. For most people, even educated people, the past is merely a prologue to the present, not merely without interest in so far as it is independent of the present, but simply inconceivable except in terms of the present.

We all suffer, he rightly says next, from 'this lack of mental perspective': 'the events of our own past life are remembered, not as they seemed to us at the time, but merely as incidents leading up to our present situation'; this leads to 'a false perspective' in which we impose the present on our readings of the past, by natural inclination. Raglan's impatience is a sign of willingness, in the post-Victorian period, to try. His generation was disposed to patronise the nineteenth century, to distort its view of eminent Victorians by judging them through the consciousness of modern emancipation, and this tendency shows another weakness in our objectivity – we define our own period in relation to the past.

The most that can be claimed for contemporary novelists is a relative degree of balance, a willingness to acknowledge the human interest of attitudes which are unlike ours, and to grant the difference in similarities. The expansion of literature in the English language has been a healthy influence. To compare

Joyce Cary's picture of the British in Africa in *Mister Johnson* (1939) with Chinua Achebe's version in *Arrow of God* (1964) can be enlightening. The forms of 'emancipation' from Victorian disciplines of mind which were achieved in the modernist period can now be seen as a loss as well as a gain. It is easy to ridicule George Grote, the historian of Greece, who (perhaps wisely) never visited Greece for fear of bandits; a contributor to the *Times Literary Supplement* remarked some years ago that Grote 'went to his grave unaware that Demosthenes was the kind of man who would have been an embarrassment at the Liberal Club'.[11] The Demosthenes portrayed in Mary Renault's *Fire from Heaven* would never have been admitted. Miss Renault is justified in complaining that Grote:

> had the fatal commitment which vitiates conscientious fact with anachronistic morality. His whole capital of belief being invested in the Athenian democracy, he was resolute in attributing its fall to external villainy rather than internal collapse. Demosthenes could do no wrong . . .[12]

Mary Renault's belief in democracy is plain from her novels. It does not interfere with her determination to occupy a Macedonian viewpoint in *Fire from Heaven*. It may be that her power to live her Macedonia was helped by twenty years in Africa. The strength of Grote's 'commitment' is lacking today, although not entirely absent. A sceptical but firm sense of values, such as that of Mary Renault or J. G. Farrell, is a good basis for looking at the past.

Praising Kipling in a lecture, 'The Sense of the Past', given in 1972, Sir Richard Southern talked about 'the pleasure of sharing the thoughts of people of the past' which he found highly developed at the end of the nineteenth century.

> It was the returned exile Kipling – in my view the most gifted historical genius this country has ever produced – who created the most vivid imaginative pictures of the successive phases of life in England going back to remote antiquity. But it was Henry James – who first used the phrase 'the sense of the past' to denote the impact of an immensely complicated and varied scene on an historically sensitive mind . . .[13]

The Jamesian sense of the past pervades Victorian fiction set in Victorian England, and much of the best fiction written today. Kipling's gift for imaginative pictures was original and exceptional. It promised well as an example for twentieth-century prospects in historical fiction.

The same could be said of the advancement of novels for children – apart from Kipling's – in the same period. A. J. P. Taylor has recently described the scorn which he felt as a child for Stanley J. Weyman, but there are scenes in Weyman which give a sense of the past – the Cardinal and his cat in *Under the Red Robe* (1894).[14] Before coming to Stevenson and Conan Doyle, one could read Edith Nesbit, at the turn of the century, who treated history as an imaginative back-garden game. Between the wars there were John Buchan's *The Path of the King* (1921) and *The Blanket of the Dark* (1931), and, later, Rosemary Sutcliffe, Cynthia Harnett, Walter Hodges and Leon Garfield. The last half-century has produced a large body of exciting, imaginative and well-researched historical fiction for the young, gradually helping to create a more demanding adult readership.

Naomi Mitchison catered for such critical tastes, preparing a way for Mary Renault. Peter Green argued in a 1958 lecture, 'Aspects of the Historical Novel', that the genre was 'undergoing a renaissance' and he saw its origin in Naomi Mitchison's *The Conquered* (1923), where the Gallic wars are seen from the Gauls' point of view. Concern to recreate an alien civilisation on its own terms, he says, is the dominant feature of subsequent work, and he praises Rex Warner, Zoe Oldenbourg (in France), Robert Graves, H. F. M. Prescott, and Alfred Duggan, among others. Accuracy and imagination are present in these novelists [as in John Cowper Powys] but their essential difference from earlier work is the power of 'empathy', Green concludes.[15] Avrom Fleishman is, none the less, justified in saying that writers between the 1920s and the 1950s were outside what was then felt to be the main stream of English fiction, and right to point to Conrad and Virginia Woolf to explain why this was felt. Fleishman quotes *The Inheritors* (1901) which Conrad wrote in collaboration with Ford Madox Ford.

> Our Cromwell! There was no Cromwell; he had lived, he had worked for the future – and now he had ceased to exist. His future – our past, had come to an end.

He comments that Conrad thought 'recent developments [had] made so sharp a break with the political values of the past that history may be said to have ended and an era of anarchy to have been ushered in'.[16] So thought Lawrence's Birkin, and W. B. Yeats, in the decades to come. Fleishman proceeds to discuss Virginia Woolf's *Between the Acts* (1941).

> The idea of history presented on and off the stage in *Between the Acts* is more subtle than any of the philosophical theories of history taken up in previous historical novels. It might be called a post-theoretical idea, for it is in tune with the attitudes towards the past that dominate the modern historian's craft . . . no longer broad causal relationships of events derived from prophetic visions of the shape of history. Neither the liberal view of progress, which was part of Woolf's intellectual heritage, nor the cyclical views of eternal return, which so many of her contemporaries embraced, is identifiable in the novel's world.[17]

Instead, *Between the Acts* is 'not a novel about history but a novel about consciousness of history which includes historiography and historical fiction itself.[18] 'Therefore the most learned historical novelists – Prescott, Warner, Mitchison – are left by their lack of methodological self-consciousness' outside the species of fiction a modern critical reader expects: 'like history itself, the historical novel must be more than its past, passing freely into new possibilities, or remain a sterile repetition of the forms doled out to it from tradition'.[19]

One purpose of this argument is to show that conspicuous formal novelty and stale repetition are not mutually exclusive alternatives. Criticism of modern British fiction in general has moved on from Rubin Rabinovitz's *The Reaction Against Experiment in the English Novel, 1950–1960* (1967), a work sadly trapped inside that assumption. Iris Murdoch, Kingsley Amis, Anthony Powell, William Golding, and Angus Wilson have exploited a wide range of the resources available from tradition, including those explored by Virginia Woolf but not limited to them. L. P. Hartley's *The Go-Between* is a subtly-told story of 1900, filled with a 1950s consciousness. Powell had published *A Question of Upbringing*, the first volume of his 'Music of Time' sequence, in 1951; Wilson's *Hemlock and After* came out in 1952. First novels by Murdoch (*Under the Net*), Amis

(*Lucky Jim*) and Golding (*Lord of the Flies*) followed in 1954. Mary Renault's first historical novel *The Last of the Wine* appeared in 1956 and *The King Must Die*, which made her name, in 1958. Golding published *The Inheritors* in 1955 and *The Spire* in 1964. Historical novelists, when Fleishman was writing, need no longer feel excluded from new possibilities if they wrote about history rather than consciousness of history. They might be as methodologically self-conscious as Anthony Burgess, but even then they need not regard realism or tradition as 'doles' to turn to when invention flagged. Realism was clearly one mode available to the most ambitious of contemporary novelists.

A revival of confidence, then, distinguishes the practice of historical novelists from the 1950s onwards. Sensing it, Peter Green said in 1958 that writers were beginning to treat the 'bastard genre' as 'a serious and legitimate medium'.[20] So they were. The following two chapters are written in the belief that Mary Renault was a better novelist than her immediate predecessors and contemporaries who treated life in antiquity: Naomi Mitchison, 'Bryher', Robert Graves, Arthur Koestler, Rex Warner, Alfred Duggan;[21] and that her novels bring a stronger talent to the same effort of showing an alien culture on its own terms. Avrom Fleishman thinks so too.

> One has only to compare her use of her scholarship with that of Mitchison, Graves, or lesser writers on classical themes (e.g., Alfred Duggan or Bryher) to sense the difference between a genuine artist and a learned entertainer. For Renault, modern knowledge is not an instrument for exposing the anthropological imperatives or political motivations of the men of the past. For the very reason that she treats Theseus as myth as well as man, she is able to rewrite his legendary exploits as history—speculative history, to be sure, but more readily approachable than the politically reduced or anthropologically expanded visions of man we are given by Graves and Mitchison, respectively.[22]

Having quoted Professor Fleishman on a general tendency in order to disagree, it is pleasing to quote his book on a particular author's talent (always more interesting than general tendencies) to agree, before parting company.

There is another feature of Mary Renault which her work

shares with that of all the novelists considered below, and that is a determination to engage the attention of readers who are not normally drawn to the history of her period, or to history at all. Graves does so in the 'Claudius' books and, perhaps, in *Wife to Mr Milton* (1942), but not in *Count Belisarius* (1938). The other novelists Fleishman names, and H. F. M. Prescott, are primarily novelists to attract historians.[23] Rex Warner and Miss Prescott could be called history-teachers' novelists – certainly they (unlike Graves) are novelists history-teachers recommend. They are both prim. Mary Renault was a best-seller; Burgess, Nye, Farrell, Fowles and Golding have enjoyed large sales. There is in all of them an element of vulgarity, in the best sense, which takes various forms. Mary Renault was a romantic and a hero-worshipper as well as a scholar and an artist. Burgess and Nye are scurrilous as well as learned and ingenious. Farrell is both very earnest and very flippant about history. Fowles's work is marked by his experience of film-making, and journalism; his style of theorising in *The French Lieutenant's Woman* is closer to journalism than to a university seminar. In Golding there are romantic and sensationalist tendencies which escape his normal austerity. It is refreshing and unusual to be able to say of a group of contemporary novelists, as we can here, that not one of them is a professional university teacher; they have made livings as writers.[24] Their 'vulgarity' is not proposed, in later chapters, as a literary merit in itself. The erotic passages in Burgess and Nye, being a-historical, have been mostly disregarded in the discussions of their work. But it is a sign of their confidence that the most ambitious kind of historical fiction can be, not only 'serious and legitimate', as Peter Green says, but lightly entertaining too. Their work is more entertaining, in the popular meaning, in excitement, wit and 'colour', than the thousands of historical adventures and romances which are aimed only at the most common tastes of the common reader. That promises well for the future of a genre which Fleishman thought should join the modern experimental movement in the direction shown by Virginia Woolf (who would probably have disapproved of most of these novelists).

The contemporary author of historical fiction works with these advantages. He is less likely than nineteenth-century writers to distort the past from an undue belief in progress, or to use it, reflecting present concerns on the past. There is a public, although not large enough, which has been accustomed, even from childhood, to accurate and imaginative work. There is no reason to believe that novels about history are old-fashioned, or a sub-genre only for specialists. There is scope to treat a past-period with regard for the integrity of surviving evidence and to address the – in all senses – 'critical reader'. There are enough talented failures among previous works to make it clear that perfection is not to be achieved in this kind of writing, that compromises have to be accepted. Given that some modern novelists complain of the paralysing effect of the great Victorian and Modernist works, the existence of *Romola* might act as a spur. Another advantage might be seen in our more relaxed attitude to levels and varieties of language, so closely tied to social class even in 1940s. English dialects need not automatically be the mark of an inferior social class, as they came to be in the nineteenth century. Spoken English can appear fluent and literate without sounding genteel-British, not at least to a British ear. The court-eunuch who narrates Mary Renault's *The Persian Boy* sounds the hellenised Persian courtier he is meant to be, not at all an English gentleman. We do not suppose there is any equivalence between the English prose he is given and whatever Greek style such a person might have used in Ptolemy's Alexandria. He would have been polished and assured, as he is in the novel. Language and style in this genre involve obvious compromises. In thirty years time the Alexander novels will be strikingly '1970s', and properly so; but they will also have a note which can be heard in ancient writing.

The argument so far has depended on the traditional assumption that perspective is possible because the past is independent of our reconstructions of it. Most of the past is lost, but more survives than we know, and we can never predict exactly how newly discovered evidence may compel us to change our ideas of it. All historical interest, including that of the historical imagination, lies in recognition of the varying degrees of what can be known and imagined. To believe all is as naive as to believe nothing. Certain facts, such as those of geography, are constant in historical times, and cannot be ignored. Between these and the most improbable wisps of legend there are countless layers of reliability in what survives, and our consciousness of a period is tiered accordingly. Historians deal with the realities of the past and with speculation. Historical novelists are privileged by our consent in their freedom to speculate but they are constrained by the real, and they will not hold attention unless they respect the past which is common to all readers.

The threat to historical fiction today comes from those who argue that all history is fiction because nothing can be known. They destroy perspective, for if the past is thought of as the creation of the present, there is nowhere to look and nothing to see. The Orwellian implications of this position are political, perhaps extra-literary. But in denying that there is any hard reality behind our sense of the past, when we put on an academic gown or cross the Straits of Gibraltar, but only individual fancy, 'culture-bound', the opponents of historical objectivity depreciate the first motive for reading historical fiction, which is to find that sense given more powerful imaginative truth than we give it ourselves. They deny too, of course, that we can learn from the past; they say that the past can only be used, to teach our standards. The implications for literature seem purely negative. The novelists considered in the following chapters are in effect combating a tendency which – whether or not it would impoverish the whole culture – would destroy the genre they practise.

A passage from Frank Kermode's *The Genesis of Secrecy* (1979) illustrates the way that interest is killed by a fashionable kind of doctrinaire scepticism. The book, based on lectures given at Harvard, is a study of Mark's Gospel which Kermode says is a pleromatic and hermeneutic system, not a history in the modern sense. His ultimate purpose is to claim that all *texts*, historical and fictional, are 'totally lacking transparency on event'. His example of a modern novelist with a proper sense of history is Thomas Pynchon and he quotes from *The Crying of Lot 49* (1966).

Let me now quote a historical, or pseudo-historical, narrative of a very different kind. It purports to describe an engagement between an American and a Russian warship off the coast of California: 'What happened on the 9th March, 1864

. . . is not too clear. Popov the Russian admiral did send out a ship, either the corvette 'Bogatir' or the clipper 'Gaidamek', to see what it could see. Off the coast of either what is now Carmel-by-the-Sea, or what is now Pismo Beach, around noon or possibly toward dusk, the two ships sighted each other. One of them may have fired; if it did then the other responded but both were out of range so neither showed a scar afterward to prove anything.' This passage describes an historical event which is held to have occurred, to have left no trace, and to be susceptible of honest report only in the most uncertain and indeterminate manner. It admirably represents a modern scepticism concerning the reference of texts to events. Events exist only as texts, already to that extent interpreted, and if we were able to discard the interpretative material and be as honest as historians, quite honestly, pretend to be, all we should have left would be some such nonsignificant dubiety as this account of the first engagement ever to take place between American and Russian forces.[25]

There are conflicting ideological interpretations of the sea-battle in the novel. Kermode wonders 'whether we do not live in a complex of semiotic systems which are either empty or are operated on the gratuitous asumption that a direct relation exists between a sign and a corresponding object "in reality"'.

The story of the sea battle occurs not in the work of a professed historian, not even as a nightmare example in a book by some distracted philosopher of history, but in a novel called *The Crying of Lot 49*. It is, for all that, a serious historiographical exercise. It illustrates the point that we are capable of a scepticism very remote from the pleromatic certitudes of the evangelists, remote even from the sober historicism of only yesterday. We can, indeed, no longer assume that we have the capacity to make value-free statements about history, or suppose that there is some special dispensation whereby the signs that constitute an historical text have reference to events in the world. That it would not be possible to discover a passage like the one I have just quoted in a genuine historical work is an indication that we mostly go about our business as if the contrary of what we profess to believe were the truth, somehow, from somewhere, a privilege, an authority, descends upon our researches; and as long as we do things as they have generally been done – as long, that is, as the institution which guarantees our studies upholds the fictions that give them value – we shall continue to write historical narrative as if it were an altogether different matter from making fictions or, a fortiori, from telling lies.[26]

Whatever the relation between the signs that constitute an historical text and events in the world, one would have to be very incurious to accept that it is the same in all cases. Interest, when one reads about Salamis or Trafalgar, is in the degrees of transparency and opaqueness on events, which can vary from the extreme mistiness of Pynchon's dubious encounter to occasional clear sightings when several independent witnesses confirm one another on points of detail while reporting from different vantage points. A modern account which is researched successfully enough to provide that may be untrue to past experience of the events because it gives a more complete view than any of the participants possessed. To allow for a character's limited view is part of a novelist's approach, and there is an interest in measuring the limits.

Frank Kermode's terminology comes from France and especially from the late Roland Barthes. Barthes's belief that realism in fiction is nowadays 'invalid' is well known, and entertainingly countered in Philip Thody's study of his work. Barthes's essay on historiography ('The Discourse of History' in its English translation) was published in France in 1967.[27] Its exact position in French structuralism of the 1960s is explained by specialist commentators in the annual *Comparative Criticism* where it was reprinted in 1981. Stephen Bann who wrote the Introductory Note concludes that:

> in the last resort, it must be conceded, Barthes's view of historiography, and indeed of History, was a sceptical one . . . [because] the linguistic and rhetorical analysis of historical narrative, as in this article, cannot grant to history, *a priori*, the mythic status which differentiates it from fiction.[28]

The last paragraph of 'The Discourse of History' makes Barthes's position clear.

History's refusal to assume the real as signified (or again, to detach the referent from its mere assertion) led it, as we understand, at the privileged point when it attempted to form itself into a genre in the nineteenth century, to see in the 'pure and simple' relation of the facts the best proof of those facts, and to institute narration as the privileged signifier of the real. Augustin Thierry became the theoretician of this narrative style of history, which draws its 'truth' from the careful attention to narration, the architecture of articulations and the abundance of expanded elements (known, in this case, as 'concrete details'). So the circle of paradox is complete. Narrative structure, which was originally developed within the cauldron of fiction (in myths and the first epics) becomes at once the sign and the proof of reality. In this connection, we can also understand how the relative lack of prominence (if not complete disappearance) of narration in the historical science of the present day, which seeks to talk of structures and not of chronologies, implies not more than a mere change in schools of thought. Historical narration is dying because the sign of History from now on is no longer the real, but the intelligible.[29]

A *sign*, according to Ferdinand de Saussure, is composed of a *signifier* and a *signified*. The signifier is a sound or a group of written characters; the signified is equally formal and relative, for the relationship is arbitrary. Nothing in a rose requires the name rose; the concept (the signified), which would not exist in a culture indifferent to flowers, is meaningful only in relation to the set of botanical species which our culture provides.[30] The 'real' for Barthes was a system of *signifiées*, separate from whatever reality may be; hence Kermode's 'language is not transparent on reality'. The 'historical science of the present day' talks of 'structures' not of chronology because it is, like Saussure's linguistics, 'synchronic' rather than 'diachronic': interested in the structure of politics at the accession of George III rather than in the evolution of parliamentary government in the eighteenth century; and partly because it seeks to imitate the theory of relativity in physics, where attention is given not to objects but to structures of activity. The historian's structures are cultural, so that the chief Italian semiotician Umberto Eco can say that 'the Battle of Waterloo was in 1815' tells us nothing except that such statements have meaning within a particular culture.[31] The consequence, for Barthes, was to celebrate the 'death' of historical narrative; and he argued throughout his career, on the same grounds, that realistic fiction was inappropriate and dishonest in our time. For him realistic historical fiction would be doubly dishonest today. Solzhenitsyn 'is not a good writer for us' he said in a magazine interview, because through no fault of his own his realistic technique is seventy years out of date.[32] Realistic fiction and historical narrative are both dying. The following chapters try to show that they are not, and that their union in historical fiction enriches our culture by protecting the past which in Barthes's theory falls away, like reality itself, leaving the dullness of solipsism to which all such reductionism tends.

Good novelists disrupt the categories which criticism tries to make for them, and it is better to say that Mary Renault, Anthony Burgess and Robert Nye, and J. G. Farrell show three varieties of historical fiction rather than three types. The variety can be seen in relation to these structuralist objections to realism and any kind of narrative history. Mary Renault's novels might be compared, in terms of methodology, to A. J. P. Taylor's history books. Taylor chose, at a time when Herbert Butterfield and others had made synchronic analysis more fashionable than narrative, to write in the old way, and do it better than the older writers or anyone else. Mary Renault brought the full resources of modern realism to the portrayal of ancient life, leaving the result to be judged on its merits. In the last resort any creative writer has to conclude, 'by God, 'tis good, and if you like it, you may!'; she also asserted that it is true. Burgess and Nye have written a more fashionable variety of historical fiction; both show the influence of Joyce; their work is more acceptable to Frank Kermode,[33] but they remain more traditional than Roland Barthes would wish; irreverent in manner, they respect the past in principle. The art of J. G. Farrell was growing in reach and subtlety when he died in his forties in 1979. It was already accomplished and idiosyncratic, and stimulating in being very difficult to place in 'traditional' and 'experimental' categories which so muddle contemporary criticism. Farrell blended realism and scepticism in new ways.

Oscar Handlin's *Truth in History* (1979) shows signs of impatience with historical fiction, but its theme expresses exactly Mary Renault's conception of her art. Professor Handlin's purpose is to protect the role of the historian from the incursions of modish scepticism. He has no serious doubts about his role.

> The use of history lies in its capacity for advancing the approach to truth. The historian's vocation depends on this minimal operational article of faith: Truth is absolute; it is as absolute as the world is real. It does not exist because individuals wish it to any more than the world exists for their convenience. Although observers have more or less partial views of the truth, its actuality is unrelated to the desires or the particular angles of vision of the viewers. Truth is knowable and will out if earnestly pursued, and science is the procedure or set of procedures for approximating it. . . . History is the distillation of evidence surviving from the past. Where there is no evidence there is no history.[34]

This reassertion of what the nineteenth century took for granted is the core of Handlin's argument. He does not probe the contentious terms ('distillation' for example), but offers instead an account of the decline in standards which has caused a Harvard professor to write the obvious so stridently. The modern discipline of history became possible because the English Civil War persuaded the English to accept a distinction between facts and their interpretation – a refinement which had meant little to the Tudor historians whose work was dramatised by Shakespeare. The distinction has been abandoned in the Soviet Union where the regime depends on a questionable ideology's immunity to questions. In the West it has been blurred by 'lazy-mindedness'. The realisation that nobody is purely objective has led to unwillingness to try to pursue objectivity. Anthropological relativism is also to blame: historians have been affected by the reluctance of anthropologists to judge one culture from within another. The study of history will continue only if the primacy of evidence is recognised and respected.[35] Frank Kermode was at Harvard in 1977.[36] It would have been instructive to have heard Handlin and Nye debate 'yesterday's sober historicism'.

Mary Renault defended the same traditional and academically embattled position, expressing herself more deftly: 'the past is a part of the human environment, and should not be polluted by falsehood'; her manifesto is a nice balance between the claims of past and present. The emphasis in all she said about her work has been on approaching (unobtainable) truth.

> Often of course I must have done through ignorance what would horrify me if I could revisit the past . . . but one can at least desire the truth; and it is inconceivable to me how anyone can decide deliberately to betray it.[37]

Academic honesty is a duty to the present since it is a defence of our integrity. In a letter to *Encounter* in 1969 Mary Renault objected to the misrepresentation of recent history in Rolph Hochhuth's play about Churchill, *Soldiers*: 'there does not exist, in any context, a higher truth than truth: truth is indivisible and interdependent'.[38] Truth in her own work means capturing a world of the past as it appeared to those who knew it – a policy of non-interference:

> people of the past should not be modernised to make an easier read, nor judged by standards irrelevant to their own day in order to make dishonest propaganda for some modern cause; the 'committed' historical novelist is of necessity a committed liar. Even the dead are entitled to justice; and the first requirement of justice is to apply to them their current moral standards, however these may differ from our own. Modernised historical characters are a bore; real ones are profoundly interesting, at least to me. I have never knowingly exploited them, but have tried to see them, as far as I am able, along the sight lines from which they might have seen themselves.[39]

Both the 'profound interest' and the 'anthropological' wish to respect the standards of an alien culture are modern in origin and ramifications. The Greek narrators of her novels seem relatively free from the author's modernising, although the literary resources of the novel are silently modernising them. The characters' 'sight lines' are those of their own time and it is intended that they should jolt and perhaps affront the reader's sensibility. But even there, as will be seen in the next chapter, there is allowance for the modern point of view. The author's selection and direction, although unobtrusive, reveal modern preoccupations, and the modern eye of a novelist. On reflection we can see her calculation of the effect her narrators will have upon us, and even of the fact that while the story is told by an Athenian soldier or a Persian eunuch, the author is a woman – a frequent source of ironic humour. When Miss Renault's Theseus speaks of fine prizes for the games, of which the second was a woman, or when her Persian boy reflects on the nuisance which results when women are let loose from the well-ordered harems where they belong, there is a well judged gap between the narrator's Greek 'auditors' who share this view and the author's reader who does not. If Miss Renault's claim to show the past from a point of view purely of the past is inevitably inexact, it is none the less justified for she achieves a remarkable degree of truth to her ancient world. She was an advanced practitioner of an art of imagining past mentalities, and as such she is a product of our time. She was determined not to 'pollute' the past, but was equally responsible about the whole of the human environment.

Her belief that 'truth is indivisible' extends to a morality which transcends the changes of custom from one period to another. 'Perhaps the only real value of history', she wrote in the final Note to *The Mask of Apollo* (1966), 'lies in considering this endlessly varied play between the essence and the accidents [of human nature]'. In the last of her fictional autobiographies, *The Praise Singer* (1979), Simonides begins (on the first page) by reminding us – soft city-dwellers in Sicily or mainland Greece – of the harshness of his native Kos; it is less barbaric indeed than people say because even in the old days men were only compelled to take the hemlock at sixty in a bad season: 'nowadays, it is just considered good manners'. It is a wry jest; characters in all the books live with a preChristian absence of fuss about suicide. That is an 'accident' of human nature. Soon afterwards the boy Simonides is put to a test when a young apprentice-poet is dying while Sim is keen to take his place. The bard says he has heard that a certain local plant is helpful in fevers; uncalculating, Sim says, no, it's a poison – passing the bard's test and ours. That is an essential good nature, and, Miss Renualt gives us to understand, an integrity essential to an artist in any age.

Anthony Burgess and Robert Nye are at a far remove from

Mary Renault; they resemble the most 'experimental' post-modernists, full of echoes of Joyce, and 'ludic' in treating historical fiction as a literary game. A Renault novel relies on willing suspension of disbelief – the conventions are given and the art which manages them is concealed. Burgess and Nye constantly jolt the reader out of passive acquiescence in conventions; the workings of the novels are on show; we are never to forget that the novel *is* a novel, or not for long. This can be called, in a Barthesian phrase, 'foregrounding the texuality of the text',[40] and the post-modernist purpose is to deny the nineteenth-century 'myth', as Roland Barthes has it, that 'narration is the privileged signifier of the real'. But their purpose, on inspection, seems to be more purely ludic, and less theoretically conscientious. They mimic Joyce for fun, liking Joyce, and not to wreck the illusions they create by 'exhibiting' the literary convention of 'the Joycean'. For literature to be ludic is nothing new; all literature is so, and a tradition can be traced back, through Sterne, Swift, and Rabelais to Lucian, Petronius and Milesian tales in Greek, in which writers turn their conventions into a game, without ceasing to be serious about the real world.[41] Burgess and Nye are comic artists who enjoy the comic possibilities to be seen in Joyce, Flann O'Brien, Vladimir Nabokov, and John Barth. Parody, puns and word-games come naturally to them. But their ludic disruptions of the narrative and their word-games do not exclude a real relationship with the world.

Anthony Burgess is the more versatile. *Nothing Like the Sun* and *Napoleon Symphony* are different in conception, while Nye's *Merlin* (1978), *Faust* (1981) and *Voyage of the Destiny* (1982) are different performances with the same stock of ideas. *Falstaff* is much the best; the others are marred by Nye's tendency to introduce copious amounts of erotic fantasy, of little historical interest and not convincingly integrated in the larger themes of the books. *Nothing Like the Sun, Napoleon Symphony* and *Falstaff* are ambitious works of historical imagination inspired by the language, literature and legends of the past. Mary Renault begins with historical evidence, with books, places and things. She was the kind of novelist Mary Lascelles has in mind in her study of historical fiction from Scott to Kipling: *The Story-teller Retrieves the Past* (1980). Burgess began *Nothing Like the Sun* with the language of Shakespeare and *Napoleon Symphony* with the writings and music inspired or provoked by Napoleon. Nye's starting-point is the Falstaff of the plays, and the fifteenth-century John Fastolf(e) from whom he took his name. Both Burgess and Nye are conscious of how legend and history interact (and support one another). They succeed, in three very curious enterprises, because of a gift for language and a relish for the literary English of the past. Language is an habitual problem for a novelist whose characters are ancient Greeks. When the character is Shakespeare, it is a great advantage to a writer who is equal to the challenge. Burgess was also equal to a series of versions of Napoleonic English. *Falstaff* deserves to be placed with Burgess's novels because it too is more than merely a literary and verbal game; it is that, but played with a knowledge of the history behind the language and literature which furnish the comedy.

Shakespeare appeals to both writers as a dominant figure of the living past. The eighteenth-century historian J. H. Plumb has argued in *The Death of the Past* (1969) that modern society has rejected 'control by the Past'. Science and technology find no answers there. In the family, in the Church, in institutions of government and even in what Plumb calls 'the bed', the Past is growing ever less relevant. He welcomes this trend and hopes that history (understanding of the past) will achieve full objectivity when it is freed in its turn from the dead hand.

> The old past is dying, its force weakening, and so it should . . . for it was compounded by bigotry, of national vanity, of class domination. May history . . . help to sustain man's confidence in his destiny, and create for us a new past as true, as exact, as we can make it, that will help us to achieve our identity, not as Americans or Russians, Chinese or Britons, black or white, rich or poor, but as Man.[42]

Plumb's book is based on lectures he gave at the City College, New York, in 1968. If it is optimistic past the point of naivety, it was in keeping with the student mood of that year, and it is ingenious in trying to exploit students' distaste for 'the past' in the cause of promoting historical understanding. But the past is neither dead nor dying; the present is made of the past and to pretend otherwise is mischievous. We cannot create a new Shakespeare, understanding his work as truly and exactly as possible, except on the basis of four centuries in which Shakespeare has dominated literature and the study of literature; nor can Falstaff be performed independently of his past fortunes in the theatre and in criticism. Nor can the political, religious and moral issues which arise in English Renaissance contexts in Shakespeare be treated purely as the property of that time. In *Nothing Like the Sun* Burgess draws on all that connects the indistinct historical figure of Shakespeare with ourselves, on centuries of interpretation and biographical speculation – there is not, indeed, one new idea in his book. In *Falstaff* Nye sets Falstaff talking in a blend of Shakespearean and modern English; this character derives from the plays but has obviously had access to volumes of Falstaff criticism, and to notes on his fifteenth-century origin. As he impersonates Sir John Fastolf, Nye elaborates a beautiful joke, and celebrates one strand – as his Falstaff keeps telling us – of the English past which is certainly still alive. Burgess insists in the 1982 preface to his novel that his WS is true to the existing evidence, and although Falstaff is the least reliable of all narrators, the fifteenth century which infiltrates his narrative is true to what we know of the real one. Burgess and Nye are concerned with real origins because they relish the ways in which the past lives on.

A false perspective appears when 'past' and 'present' are too drastically opposed, which is what happens in Plumb's *Death of the Past*. It occurs too in a line of thinking which derives from Benedetto Croce, is best known in the English-speaking world from R. G. Collingwood's *The Idea of History* (1946), and is often crudely summarised in a catch-phrase, 'all history is contemporary history'. Here is Collingwood on Croce:

> Let us look in some detail at the conception of history which emerges from this point of view [Croce's later position]. All history is contemporary history: not in the ordinary sense of the word, where contemporary history means the history of the comparatively recent past, but in the strict sense: the consciousness of one's own activity as one performs it. History is thus the self-knowledge of the living mind. For even when the events which the historian studies are events which happened in the distant past, the condition of their being historically known is that they should vibrate in the

historian's mind, that is to say that evidence should be here and now before him and intelligible to him. For history is not contained in books or documents; it lives only, as a present interest and pursuit, in the mind of the historian when he criticises and interprets these documents, and by doing so relives for himself the states of mind into which he inquires.[43]

The extent to which Collingwood agreed with Croce is difficult to discover. (Oscar Handlin berates them together.) But although Collingwood as a responsible historian and archaeologist, respected evidence from the past, assigning it only in his role as a philosopher to the vibrations in his mind, the formula 'all history is contemporary history' is dangerous when released from its context in Collingwood's careful thinking. History may need to be rewritten in every generation – although that is not entirely true – but it does not come fresh to every generation. The process is rather that history accumulates; we read Livy, Gibbon and Macaulay. When we read Gibbon two minds are reliving Roman experience, and since Gibbon's is usually the more powerful, it may be hard to say exactly where the events are vibrating more vigorously. That leads into questions which need not arise here. The danger to perspective is in the emphasis placed on 'contemporary' and 'the historian's mind'. In Roland Barthes, and perhaps in Frank Kermode, the emphasis allows the past to be regarded as the property of the present; what happened is subordinated completely to what is thought to have happened.

It might be objected to Collingwood that much history is contained in language and that the vibrations in the historian's mind may be in the language of his documents. Is the present consciousness of an historian who is reading a Latin author 'purely' present? It might be objected to Plumb that 'a new past' would involve the destruction of existing language for the past lives most strongly and intimately there. George Orwell repeatedly made this point. Anthony Burgess is among many things a linguist and historian of language. Geoffrey Aggeler's book about Burgess records the anxiety the novelist has expressed about present disregard for the past and especially for the past life of language.[44] *Nothing Like the Sun* is not a novel which puts the past at the disposal of present interest, if only because it respects the history of English and literature in

English. Burgess has a disciple in the Nye of *Falstaff*.

David Lodge's survey of the state of the novel in 1971, *The Novelist at the Crossroads*, borrows Robert Scholes's term 'fabulation' for the type of fiction Barthes called 'ludique',[45] and said that this was one of the roads which might be taken in preference to realism. In the opposite direction was 'the non-fiction novel' of which Norman Mailer's *The Armies of the Night* (1968) is an example. The 'fabulation' abandons the realistic novel's commitment to history, and the 'non-fiction novel', sometimes called 'faction', abandons or reduces its commitment to the private experience of history.

> Literary realism, we may say, depicts the individual experience of a common phenomenal world, and . . . both parts of this undertaking are under pressure in modern culture.[46]

Lodge did not raise the question of historical fiction, which needs both the private experience and the common world if it is to find a real perspective. Mary Renault was in no doubt about either. Her invented and her recreated characters (such as Alexander) experience directly in her imagination the history which an ancient-historian can piece together. Burgess and Nye use the conventions of ludic fiction to explore the past, especially through its language; but their characters – however oddly conceived – are living through history which we can verify. They belong to their own times. J. G. Farrell was not tempted by ludic possibilities, but his 'Empire' novels are increasingly weighted with non-fictional material. He worked with an urge to document which might have overwhelmed the fiction in a writer less fascinated by the private experience of his characters. It did not, although in reading the last completed novel, *The Singapore Grip*, one may feel that Farrell would have had to write novels and history-books in future. The unrevised fragment he left at his death, published as *The Hill Station*, seems a more conventional, although not less idiosyncratic, sort of novel.

'Faction' is an unsatisfactory as well as an ugly term because almost all novels turn fact into fiction. The traditional criterion requires that sources be absorbed and digested. In Mary Renault there is a failure in artistry when – in the last chapters, in *The Mask of Apollo* and *The Praise Singer* – the writer's duty to history has got the better of her duty to fiction. A novel in which this criterion was not felt to apply might be called a 'faction'. In *Troubles* the story is frequently interrupted by quotations from newspapers. Had Farrell deleted them all before sending off his manuscript we should not have felt their absence. But we come to see that these lumps of fact are deliberately disconcerting, and that the problem of their interpretation is a part of the novel's meaning. The news in the *Irish Times* for 1920 was and is difficult to take in. Historical facts and private experience coexist uneasily for the characters here and in the later novels.

The Singapore Grip draws heavily on secondary sources, incorporating a history of the rubber industry in the Far East, and an account of the Japanese campaign through the Malay peninsula, parts of these sections entirely unrelated to the immediate experience of the characters. One reviewer noted that the passages dealing with the destruction of old communities by forces let loose by Western capital could be 'the work of a professional left-wing academic'.[47] Farrell constantly crosses and recrosses the line between history and fiction. He also constantly subverts the 'left-wing' drift of his documentation by his fascinated and affectionate treatment of his characters, however villainous in economic terms, or incompetent in military practice. Norman F. Dixon's *On the Psychology of Military Incompetence* (1976) argues that understanding the fall of Singapore is 'essentially a human problem'.

> No explanation in terms of geography, climate, broad political or military considerations can possibly do justice to the facts.[48]

Farrell's presentation of the facts in such copious detail, weighing heavily on the narrative but usually under control, adds to the effectiveness of his portrayal of 'the human problem', the plight of his characters. The worst aspect of their plight is that they cannot understand, and Farrell does not substitute Dixon's psychological solutions (the military commanders are background figures) for any others. He contemplates them with a sympathetic scepticism, not explaining the past to the present, but showing the greatest defeat in British history, forty years back in time, as a dreadful, infinitely debatable, ultimately perplexing event. 'No explanation can do justice to the facts' summarises Farrell's vision of history, but it increased rather than otherwise his fascination not only with facts but with the nature of facts in human affairs. His own work as a novelist is a sadly incomplete story, but it is a large demonstration of the potential life historical fiction has in it.

The last chapter of this book looks at John Fowles's *The French Lieutenant's Woman* and William Golding's *Rites of Passage*. The first is a mixture of a novel. It is a pleasing social comedy set in the 1860s; it is an exercise – sometimes entertaining – in the sabotage of realism; and it is a thoroughly documented history lesson. Such a work could only have been written in the present period, and probably only in England. It is saturated with contemporary kinds of anxiety and earnestness although less satirical about them than about their Victorian equivalents. It is a success, but not one that could be repeated, and it seems to have been a success which its author could not repeat. The second novel is mature Golding. It is obliged to no fashion of our time for its form or for the quality of its imagination. Its sight lines are those of the early nineteenth century and its pessimistic, sour humanism is modern and British. Perhaps Golding's Nobel Prize will help draw attention to the steady, methodologically unfussed control of perspective which is possible in an up-to-date historical novel.

Like other genres of the novel, historical fiction includes subgenres, and divisions within them. The novels chosen for study here illustrate various possibilities. The challenge of rendering ancient life is obviously different from that of dealing with modern history; the period immediately preceding the author's lifetime is 'historical' in that a world has had to be created at second-hand, but since this can include oral evidence such a novel as *The Singapore Grip* is a borderline case. Novels such as *Fire from Heaven* and *The Persian Boy* are different in kind from those in which the central character is an invented, typical figure of the time portrayed. These novelists are all, except Farrell and Mary Renault, still writing; all have published fiction, and, all except Fowles, historical fiction in the last five years.[49] This criterion has excluded Alfred Duggan who died in 1964. The term 'British' has excluded the Irishman

John Banville and, of course, Gore Vidal. All those selected have established critical reputations, although Mary Renault is still regarded as *merely* an historical novelist. All have written novels about the modern world, although Renault and Farrell became known only when they turned to historical fiction. Only one of Mary Renault's earliest books, *The Charioteer* (1953), is still in print. Bernard Bergonzi's assessment 'that Farrell did not become an important novelist until the publication of *Troubles*' is correct in every sense.[50] These are both, for reasons which are probably beyond explanation, writers who found their talent when they came to write about the past. That could be said of Fowles. No explanation is offered here, and only occasional mention is made of the writers' work outside the genre being considered. All have had considerable popular success. Burgess calls *Napoleon Symphony* 'a lump of minor art', not to be fairly judged in relation to Tolstoy on the same subject.[51] In that comparison these are all minor novels, but they are meant to be judged as art. Time will tell.

2 Mary Renault: The Earlier Novels

Mary Renault [Eileen Mary Challans], who died in December 1983, wrote eight historical novels. Three of the last four make a sequence about Alexander the Great: *Fire from Heaven* (1970), *The Persian Boy* (1972) and *Funeral Games* (1981). *The Last of the Wine* (1956) is set in Athens in the period of the Peloponnesian War; *The Mask of Apollo* (1966) is set partly in Athens in the next generation, partly in Sicily under Dionysios the Younger and afterwards Dion. *The King Must Die* (1958) and *The Bull from the Sea* (1962) retell the story of Theseus. *The Praise Singer* (1979) is a fictional life of the poet Simonides. These books are traditional in their use of the formal and linguistic resources at the disposal of a modern novelist, which is not to say that they are unadventurous in technique. Six are autobiographies which proceed from childhood onwards without dislocation of the time-scheme or variation in the perspective of a lifetime remembered in orderly detail. The novels follow ancient sources closely and where gaps occur in what is known, the author's reconstruction is based on rational discussion of probability. Historical materials very rarely intrude. Herodotus, Thucydides, Plato and Arrian have been absorbed into the Renault world, and although she sometimes incorporates her translation of a portion of an ancient text the unlearned reader is unlikely to notice.[1] She infiltrates history into her story so that a newcomer to ancient affairs quickly feels at home. Historical interest is usually subordinate to the personal interest of people involved in the history. The recreation of their daily experience is realistic: the artificiality of the undertaking is not offered to the reader's attention, except in occasional jests. These novels are serious attempts to retrieve the past through study and imagination and to relate her past to the reader's present. Christopher Ricks summarised her achievement in his review of *Funeral Games*. 'Miss Renault's accomplishment is simple, though not easy: she knows, she cares. She knows not only the ancient world, but the modern world to which these "Old, unhappy far off things/ And battles long ago" must be responsibly accommodated. She cares not only for the spirit of the past but for its letter'.[2] To be true to the past, for Miss Renault, is to be true to our own time. She wrote from a full and intelligent sense of both.

The novels are at their best where they are closest to good historical evidence. In the two novels about fifth- and fourth-century Athens ancient sources are relatively reliable, for the chronology and for the characters known from Greek history. Alexias [Greek names are in the spelling they are given in the novels], the fictional narrator-hero of *The Last of the Wine*, is born at the start of the Peloponnesian War in the year of the plague at Athens in 430 B.C. He is a schoolboy on the day of the mutilation of the Herms in 415 and he sees the Athenian expedition sail for Sicily in the same year. When news comes of the Athenian disaster after the battle of Syracuse in 413 he believes his father to be among the dead. In 412, at the age of eighteen, he competes in the Isthmian Games. His father returns and becomes a moderate in the oligarch cause when the Council of Four Hundred is established in 411. Alexias goes to Samos where he takes part in the democratic naval coup against the oligarch party which results in the deposition of the Four Hundred later in 411. He sees Alkibiades proclaimed leader of the Athenians in 407 and serves under him in the war against Lysander. He is at Athens when the news arrives of the slaughter of the Athenian forces at Aegospotami (Goat Creek) in 405 and he is in the City throughout the siege, the capitulation, the Spartan occupation and the destruction of the Long Walls in 404. His father who has supported the Council of Thirty is a moderate and is murdered by its extremist leader Kritias. Alexias escapes to Thebes and fights at Piraeus with the liberation army which ends the tyranny in 403. At the close of the novel, under a newly restored democracy, he can foresee the trial of Sokrates. Alexias's friends include Sokrates, Xenophon, Phaedo and Plato. He knows Euripides; and he is an almost life-long enemy of Kritias, whom he kills to avenge his father. Miss Renault follows Thucydides for events down to 411, and Xenophon's *Hellenics*. Her description of the war in

Sicily closely follows Thucydides. Her portraits of the famous are drawn from Plato and from Plutarch. Avrom Fleishman remarks that these never lose their 'statuary pallor',[3] and the same could be said of Plato and Dion of Syracuse as they appear in *The Mask of Apollo*. Alexias's father, an old-fashioned gentleman, proud and irascible, a very decent conservative baffled and outraged when he goes into politics, is a more vivid character than the ex-stonemason with wisely twinkling eyes socratically questioning young men, whom we know too well from schoolbooks.

The Mask of Apollo covers events in Athens and Sicily between about 390 and 340, especially the reign of Dionysios the Younger and Dion at Syracuse between 367 and 354. Nikeratos, a (fictional) tragic actor begins his adult career touring in the Peloponnese in the 370s and meets the Sicilian philosopher-prince Dion at the Delphi Congress in the summer of 368. He is protagonist in the elder Dionysios's prize winning *Ransoming of Hector* at the Lenaean festival in 367, and he arrives in Syracuse just as the tyrant is dying from his excessive celebrations of that last victory. (Like so many good turning-points in Mary Renault's stories this is based on evidence.[4]) He speaks the funeral oration, winning the approval of Dionysios II, and returns to Sicily during Plato's second and third visits as an unsuccessful philosophical adviser to the feeblest of tyrants. He is there to see the disastrous consequences of Dion's well-meant invasion of Sicily in 357 and he revisits Syracuse at the time of Dion's murder in 354. In Athens during these years he has moved on the fringe of Plato's circles at the Academy. In 342 he visits Pella and meets Alexander. The principal events and personalities are based on Plutarch's *Lives* of Dion and Timoleon, Plato's *Letters* and Diodorus Siculus's *History*. Plato's views in the novel paraphrase those of the *Republic* and *Symposium*. The celebrated actor Theodorus appears as a minor character; Mary Renault's Note to the novel tells us that she has 'inferred the character' of Thettalos, Nikeratos's apprentice, fellow-actor and lover, from his role as a political agent for Alexander in 337 (as recounted in Plutarch's *Life* of Alexander). These novels cover a relatively well documented hundred years of Greek history. The surviving evidence has been analysed and debated in great detail; the novelist's purposes do not require her to depart from established chronology and established character out-lines.

For the story of Theseus in *The King Must Die* and its sequel *The Bull from the Sea* she goes almost a thousand years back into the Mycenean and late Cretan civilisations which were un-known, except from Homer, until late in the nineteenth century. Her story of Theseus follows Plutarch's account almost exactly and attempts to reclaim for history the legend which, as she says in the Author's Note to *The King Must Die*, had 'by classical times acquired so fabulous a garnish that it has sometimes been dismissed as pure fairy tale, or, after Frazer, as religious myth'. By the 1950s it was possible to re-examine the myth with more confidence in the later Greek tradition, although there was still considerable scope for the imagination; there is no hard evidence that Theseus ever existed. Mycenean archaeology, since Schliemann's excavation in 1876, has un-covered a period of history only less dazzling than the Crete unearthed by Sir Arthur Evans at Knossos in the first three decades of this century, and at other palaces by his colleagues and successors. Miss Renault notes that

> the rationalists [of the Theseus story] had their first setback when Sir Arthur Evans uncovered the Palace of Knossos, with its labyrinthine complexity, eponymous sacred axes, numerous representations of youths and girls performing the Bull Dance, and seal-carvings of the bull-headed Mino-taur. The most fantastic part of the story having thus been linked to fact, it becomes tempting to guess where else a fairy-tale gloss may have disguised human actualities.[5]

In *The Archaeology of Crete* (1939) John Pendlebury, a colleague of Evans's, allowed himself the kind of guessing which all but the driest of scholars presumably enjoy at times.

> Now there is a name which is always associated with the sack of Knossos, at least with the liberation of its subjects—*Theseus*. Names have a habit of being remembered when the deeds with which they are associated are forgotten or garbled. . . . It has already been suggested that the seven youths and seven maidens may have been the mainland quota for the bull-ring at Knossos. This is just the type of detail that would

be remembered, the more so in that it may well have been the sentimental reason without which no purely commercial war can ever take place. . . . And in the last decade of the fifteenth century on a spring day, when a strong south wind was blowing which carried the flames of the burning beams horizontally northward [as the remains suggest], Knossos fell. . . . The final scene takes place in the Throne-Room. It was found in a state of complete confusion. A great oil-jar lay overturned in one corner, ritual vessels were in the act of being used when disaster came. It looks as if the King had been hurried there to undergo, too late, some last ceremony in the hope of saving the people. Theseus and the Minotaur! Dare we believe that he wore the mask of the bull?[6]

He wears it in *The King Must Die*. Mary Renault accepts Evans's view that an earthquake destroyed Knossos and provided the opportunity for an armed rising of bull-dancers and native Cretans against the Greek-speaking aristocracy. Michael Ventris's demonstration that Greek was the language of the 'Linear B' tablets in Crete had been published in 1953. Her 'Minotaur' is an ambitious Cretan prince and her Minos an ageing king and scholar who wears a bull-mask to conceal the effects of leprosy. These are reasonable guesses on which to hang a realistic novel in place of the tale of a bull-man monster who fed on the girls and youths supplied as tribute from Athens. Another guess gives Theseus a foresense of earthquakes, to explain his supposed relationship to Poseidon. The best part of *The King Must Die* is Theseus's account of his life in the bull-ring where he and his team of Athenian teenagers vault and ride the bulls. This spectacle, a sport and a religious ceremony in honour of Poseidon, may be seen in the paintings in Crete, as may the lively, gossiping, uncannily modern-seeming faces of the Cretan ladies who watched.[7] This section of the novel, which made Mary Renault's reputation, is probably the best imaginative recreation in English literature of past life from purely archaeological evidence.

Judged by that high standard, *The Bull from the Sea* is disappointing, and the brilliant failure of its attempt to make Amazons, Centaurs, the sea-bull of Poseidon, and the story of Hippolyta, Hippolytos and Phaedra into a plausible world suggests that historical fiction is bound to fail when it has so very little history to work with. Mary Renault was good at guessing whenever history left her with gaps to fill but the later Theseus legend is all empty space. Theseus's love-affair with Hippolyta comes closer than anything else she wrote to the kind of historical novel which gives its author's mind a holiday. The reviewer in the *Times Literary Supplement* rightly complained, furthermore, that the book is 'a string of interesting anecdotes rather than a shapely novel'.[8] The introduction of Oedipus and (at the end, briefly) the boy Achilles at Skyros is true to the legend, but seems inartistic as well as unlikely. Theseus's dream, in the last pages, of his ghostly part in the Battle of Marathon is again true to later Greek tradition – the Athenian soldiers saw him leading them to battle, as an angel was seen in 1914 at the battle of Mons. But chronology, fictional method and language go wrong in this last section. Theseus resolves to die, throwing himself from the cliff in the Erichthid kingly custom, sooner than disappoint the hero-worshipping Achilles who is to meet him next day. This brings the destruction of Knossos and the fall of Troy closer than most archaeological opinion allows. Up to this point we can accept a Theseus narrating his life's exploits, perhaps (since he offers much advice on ruling) to young princes; the last chapter, in the present tense, comes direct from the mind of the dying man and the change of narrative convention makes it look even more contrived. Perhaps the author felt a strain in what she was writing because the style for once falls into the slacky rhythmic prose which is the curse of historical fiction: 'while the bard sings and the child remembers, I shall not perish from off the Rock'. Mary Renault was at her best artistically when she was closest to hard evidence about what actually happened.

'Don't ever pretend you live in 1867', John Fowles told himself when working on *The French Lieutenant's Woman*.[9] Reading Miss Renault we are addressed as though we were ancient Greeks. There are several aspects to this pretence besides suppression of hindsight: the use of English; the use of the novel, a genre which scarcely existed in the ancient world, with its concentration of interest in character and incident which is not to be found in ancient literature; and the fact that we see the illusion as we submit to it. Hearing a narrator who takes his past for granted, we are conscious too of a novelist for whom it is the past. Management of 'voice' is the secret of Mary

Renault's success. Several recent critical studies of the art of fiction have discussed the sense in which the text 'creates' its reader, in so far as it can persuade him to yield to its assumptions and point of view.[10] Mary Renault invented a role: that of a fourth-century Athenian novel-reader; for the sake of plausibility we can suppose him to be speaking; talk must always have employed some of the techniques which first appeared in literature in the novel.

The first chapter of the first of the Greek novels illustrates the role we are asked to borrow. *The Last of the Wine* begins:

> When I was a young boy, if I was sick or in trouble, or had been beaten at school, I used to remember that on the day I was born my father had wanted to kill me.
>
> You will say there is nothing out of the way in this. Yet I daresay it is less common than you might suppose; for as a rule, when a father decides to expose an infant, it is done and there the matter ends. And it is seldom that a man can say, either of the Spartans or of the plague, that he owes them life instead of death.

We are adjusted in this opening passage to the imaginative part we are to play in reading. The writing is deceptively simple. Juxtaposition of the commonplace and the exceptional keeps us unsure of how to make the called-for response. 'You will say' makes us ask who is meant by 'you'. The surprise of the first sentence is annulled by the second, and the next reminds us of what we are supposed to know, without seeming to do so. Few unwanted infants live to tell the tale, but the upsets of war and calamity can blow somebody good. The speaker knows we accept the custom unsqueamishly – that's life; but a surviving son may feel aggrieved that he wasn't loved from the first. The childhood troubles, commonplace at any time, jolt against 'to kill me'; but then it is implied that we object to his mentioning something so commonplace. 'Out of the way' is nonchalant, light, demurring. 'Less common than you might suppose' hints that one rarely gives much thought in a busy life to infanticide, and implies that this unfatherliness is perhaps noteworthy; but then that implication is reversed by the remainder of the sentence: 'it is done' has finality and unconcern (a slave bearing a bundle away). 'It is seldom' shifts into a wider range of normal events. Spartans and plague are normal too and death is their normal consequence; they help to explain why babies have to be exposed; no one has the right to expect to live long. What is out of the way is the tale to follow, one of unusual good fortune. Adjusting to the norms behind the words, the reader is jostled out of his habitual reactions.

The style helps. Any trace of indignation in the first sentence, meant to catch our 1956 attention, is brushed away in the relaxed familiar voicing of the next reflections. Without archaism, in a neutral (classless, regionless) English without idiom that can be easily placed, the writing makes us at home with itself. There is a deftness which prompts confidence in the speaker – it is a speaker's voice. 'You will say' seems to gesture with a finger or a wine-cup. At the same time we are located in a new setting – we are men ('seldom that a man can say') and (a note of bitterness sets the Spartans beside the plague) Athenians.

The next paragraph places us in time. That day saw the start of the Great War. The Spartans were burning the farms and Pericles advised retreating to 'the City, and Piraeus, and the Long Walls between'. That Pericles was still alive 'is no reason for foolish youths to ask me, as one did lately, whether I remember him.' We are, therefore, a fair part of a lifetime on from the beginning of the Peloponnesian War; the familiar phrase ' the Great War', besides bearing a tacit reminder from the novelist of how many generations have looked back to one, helps to place the distance in time from this mature speaker who is irritated by foolish youths with no proper sense of modern history. It is approximately equal to the distance between 1956 and 1914. Some readers will know that Sparta decided on war in 432 BC, that there was plague in Athens in the second year of the war, in 430, and that Pericles died in 429, so that the narrative comes from early in the fourth century. If the speaker sounds testy about foolish youths, having lived through the war, that is understandable. If we have forgotten the history when we start reading for the first time, we are made to feel that we ought to know about this Great War and what came of it by the familiar mode of address which implies 'you know', and we are prepared for the recounting of it by the note of melancholy, sounded in the first chapter, which will pervade the novel.

The plague came after the peasants crowded into the city for protection and lined the walls with their stinking huts. The opening passage continues:

Some of the women, I believe, blamed the country people for bringing in a curse; as if anyone could reasonably suppose that the gods would punish a state for treating its own citizens justly. But women, being ignorant of philosophy and logic, and fearing dream-diviners more than immortal Zeus, will always suppose that whatever causes them trouble must be wicked.

The plague thinned my family as it did every other.

There are several assumptions here which are likely to distance the reader: that a plague has nothing to do with bad hygiene and overcrowding; that the gods exist and are just; that women are innately foolish; that their ignorance is somehow blameworthy or contemptible; and that immortal Zeus, being a god, is beyond their religious capacity. The irony from hindsight — women's intuition was right on that occasion – helps to deflate indignation, and so does the fact that the novelist is a woman. The sudden outburst of annoyance sounds so real that it humanises the incorrect opinions, drawing us closer not to agreement or even perhaps to sympathy, but to understanding. The justice of the gods and the injustice of the plague are irreconcilables, not faced by the narrator, which we cannot patronise by hindsight. We are manoeuvred into accepting our role as audience, while seeing our distance from the intended audience at the same time.

An uncle died of the plague after nursing a dying youth, with whom he was in love.

From the way they were lying, it seems that in the hour of Philon's death Alexias had felt himself sicken; and knowing the end, had taken hemlock, so that they should make the journey together. The cup was standing on the floor beside him; he had tipped out the dregs and written PHILON with his finger, as one does after supper in the last of the wine. . . . Every year at the feast of Families we sacrificed for Alexias at the household altar, and the story is one of the first that I remember. My father used to say that all over the City, those who died in the plague were the beautiful and the good.

The story is potentially awkward, not because it belongs to an alien society as it does, but because we are familiar with the feelings involved from much poor late-Romantic literature which has made them seem artificial and cheap. The cadences help to rescue it from triteness. The even tone of the sentences mellows the very romantic anecdote, hoping to win an unsentimental reader, who might scoff at *Yellow Book* love-in-death Hellenistic morbidity, by its matter-of-fact freedom from modern sentimentality. 'Make the journey' sounds unfussed, as does 'we sacrificed for Alexias'; his was a good death, rightly honoured in the family. Approval of timely suicide, and of the 'Socratic' kind of romantic love, is assumed with no flicker of suspicion that we might disapprove of both. The fluency, which is not quite glib, catches exactly a speaker who recalls a story often heard and often told, used to it but still touched by it and by its place in his earliest memories. He is quite sure of his audience's correct appreciation of Uncle Alexias's virtue and the fate of the beautiful and the good. The voice is heard to soften at 'as one does after supper in the last of the wine'; he knows that his audience have tender wine-mellowed moments, and probably beloved youths to remember: who has not traced a name, 'as one does'? That the effect sounds practised makes it seem all the more sure of our response. A modern reader who knows what happened to Athens in the Peloponnesian War is more susceptible to the concealed force intended in the last words: on a second reading the plague is plainly a metaphor for the contamination of the best in Athenian life; by the end of the book the title phrase makes a symbol, fully exploited. The novel's opening passage attunes us to a mood of acquiescence in disaster, and to the reader's role the narrator expects of us.[11]

Born small, wizened and ugly, the new baby arrived too soon. 'My father decided at once that . . . it would be better not to rear me'. At the crucial moment of decision, however, the father was called to arms; finding, on his return, his wife and eldest son dead of the plague, he relented. Putting on weight and seeming worthier, the remaining child took the name Alexias after all.

This first chapter of only twelve hundred words introduces a narrator whose conception of life is blatantly unlike our own and who is undisturbed by our kind of misgivings. The reader of 1956 would probably be reminded of Naomi Mitchison's

Black Sparta (1928) and *Barbarian Stories* (1929) which are very frank about the least glamorous aspects of ancient Greek life. But even in the most appalling incidents of those books, allowance is made for a modern sensibility; in the story 'Krypteia' in *Black Sparta* a helot-boy is killed for his part in a plot against the Spartan citizenry and a young Spartan who has befriended him is inconsolable. 'Oh, I wish we'd let him go! I don't want to be a good citizen!' The proper Spartan view ['why we did it made it right'] is expressed, but the story ends with tears shed for unrighteousness 'soaking down to the earth of Sparta'.[12] There is the eternal human heart working in the way we know. In a later story in the same book 'Who Will You Have for Nuts in May?' an Athenian in Persia puts himself to trouble, cost and danger to free a young Spartan slave whose owners keep him insultingly chained, discovering charity in himself, despite his former hatred of Sparta during the occupation of Athens. Where ancient customs – helotry and slavery – offend now, they are registered as offensive by one of the characters. A reviewer in the *Times Literary Supplement* commented on Naomi Mitchison's early historical fiction that 'one is often on the point of taking these charming creatures for our own contempories but one is always recalled to the barbaric shadow that lies on them – unknown rites and superstition'.[13] One cannot take Miss Renault's Alexias for our own contemporary. He never considers that infanticide might be wrong; he is grimly amused by the chance that saved him. Later in the novel, during the siege of Athens, he exposes a new-born brother, regretting that the gods and The Kindly Ones will not allow him to make a quick end. The gods of Olympus, and the Eumenides – with whom Alexias brushes when bad relations with his father reach a crisis – inscrutable, hard to placate and quick to anger, are never far from his thoughts. Suicide can be seemly; animal sacrifice is a fact of life. Women are inferior because the gods made them so; homosexual love is the noblest and most dependable bond for men.

The method which presents Alexias and his world in these three pages is followed throughout *The Last of the Wine* and the next three Renault novels. A Hellenic view of Hellas is sustained without any protective shield of authorial comment, explanation or apology interposed to reassure, and with little or no undercutting irony to allow a comforting sense of superiority. Sokrates in this novel challenges all his contemporaries' beliefs in the same spirit (often in the speeches) in which he challenged them in Plato's dialogues, and Kritias arrives at a total cynicism which might sound modern to us, except that here it is a new attitude. The best and the worst of men can remove themselves from their culture but we see them through the eyes of Alexias who is a very normal gentleman of his time, wondering at Sokrates's virtue and Kritias's vice though troubled by the ideas of both. Her power to make these Athenians real to us has been amply acknowledged. 'The most vivid and convincing reconstruction of ancient Greek life that I have ever read', said Raymond Mortimer of *The Last of the Wine* (in the *Sunday Times*);[14] 'an unforgettable picture of the peak of this civilisation and the beginning of its decline . . . [it shows] what it must have felt to be an ancient Athenian', wrote the *Times Literary Supplement* reviewer.[15] Mary Renault makes ancient Athenians of us while we read; we acknowledge the supreme elation of going to war for the first time, the ecstasy of winning a foot-race, the serenity which comes from the love of an older man, the awe inspired by the carved face of a god, the occasional poignant pity one feels for women and slaves, the pride in being a free Hellene, the beauty of ideals proved by logic. We are asked not so much to suspend disbelief as to suspend all that distinguishes our culture from theirs. Some of these emotions have their English counterparts, from what persists in human nature and from the Greek influence on education in the last hundred years; and some readers will have less reluctance to yield than others in accepting the role of the reader Alexias expects. A patriotic, upper-class, religiously inclined, homosexual soldier and cricketer might find Alexias more congenial than the next man or woman will. But he might be even more sharply conscious of difference. We cannot approach the Greeks' religious and civic satisfaction in athletics, performing best 'in honour of the god'; and a modern homosexual who believes himself to be 'natural' knows that most people do not agree. C. S. Lewis's claim (discussed in Chapter 8, below) that his Christian faith takes him closer in sympathy to paganism is fanciful; his theology puts the Devil in his place, Alexias's leaves the Furies loose. The Olympic wreath, the boy's name written in the lees, and the cock due to Asklepios belong to the past. Mary Renault's technique denies the consolations of Hellenophile fantasy and engages her reader in the otherness of the Greeks.

Presenting ancient Greeks in modern English narrative and dialogue can be easier than dealing with Medieval or Renaissance characters, because English is further from the language we know they would have spoken. The alternative options are to use distinctly contemporary and colloquial English, as in Naomi Mitchison, in John Arden's *Silence Among the Weapons* (1982) and in Arrowsmith's translations from Petronius and Aristophanes – or to attempt a plain English style which minimises modern connotations, as in Mary Renault. According to some reviewers she wrote 'unadorned' English; in fact she wrote a deceptively simple, flexible prose which is discreetly adorned in a variety of ways. One modification is a carefully regulated use of old-fashioned, slightly stilted phrasing. It gives an impression, at times, of foreign idioms showing through a translation, and it excludes any unsuitable impression of smartness in the English. The writing is usually crisp but diverts attention from its good English style with small, quaint additions, as in the following lines which could be a translation from Herodotus in the 'Loeb' manner which has caused 'Made . . . to be', 'and other swine' and 'all sorts of men' to sound vaguely 'classical' in this passage from Chapter 3 of *The Last of the Wine*:

Once long before, I had asked my father why Zeus made some men to be Hellenes living in cities with laws, some barbarians under tyrants, and others slaves. He said. 'You might as well ask, my dear boy, why he made some beasts lions, some horses, and other swine. Zeus the All-Knowing has placed all sorts of men in a state conformable with their natures; we cannot suppose anything else. Don't forget, however, that a bad horse is worse than a good ass. And wait till you are older before you question the purposes of the gods.'

Renault Greeks use English without fear of triteness, as though it were fresh to them; they form images a contemporary English writer would think banal without any sense that they may seem stale. We quickly grow accustomed to this adaptation, which does not disturb the illusion of sharing a Greek point of view. We are supposed to have heard fathers speaking as Alexias's father speaks. Sometimes there is a discreet borrowing: Alexias says of Socrates: 'but to him everything that is in the world was full of gods' (Chapter 7); Plato asks 'Can we then deny that everything is full of gods?' (*Laws* 896b). Sometimes a proverb or tag suggests Mary Renault's knowledge of Africa: 'after the rain has fallen, you cannot put it back in the sky' (*The Last of the Wine*, Chapter 7); 'a ghost has spoken' in *The King Must Die* is a Cretan saying when there is no witness ('Crete': Chapter 9). Characteristically, the writing alternates terse, pithy remarks, easy to imagine spoken, with vivid images, and a subdued lyrical note. Recalling the story of the Spartan boy and the fox, Alexias says that 'not the least remarkable part of [this] is that the boy was hungry enough to have intended eating a fox' (Chapter 12). Alexias reflects on Aristophanes's *The Birds*:

> Yet in this comedy was a song about birds so beautiful that it made the hair prickle on one's neck. Indeed, while he is singing, he makes his own heaven and earth: the good is what he chooses, and where he sets their altars, there the gods alight. Plato says that no poet ought to be allowed to do this: and he is too distinguished now to be argued with any longer. I notice, however, that he goes himself.   (Chapter 6)

The wry brevity of the last sentence is typical of the narrators of all the books. Alexias is occasionally, and justifiably, 'classical': 'as, when great Helios shines upon a frost-bound pool, the birds begin alighting, and at evening the beasts come down to drink, so I, being happy, instead of suitors began to have friends' (Chapter 11). Simile is usually more matter-of-fact in phrasing as well as in content. 'Samos is an old and noble city. Even its ancient tyrants hung gifts upon it, like jewels on a favourite slave' (Chapter 20) – an appropriate thought for a democrat at a time when democracy is threatened. A simple image can be elevated at a moment of very strong feeling, as when it turns out that the model for a startlingly beautiful sculpture of young Apollo was Alexias's father, now physically ruined by slavery in Syracuse. 'My mind was silent, like fallen snows in a still air. I stood and gazed. Then, as winter's white comes crashing down the mountain-side and runs away in water, grief fell upon me for all mortal men . . . ' (Chapter 18). The simile does not seem decorative. It avoids the mannered pastiche of some modern writers and the effect of Edwardian 'fine-writing' as in Lawrence Durrell at his worst. In Alexias it sounds innocent of modern-English prose-poetry and right for his sudden inner collapse of feeling. His usual tone is that of a quiet speaking voice, articulate and unconscious of anything stale in its literary departures from normal educated modern English speech. 'So we laughed, and shared the last of our wine, and fell to telling bawdy tales and then to sleep. I daresay I remember the night so well because soon afterwards there came an end to laughter in the City' (Chapter 14).

The novels open well, fixing their narrators in the mind at once. 'It was dolphin weather when I sailed into Piraeus with my comrades of the Cretan bull-ring', Theseus remembers in the first line of *The Bull from the Sea*, catching the exuberance of youthful homecoming and picturing the Bay of Salamis and the murals of Knossos in which dolphins can still be seen. *The King Must Die* begins with proud formality, proclaiming its speaker a king.

> The citadel of Troizen where the Palace stands was built by giants before anyone remembers. But the Palace was built by my grandfather. At sunrise, if you look at it from Kalauria across the strait, the columns glow fire-red and the walls are golden. It shines bright against the dark woods on the mountain-side.
>
> Our house is Hellene, sprung from the seed of ever-living Zeus. We worship the Sky gods before the Mother Dia and the gods of earth. And we have never mixed our blood with the blood of the Shore people who held the land before us.

These lines are performative, the romantically stirring English reproducing the authoritative role of public utterance in a predominantly oral culture. We are to attend, to acknowledge, not to interrupt. Setting and themes are being established: the splendour of a palace in the wilderness, the Dark Age mentality whose history goes back two generations and whose god is the founder of the tribe; the patriarchal culture which the Hellenic conqueror Theseus will represent in his conflict with the indigenous cult, in his passage through Eleusis on his way to Athens. The second sentence's relaxation of style prepares for

Theseus's practical, frank story-telling; but the strident heroic note sounds clear. We are not to think ourselves the narrator's social equals.

Theseus can sound prissy, occasionally, when a phrase is ill-chosen: 'my mother hung her girdle up for the Mother Dia, and so I was conceived' ('Athens', Chapter 2). But he more often makes modern English serve his own purposes, referring neatly to 'god-got men' or praying to Poseidon:

> Earth-Shaker, Father of Bulls, you know us all. We are your children, your little calves who danced for you. You have heard our feet, you have tasted our blood in the dusty sand. We have taken the bull by the horns . . . '
>
> ('Crete': Chapter 10)

He speaks with pungency: 'Poseidon is coming in black anger, stamping on the cities', before the earthquake; 'the strong-laid floor of Daidalos broke like water and surges in waves', as the earthquake strikes ('Crete': Chapter 10). Titles convey the special power which names have always possessed in oral cultures. 'I was once more Kouros of Poseidon, Kerkyon of Eleusis; Theseus, son of Aigeus, son of Pandion, Shepherd of Athens'; 'I opened my heart in this small, close room to Star-Born Minos, Lord of the Isles' ('Crete': Chapter 10). 'Lord of the Isles' is a good borrowing, and 'the House of the Axe' (*passim*) Englishes 'labyrinth', since '*labros*' is the two-headed axe of Crete. Poseidon's titles resound, as in Greek; he is 'Lover of Bulls', 'Earthshaker', 'Hippios', 'Blue-Hair'; Apollo is 'Paian Apollo', 'Slayer of Darkness', 'Apollo Longsight'. There is no doubt that Miss Renault relishes such titles, but so no doubt did Theseus.

Nikeratos is an actor thinking aloud in the opening lines of *The Mask of Apollo*:

> Not many people remember Lamprias now in Athens but his company is still remembered in the Peloponnese. Ask in Corinth or Epidauros, no one will have heard of him; but down in the Argolid they will go on about his mad Heracles, or his Agamemnon, as if it were yesterday. I don't know who is working his circuit now.
>
> At all events, he was in Athens when my father died, and

owed him more money than anyone else did; but as usual was nearly broke, and trying to fit out a tour on a handful of beans. So he offered to take me on as an extra; it was the best he could do.

As usual, we are involved. 'Ask in Corinth . . . ' But here there is no special distance from the narrator, whose style is more briskly modern English than Alexias's or Theseus's. Change the names and this might be the start of a modern English first-person novel (perhaps Iris Murdoch), unaffectedly colloquial with easy cadences pleasantly controlled. Lamprias, and Nikeratos's early struggles are comfortably away in the past; this Athenian is now professionally well enough established to speak lightly of tight budgets and smile at provincial reputations. Herakles and Agamemnon, as dramatic subjects, are brought into the same world as a touring actor-manager making the best of being 'nearly broke' – a rare instance of slang in Renault, calculated here to help to free the subject of Greek tragedy from pompous schoolbook connotations. An actor moves in all social circles but the novel contains actors, scene-painters, mask-makers, mercenary soldiers, sailors, innkeepers, couriers, and people in bars, besides Dion, Plato and Dionysios II, and the dialogue is appropriately comprehensive with a variety of English registers. Nikeratos is the least restricted of Mary Renault's narrators in his linguistic range; one reviewer objected, perhaps rightly, to the anachronism of 'camp' terms in the actors' talk among themselves – but that register is not over-indulged, and it is likely that ancient actors used some equivalent; any privileged guild has its private language. Dion is shocked by backstage talk. Nikeratos says of Theodorus that his dignity could be freezing with rich sponsors or with kings; 'he kept this sort of thing ['camp'] for equals' (Chapter 13). Nikeratos has a fund of attractive and timeless similes. Aristotle regards Alexander 'with dissatisfaction, like a hen that has hatched an eagle-chick' (Chapter 24). A studious girl pauses 'for a feed-line, as philosophers do; just like comic actors, though one must not say so' (Chapter 4). Plato recalling the humiliation which followed his first trip to Sicily is 'an old hand who had played, so to speak, Sophokles in Boeotia, and had been hit with half an onion' (Chapter 8). Dionysios II, beginning to respond so far as he is able to Plato's teaching, looks 'better-favoured, like a plain girl pleased with her marriage' (Chapter 9). Such images, better than description, put familiar unstatuary expressions on ancient, sometimes distinguished faces, and help to bring them to life.

In so far as we yield to the point of view and to the style, we succumb to Miss Renault's illusion. There is great pleasure to be had from succumbing; this has made her a best-seller. Auberon Waugh declares that she offers the best that literature can offer – to be taken out of ourselves and our own world and enabled to live in one of a writer's imagining;[16] that might be called escapism because Waugh is a critic who finds the present era distasteful. This aspect of what the Renault novels offer is at least a very superior form of solace. But we are likely to dissociate ourselves from a point of view so unlike our own, when we set the book down, and think about its implications. When we do so it is plain that Mary Renault's vision includes the life of our time. She said that she believed the introduction of moral judgements from a modern perspective to be wrong – a form of interference with the past. Instead, she brings Greek morality to bear on us. All her narrators in the first-person novels are impressive in the moral sense and in their codes of conduct. All eight books explore an approach to life which is religious, social and aesthetic, and which arises from a spirit in Greek culture which Miss Renault admires and celebrates, very memorably in a spectacular scene in the second chapter of *The Mask of Apollo*.

Nikeratos is protagonist in *The Myrmidons* at the festival at Delphi during the Congress there in the summer of 368. 'Flown on' as Apollo for the prologue, and hanging thirty feet above the stone, he hears a strand of the rope part; a former actor now reduced to odd-jobbing has borne him a grudge. Through the mask he speaks the words of Apollo ('For I am Phoebus, zenith-cleaving, sun-shafted archer,/Unforsworn tongue of truth') and reckons that a call for help might still save him. Then he thinks of the bathos of 'a human bleat' coming from the mask of the god. An eagle up in the Phaidriades cliffs shrills as if in scorn. He tells himself that his father would have gone on. When the audience see his danger and call out he stills them, and the crane-man lowers him to safety on the one remaining strand. Such moments test the quality of other characters in other books. Plato in *The Last of the Wine* goes to Kritias to plead for Sokrates's life in the same spirit, and in *The Mask of Apollo* the girl Axiothea who studies with Plato resolves to visit Dion's Sicily disguised as a youth. In *The King Must Die* Theseus goes through a similar crisis when he chooses to go to Crete with the tribute-party; some of his own subjects from Eleusis have been included in the lottery and he takes his place with them while his father calls the names. When he guesses from Aigeus's calm that his lot has been left blank, so that he has lost his chance of honourable escape, he is tempted to bribe Poseidon with a gift of horses, but knows that the gods wants him, the king-to-be, as a volunteer. The bull-leaping in the labyrinth is a submission of personal will to the god; death comes soonest to those who fear to risk their lives. 'When you love your life too much in the ring, that's when you lose it.'

Honour, courage, dedication to one's calling, and a pride in excellence are combined to form this quality which is possessed by all Miss Renault's best people. They also accept human limitations. This is the part of their religion which can be explained. The rest is awe (fear and delight) inspired by 'the presence of the god', in a temple, before a sculpture, in an earthquake or a storm, during a play, for Sokrates everywhere. 'We servants of the god have our honour too' says Nikeratos (Chapter 3) who as an actor is a servant of Dionysos. Honour for Theseus is an aristocratic code to which he adds the kingly duty to 'stand before the gods' for the people, and to die for them if the god calls; the Erechthids go willingly to their deaths, like men not oxen, leaping from high rocks. They are aware that kings were sacrificed in former times, to ensure the next year's harvest, as kings still are among the matriarchal shore-people, but Theseus is shocked at Eleusis to see that Kerkyon, the 'year-king', is not willing when his time comes to die. Willingness is a form of honour which the gods acknowledge. Something of that survives in Nikeratos's instinct at Delphi. Responsible to the god, Renault's Theseus is a king 'dedicated' in the ancient and modern senses, bravely disposing of boars, bulls and brigands. Plutarch says that Theseus's tomb is a sanctuary for runaway slaves, because Theseus defended the oppressed. This belongs to the tradition which made Theseus the model of the good king, of individual virtue and piety. A Bronze Age ruler, we might object today, would probably have been more completely bound by religion and social custom, by the established rites of the gods and the tribe, than Plutarch's or Miss Renault's character. If he joined the tribute-slaves the explanation would be found in some aspect of ancient Athenian lore rather than individual choice or a private religious experience. But Theseus, Mary Renault presumes, became a legend because he was uniquely gifted.

Something of the light of Apollo reflects on Theseus, Nikeratos thinks, when he looks at a bas-relief of god and hero. It might be argued that for Theseus the gods are transcendent, Poseidon a cosmic bull tossing the islands on his horns and shaking the sea, while for Nikeratos Apollo is imminent, integrity prompting him whenever he is tempted to betray his art or his loyalties to a lower self-interest. There is no general agreement among the Greeks of Nikeratos's time about the nature of the gods. Intellectuals find Homer's gods unholy. Nikeratos is shocked by the younger Thettalos's outspokenness: 'half the modern writers don't believe in them; the rest think like you and me, that they are somewhere or everywhere, but in any case not sitting in gold chairs on Mount Olympus, feuding and meddling like a brood of Macedonian royalty' (Chapter 15). A generation ago (in Sokrates's lifetime) such talk had been 'a hemlock matter'. *The Mask of Apollo* illustrates other attitudes, and the way different views coexist in thoughtful, undogmatic minds in periods of religious uncertainty. When Nikeratos becomes involved in a faction fight while he is costumed and masked for the role of Apollo, some of the onlooking countrywomen think it really is Apollo — and that amuses the actors. At the other extreme from popular belief, Plato reasons his way towards belief in God; numbers 'have the constancy of God' and cannot lie; in everything else 'we must test each step, learning never to love opinion more than truth' (Chapter 16). Advances in geometry had given Academicians an undue faith in reason. To a political philosopher, Nikeratos observes, life 'must be like a diagram of Pythagoras; but to me, man's life is a tree with twisted roots' (Chapter 11). He knows that in an actor of genius 'feeling can work like intellect, so clearly it forms its concepts' (Chapter 14). For Plato 'the gods' and 'God' are often interchangeable. For Nikeratos, as Thettalos says, the gods 'somewhere or everywhere' are powers and presences. Plato tells him that 'men see as much truth as their souls are fit to see' (Chapter 16); this, together with the theme of self-sacrifice, suggests a Christian interpretation of pre-Christian belief. Plato is a reminder of how Christian doctrine was to coincide with traditions of Greek thought. Nikeratos is closer than Plato to traditional belief. His Apollo mask can speak to him in the quiet of his room, and by dedication to his calling he can approach the divine nature as far as a man may. But his gods are no more human than Theseus's. Discussing *The Bacchae*, Nikeratos admits that Euripides may have set out to show 'that the gods are not' (Chapter 11). 'If so, someone crept up behind the poet and breathed down his neck when he wasn't looking. One thing I take it we may agree upon: the god of *The Bacchae* is not supposed to be like men.' Nikeratos's Apollo shares his delight in theatre and in excellence – but he belongs to a different order of being.

> The god is that which is. He is stern, radiant, gracious and without pity. A perfect chord is the friend of him whose strings are tuned to it. Can it pity the kitharist who fumbles?   (Chapter 1)

Thettalos asks Nikeratos if Apollo cannot be grateful. The answer is that 'he cannot change his nature which can light or burn' (Chapter 14). Men suffer from the gods when they ignore the fact that their humanity is not godlike: like Pentheus in *The Bacchae* (which is performed, with a beautiful commentary by Nikeratos, in Chapter 11) Dion suffers, ending as head of a police state, killed by his police.

Better in a novelist than the disposition of ideas about God is the character's feeling for the divine which arises from his calling. Nikeratos likes the Apollo mask which is old work, heavy olive wood carved to last, unfashionably severe with dark lidless eyes, because it seems right for the role: 'no one would say as they do before a modern Apollo, "Delightful! What a nice young man!"' (Chapter 1). Sponsors object that it 'lacks grace and charm'. Nikeratos's response is merged with his feeling for drama: 'I did not ask them what Apollo needs charm for, coming to speak of doom in words like beaten bronze' (Chapter 2). A mask-painter agrees with him, admiring the art of the last age ('What was it like when men had certainty like that?'), rubs it down to the wood and repaints, finding traces of lost features. The passages in which actor and painter 'restore' the god convey the particular religious sensibility for which a mask is a work of art and a supernatural presence – one might be reminded of the Nigerian Wole Soyinka's writings about the gods of the Yoruba;[17] something of this sense has survived, of course, in Mediterranean Christianity. Nikeratos's description of the temple-road at Olympia catches the way that several phases in the life of Greek religion coexist in his time.

> The great altar of Zeus, uncleaned since the morning sacrifice, stank and buzzed with flies. But there are always sightseers for the temple. The porch and colonnades were noisy with guides and cheapjacks; pedlars sold copies of Zeus's image in painted clay, quacks cried their cures, kids and rams bleated, on sale for sacrifice; a rusty-voiced rhetor declaimed the Odyssey while his boy passed round the plate. I went in from the hot sun to the soft cool shadows, and gaped with the rest at the great statue inside, the gold and ivory, the throne as big as my room at home, till my eye travelling upward, met the face of power which says, 'O man, make peace with your mortality, for this too is God'.

Apollo's warning is predictable. Its effect is in its climax to the sequence of images: seamy primitivism, mass-produced art, tourism and the peddling of culture, the sudden religious cool. Some scenes and sensations for which we have ready equivalents mingle with others – the morning sacrifice to Zeus – which we normally think remote, so that we share the impact of the god's expression on Nikeratos. Reviewing *Funeral Games* in 1982 Peter Green correctly said that 'the reader's extraordinary suspension of disbelief' is induced 'not (as with so many historical novelists) through her power to evoke people and places visually. . . . Miss Renault may not *see* the world of fourth-century Greece and Anatolia vividly but one suspects she can *feel* it, even smell it.'[18] That is true of all the novels. One of the best scenes in *The Mask of Apollo* is Nikeratos's supper with Dion and Plato at Delphi. Even after several readings nothing visual is recalled except the white Italian cup with a painted Eros which he is given as a souvenir, but every stage of the evening's moods and conversations comes back; a check shows that that is how Nikeratos has remembered it. His visual descriptions are dutiful and vague. Even the cliffs around Delphi are *felt* more than seen. As Nikeratos approaches the temple we sense rather than see the commonplace brightness and heat, filth and squalor, and the aimless crowds, as he is aware of them, and then sense with him the moment of awe.

The Last of the Wine shows the beginning of the breakdown of traditional morality in Athenian culture in the time of Sokrates. Kritias and more attractively Alkibiades have thought their way out of the good conduct of a citizen who puts the City's interests before his own and who fears the gods enough to respect a conventional communal morality and Greek moderation in everything. Kritias's position is expounded (Plato thinks rebutted by Sokrates) by Callicles in Plato's *Gorgias*; Callicles holds that morality was invented by the feeble-minded majority as self-protection from the able few who ought nowadays to see through the deception and act accordingly. The speech of the Athenian envoy at Melos, given in Thucydides, is the usual example of how such thinking worked in practice; it is a law of nature, the Melians were told, 'that the strong take whatever they can and the weak give it to them'; when Melos was taken the fighting men were killed, everyone else sold into slavery. Plato's Sokrates argues in *Gorgias* that it is better to suffer wrong than to do it (as Plato and Dion argue in *The Mask of Apollo*), but ends by recounting a Platonic myth of judgement after death, ordained by Zeus. In Renault's ancient world the immoralists are usually those who lack the true religious sense, which need not belong to an unthinking piety, or be lost with agnosticism. Nikeratos's happy childhood, his gifts and early success have helped to make him kindly, trustworthy and tolerant. At moments when good-nature is not enough, the mask on his wall alerts him to his moral duty. He suppresses his instinct to discourage young Thettalos, for example, whose talent he knows will surpass his own, and later overcomes his wish to keep the now beloved apprentice with him when Thettalos is ready to move on to another company, because the black eye-sockets of the mask rebuke him. Nikeratos is a better actor and a better man because he believes himself transcended; he is not quite his own master. That is a very feasible state for an intelligent and imaginative fourth-century mind.

Miss Renault's emphasis is on the integrity of the past which needs to be protected against our instinct to make it serve our present interests. The données of her Greek antiquity are buried deep in the story-telling. The narrators describe what catches their attention. What is strange to us is seeped through their familiarity with it. They occupy their modern world, conscious of a historical and a legendary past, and the reader gradually adjusts to their perspective. The dictators in Sicily are tyrants in a new style; Polycrates of Samos was another sort of *tyrannos* in different conditions. Simonides in *The Praise Singer* looking back from old age in the fifth century to Polycrates's regime, has already seen the meaning of 'tyrant' change. The author is concerned to guard against unhistorical reading by analogy, against facile translation of Greek terms into English. Passages are frequently introduced to shock us out of these almost irresistible bad habits. In Italy Nikeratos sees a play put on by Etruscans who perform bare-faced. He is indignant at this barbarism; and he expects us to agree, unconscious that we are barbarians. If we are beginning to read about his acting in the light of our own, here is a check. Another comes when Nikeratos says of a winsome but untalented colleague that 'some mocking god had given him a handsome face, the one beauty an actor can do without' (Chapter 1). The players in Arden's *Silence Among the Weapons* imply that not only bare faces, but also actresses are a natural result of progress in the history of the theatre. Nikeratos has scarcely dreamed of such a degeneration. His world, protected from the author's knowledge, finds its own fulfilments; art, religion, political systems are mature, sometimes declining, products of an old civilisation, not early stages in the evolution of our own. Marx thought ancient Greece to have been the childhood of mankind; Renault's ancient Greece is like the real one in being no more and no less childish than we are.

The Author's Note to *The Mask of Apollo* ends with a warning against looking for modern analogies.

No true parallel exists between this passage in Syracusean history and the affairs of any present-day state. Christianity and Islam have changed irrevocably the moral reflexes of the world. The philosopher Herakleitos said with profound truth that you cannot step twice into the same river. The perpetual stream of human nature is formed into ever-changing shallows, eddies, falls and pools by the land over which it passes. Perhaps the only real value of history lies in considering this endlessly varied play between the essence and the accidents.

Every sentence there invites a number of obvious objections. The drift is justifiable in the cause of protecting the past, but it is considerably modified by other remarks Mary Renault made about her work, and it is not entirely true to *The Mask of Apollo*. The author is occasionally noticeable in the background.

There are, for example, occasional jokes of which the narrator is unaware. Recovering from the shipwreck Nikeratos has a feverish dream in which he is playing the son of a king whose ghost calls for vengeance – but he is not Orestes – and he stands by a stage-grave with a skull in his hand: 'it would be nonsense, I suppose, like most dreams, if I could recall the whole' (Chapter 8). The realist illusion is not broken by such rare 'ludic' moments; Shakespeare seems to have indulged in them as a display of the strength of his illusion (Cleopatra foreseeing herself as a stage-character, *Antony and Cleopatra*, v.ii. 215, is a good example). In Renault's works, the author's sense of humour is lent to the characters, but in some passages of a different kind it creates a parallel with the modern world. Theseus is taken to a potter's workshop in a Knossan nobleman's house, and bored with the high-brow talk he fingers a lump of clay into the rough shape of a bull – the kind of artless work one sees from children or in markets in rural mainland Greece. His hosts are delighted: 'how he has understood the clay'. He has achieved what the latest craftsmen are attempting; after a thousand years of art, Theseus thinks, 'even beauty wearied them, if it was not new': '"You see", they said, "how we learn strength from the early forms"' ('Crete': Chapter 5). Sir Arthur Evans found periods of development, maturity and decline in all three eras of Cretan civilisation.[19] There is more than a hint, though, that we are awaiting our earthquake, bored with art and talking nonsense.

The Mask of Apollo, too, contains at least one scene in which Nikeratos's sense of Athens's decline seems to reflect the author's sense of a modern parallel. Thettalos is a new man of the theatre eager to experiment. When he suggests that a new play called 'Achilles Slays Thersites' should be played 'against the text' he speaks in terms which were common in drama circles in the 1960s. He argues with Nikeratos that it would be in the spirit of the times to play Thersites for sympathy. 'Thersites spoke for the common people. . . . It's anti-oligarchical. Let us show the common man rebelling.' Nikeratos thinks that Thersites spoke only for the mean and envious who 'hate great good worse than great evil'. 'God help the Syracusans if they recognise themselves in Thersites. They have forgotten greatness; all the more reason to remind them of it.' Nikeratos could play an Achilles to that Thersites, but he won't: 'I suppose because men could be more than they are. Why show them only how to be less?' (Chapter 16). He wonders afterwards how much of what he has said he has learned from Plato. Christopher Ricks's 'she knows not only the ancient world, but the modern world to which . . . it must be responsibly accommodated' comes to mind here because the presentation is clearly meant to comment on the modern world.

The search for parallels can go too far. Peter Wolfe's book on Mary Renault compares *The Last of the Wine* and Christopher Isherwood's *Berlin Stories*. They share the idea that unjust government turns people into beasts. Under the Council of Thirty, Renault's Athenians surpass the Spartans in wickedness and Wolfe is reminded of Isherwood's picture of Berlin in the 1930s; the attempts of the envoy Theramenes to appease Sparta suggest Chamberlain at Munich. Both books show the excesses of false 'democracy': contempt for excellence and a mean levelling of standards. Then Wolfe claims that 'like the death of Sokrates, the Bomb has introduced an age of commonness and collective impersonality, which has all but ruled out any dignified search for transcendent values'.[20] Wolfe's analogies put us in mind of the innumerable differences between the two books and the two worlds involved, but it is hard to read *The Last of the Wine* without some such reflections. It is a journalistic commonplace to talk in his terms about 'the Bomb' and about German and Russian atrocities which in some extreme views have paralysed all literary endeavour. Nathalie Sarraute asks: 'What invented story could compete with the accounts of the concentration camps?'[21] There are many possible answers. One is that a modern sense of the problem of evil can be reflected in a story based on real events, removed in time but still a part of our culture. In

Athens, in the period of *The Last of the Wine*, an enlightened sense of human opportunities was combined with horrific evidence of the deep instability of human nature. The life and writings of Plato are the most lasting result. Plato continues to occupy modern minds. His role in Mary Renault's Athenian novels could be read in the light of a study by a novelist and philosopher who is fully alive to the contemporary world: Iris Murdoch's essay *The Fire and the Sun* which discusses Plato's view of art and artists.[22]

'Plato temperamentally resembles Kant in combining a great sense of human possibility with a great sense of human worthlessness',[23] Iris Murdoch writes, and, 'of course the Greeks always took a fairly grim view of the human situation'; 'human life is not μέγα τι, anything much'.[24] Her formula for Plato's basic position is that 'human affairs are not serious, though they have to be taken seriously'.[25] In the closing chapters of both Mary Renault's Athenian novels human affairs come to seem almost hopeless. The rule of the Thirty with its gradual diminution of freedom and suppression of the forms of justice 'during the emergency', is eventually overthrown. Moderate oligarchs such as Xenophon and Alexias's father are shown to be wrong—the father is killed by the regime he has supported. But power corrupts the people, too; most are pleased at the banning of logic and the threat to Sokrates. Plato is obliged to go to his kinsman Kritias to save Sokrates—a tyrant can spare a just man, although for the wrong reasons, where a public trial would not. At the close of the novel Alexias can see that the now victorious democrats will be less merciful to this dissident, and we can see why Plato decided after Sokrates's death that an ideally just man would be a dissident under any then-existing form of government. His failure to create a new one with a philosopher-king, in *The Mask of Apollo*, is predictable in the case of Dionysios II; the scenes in which the young man shows off his half-learned Platonic wisdom, while the mercenary army frets under the fortress walls, leave Plato looking more impressive because he perseveres when his situation is ridiculous. Nikeratos sees how close to the absurd Sokrates is in Aristophanes, and Plato is when sold as a slave after his failed mission to Dionysios I, but he does not laugh at them. Dion's failure to make the Syracusans constitutional subjects, and his resignation to dictatorship, are predictable too: the people are accustomed to tyranny. A philosopher's rule can no more be installed by decree than democracy; although the fact that even moderately successful institutions take generations to develop is one which our own age finds very uncomfortable. Mary Renault is bleakest in her implication that the strength of Plato's vision is inextricable from its weakness. 'Plato', says Iris Murdoch, 'is a moral aristocrat, and in this respect a Puritan of a different type [from Kant] who regards most of us as pretty irrevocably plunged in illusion'.[26] Because the theatre fosters illusion, Plato banishes the artists. *The Mask of Apollo* contrasts two aspects of Greek culture: Plato represents the Puritanical, elitist, idealist Academy; and Nikeratos the festive, communal, open-minded theatre. Most people prefer the theatre and Nikeratos fears that Plato and Dion do not understand a crowd. His reading of *The Bacchae* makes Pentheus a moral aristocrat stricken by *hubris*; rejecting Dionysos he loses touch with humanity and with his own nature. Dion's features have been painted on the Pentheus mask at the performance at Syracuse; that is done on the orders of a political enemy, whom Nikeratos despises, but the connection is meant to remain in the memory.

The melancholy in which both Athenian novels end is the product of a realistic but not embittered scepticism. Only the gods are wise and happy; man's aspirations to wisdom and happiness have to be grimly regarded. They have to be taken seriously because 'men could be more than they are' and that determination is frail enough when set against the novels' background of overwhelming political failure to satisfy the postwar mood of disillusion. 'Sing of human unsuccess!' wrote Auden. Mary Renault did. She could see too that Thersites can be played for sympathy, in a theatre of the absurd; her characters Alexias and Nikeratos remain stubbornly resolved not to. They are unexceptional, but they have the dignity of the minor hero because they decline to be victims of events. Mary Renault has often been called a hero-worshipper and, in this sense, she was. It is not a Carlylean or a Nietschean adulation; it maintains only that one can, without illusions and more observed than aided by the gods, resist the indignities of the human situation. Nikeratos's respect for Apollo belongs to an imagined world which tries to be true to the past. For Miss Renault that meant truth to the present also. His precarious dignity in the theatre at Delphi is rightly admired by Dion and Plato, and by the modern reader, as he hangs by the single thread.

3 Mary Renault's *Fire From Heaven, The Persian Boy* and *Funeral Games*

Alexander the Great, admired and denigrated in his own time, has prompted imagination and provoked debate ever since. Every age comes to its own terms with him. The evidence allows for extreme and opposed views of his character and influence on events. Mary Renault was an admirer; and her novels about Alexander are full of her sense that he *must* have been as she interprets him. They are her most ambitious attempt to reflect the distant past in present consciousness and to make fiction from both.

Because it encompasses several civilisations, the story of Alexander offers a broad view of how peoples are divided, across frontiers and within, by the uneven pace of change. The 'fish-eaters' of the Asian coasts whom Alexander's admiral Niarchos discovers in *The Persian Boy*, live, as he thinks, like beasts, while city-life in Mesopotamia is millenia old. Babylon has settled down to a sense of its own history while Athens has changed in every generation for two hundred years. In Macedon Philip has recently created a modern army and an organised state from tribes who have herded and fought in the hills for centuries. Alexander is tutored by Aristotle; but reading the *Iliad* as a child he finds that the story 'could have happened any day in Macedon'. All the Renault novels present their characters' world in relation to its past; her people have a lively sense of how the modern coexists and mixes with various stages of the living past, and they feel appropriate awe and exasperation. Theseus is impressed by the age of the House of the Axe, Nikeratos by the old Apollo statue at Delphi, and Bagoas in *The Persian Boy* by the Egyptians, 'the oldest people, scornful in their long history' (Chapter 27). But the Matriarchy at Eleusis is social backwardness to Theseus, Boeotia to Nikeratos is a land not yet civilised enough to appreciate drama, and Alexander finds Epirus backward; the court there is typified by a royal bath of clay which is tiresomely antique, 'much mended and prone to leak' (Chapter 8). This is realistic, and by showing things in relation to earlier periods it complicates their relation to ours. Alexander experienced his time in its most recent and in its oldest characteristics; and his life touches our most modern interests.

When we relate the world Alexander knew to present day Europe, we are struck by the unevenness of our modernity. Aristotelianism and Buddhism (which Alexander encountered in Cashmir) are still with us. Warfare has become more efficient and is still ineffectively modified by human restraints. The idea that war is wrong was first publicised by Stoics a century after Alexander's lifetime; and it has made little progress. If we judge Alexander by the standards of his contemporaries we cannot consider the fact that he made war but only his standards of conduct. The social position of women has changed and is changing further in Europe, and the author's approval is apparent in her portraits of the women frustrated in their roles – Alexander's sister Kleopatra, Queen Sisygambis of Persia who, Alexander acknowledges, would have given him a harder fight had she been Great King, and the warlike princess Eurydike in *Funeral Games* who tries unsuccessfully to live with the freedom of action then available only to men. Homosexuality, a subject of special interest to Mary Renault, is now accorded a measure of public tolerance for the first time since pre-Christian antiquity. There is no general agreement on any of these matters today – religion, war, the role of women, sexual behaviour – in the world or even in England. The story of Alexander's conquests ought to be particularly interesting to us because they brought such a wide variety of cultures and stages of civilisation into close co-existence in an era remote enough for relatively unprejudiced consideration.

Alexander was a soldier of genius. His most committed detractors find it hard to dispel that reputation. He was a brilliant and tireless general. It can be objected that he did not live to show that he could rule the lands he had conquered; but while he lived men he had appointed ruled from the Danube to the Indus; when he died the empire fell apart. Miss Renault claims more; her case for his greatness agrees with Sir William Tarn's verdict:

> He was a great dreamer. To be mystical and intensely practical, to dream greatly and to do greatly, is not given to many men; it is this combination which gives Alexander his place apart in history.[1]

On this view, the first dream was to gain personal glory by conquest and by ruling magnificently. Since that involved ruling well and since his ideal of just rule derived from Xenophon's portrait of Kyros, he overcame the ancient apartheid between civilised (Greek or Persian) peoples and (Persian or Greek) barbarians, and created, in the hellenised Asia he brought about, the concept – and something of the practice – of a civilised world. This summarises the final tribute of Tarn's book.[2] Mary Renault's biography *The Nature of Alexander* objects that Tarn distorts the truth: Alexander's 'unprejudiced regard for quality in friends or enemies is expanded into an idealistic faith in the unity of all mankind'.[3] She is concerned as always to avoid ideological anachronism. But her character rejects the Greek view that non-Greeks are necessarily inferior to Greeks and acts accordingly in Persia. He escapes the confines of his own culture. Tarn rightly said that Asia 'felt' Alexander as no other Westerner in history.[4] That is an essential part of his nature as it is revealed in the novels. Whether any higher unity can allow for cultural differences, whether in fact peoples can come to live easily with the otherness of aliens is a question still unresolved. Edward W. Said's *Orientalism* (1979), which assumes that hostility between East and West began with the wars between the Greeks and the Persians, is pessimistic.[5] Mary Renault shows the difficulties which confronted Alexander's biracial policy and its failure after his death, with her usual blend of idealism and scepticism.[6] Napoleon complained that the world he knew was too old for great deeds, and envied Alexander. The world of these novels is old and complex, and as recalcitrant to human will as it has always been. Alexander's ability to act upon it and above all his willingness to dare the impossible made him a hero for the author. Some readers are likely to find her Alexander less agreeable than he is to her, but the issues of his life and the manner in which he lived them are both convincing as a story of the past and compelling as a story for today.

The story which emerges from the most sceptical reading of the ancient histories is a remarkable example of how much stranger fact can be than fiction. If Alexander had not existed no historical novelist who wished to be taken seriously would have dared to invent him, and the boldest flights of Miss Renault's imagination, where she is inventing, do not equal what is known to have happened. Tarn complains that many of Alexander's achievements are not fully appreciated because he was too successful – he concealed his art.[7] Even a novelist delighting in scenes of action is embarrassed by these riches. The Renault trilogy omits entirely the European campaigns and reintroduces Alexander as King in *The Persian Boy* after the death of Darius. Issos, Tyre, Gaza are reported briefly in the talk of Persian courtiers and Macedonian soldiers. 'Then the great cities fell.' Understatement and summary are essential to avoid overwhelming the reader with military achievements. Alexander's reputation as a general could have been illustrated from many more campaigns than are treated in the trilogy. The author concedes that she has been unable to detail all aspects of her Alexander's genius.[8] Given her commitment to telling the history of a period, *Fire from Heaven* and *The Persian Boy* are impressively effective books in their willingness to exclude history for artistic purposes. Direct narration of Alexander's conquests is restricted to the second half of the second volume of the trilogy.

More selective than before, Mary Renault is loyal as always to the past. None of the records made by Alexander's contemporaries has survived, although historians of the Roman period had access to them. Arrian's *Campaigns of Alexander*, written in the second century A.D., draws upon books by Ptolemy, the king's half-brother, and Aristobulus who was also with him in Persia. Plutarch's 'Life' of Alexander (and other writings) drew upon the large corpus of Alexander-books, some unreliable, in existence at the end of the first century AD; his approach to their relative values was less intelligent than Arrian's. Quintus Curtius, whom Mary Renault calls 'an unbearably silly man'[9] provides further, unreliable, information in his Latin *History*. The novels also draw on Athenaeus, for anecdotes, on

Diodorus Siculus for the lives of Philip and Alexander and for the events after Alexander's death covered in *Funeral Games*, on letters and speeches by Isocrates (who urged the case for Philip as war-leader of Greece), Demosthenes and his opponent Aischenes who both figure in *Fire from Heaven*. From Plutarch's 'Life of Demosthenes' Mary Renault takes the unflattering details with which she builds up a cruel picture of him. Plutarch's 'Alexander' is the main source for his early life in *Fire from Heaven*, for the want of any other. Scenes in Plutarch, such as the child Alexander's reception of ambassadors from Persia, and his taming of the horse Boukephalas ['Oxhead' in the novel][10] are interspersed with others invented on the basis of what must have happened – he must, for example, have had experience of war before being appointed Regent at the age of sixteen and cavalry commander, at eighteen, at the battle of Chaironeia. The third-person narrator shares the author's modern grasp of history and her psychological insight, which would not have been available to any of the characters; but there is no conspicuous intrusion of this 'omniscience', and the story often borrows the point of view of one of the main characters – Philip, Demosthenes or Hephaistion. Elsewhere, one reviewer put it, we look over Alexander's shoulder;[11] we are close to him and sense his thought and feelings but only rarely enter them. The first-person of the earlier novels was presumably abandoned for this book because there was no suitable narrator. Only Alexander knows enough to tell the story and he cannot be allowed a sufficient degree of foreknowledge to tell it.

Fire from Heaven, like all Miss Renault's books, offers various pleasures. It is an adventure-romance, an historical documentary, and a vivid study of character. It is as full of incident and emotion as any popular work of fancy, more exciting and passionate than most, and far better written. It is also a charming introduction to a phase of ancient history: we learn about Macedonian kingship and the Macedonian army, the tactics of the phalanx and the handling of the sarissa; of Philip's foreign policy, Demosthenes's opposition and the feuds between the city states which Philip exploits. The novel arouses and feeds such interests and it is natural to go on to read Tarn's biography or (since its publication in 1981) N. G. L. Hammond's *Alexander the Great*, and to the analytical studies, cited in their bibliographies, where everything becomes a question for debate. Mary Renault caters for kinds of curiosity they do not satisfy, showing the dusty old-fashioned Zeuxis décors of the palace at Pella, and giving the feel of its chill at night, its sounds and silences, the reek from the slave-pens when a city has been punished, dust in the air when the King holds manoeuvres. She conveys the differing moods of Pella, still in part a tribal chief's headquarters, barbaric to Persian or Athenian eyes, but becoming the power-centre of Greece, visited by statesmen, artists and philosophers. Few historical novelists are so good at setting a scene. The former study of King Achelaos (at the start of Chapter 3) contains a chair from Egypt where in their day sat Agathon and Euripides, and an old bronze of Hermes from Athens; the painted walls are obscured by racks of administrative documents, and a secretary labours at letters, shivering in the draughts, while the King sits relaxed, brooding on hegemony; the voice of his ten-year-old son is heard outside, greeting the guard by name. Alexander comes in resentfully, but is won by Philip's gift of a Scythian sling from Thrace; and they talk politics. The details are all correct. Set floating in the currents of the characters' minds — Philip's confidence nagged by anxieties, Alexander's curiosity overcoming suspicion, — they seem familiar.

Although the characters in *Fire from Heaven* are seen in a perspective which is larger than their own, the author directs our loyalties to Macedonians. This Philip is formidable. His vigour shows in his charm and intelligence and in his sensual coarseness. His barbed wit fuses a Macedonian contempt for southern pretension with a cultivated Greek's superiority towards ignorant hillmen: here he gets the best of both sides of his background. He plays a number of roles well — chieftain, diplomat, comrade, statesman, and, away from his wife, father; they suit him and he has learned to live them. In none of them is he the tyrant Demosthenes calls him and the novel persuades us that he must have charmed as often as he infuriated Alexander. As a husband he is a would-be tyrant and Olympias is not to be tamed. He wins sympathy because we often share his point of view. But Olympias's schemes, her rages and her almost destructively possessive love for her son are related to her impossible situation. She has a measure of the author's sympathy. Little is given to Demosthenes who appears to us as though to Macedonians, no soldier but a creature of mere words, and in Persian pay. This interpretation makes him a fanatic for a lost cause, not the devoted servant of a true one; his power is a proof that free city-state democracy has failed, and it is more a weak man's compensation than a strong man's devotion to duty. It is a defensible view, but there are passages depicting his inner life where the author's distaste for modern demagogues appears to have provoked her.

The novels' conception of their hero is contained in the first three scenes of *Fire from Heaven* (all in Chapter 1). The story begins with a very early adventure. The four-year old Alexander wakes to find a snake in his bed and takes it to his mother's room. He is already tactician enough to evade the guard at the door, and sharp enough, knowing what happens to slack guards at Pella, to conceal the man's name from his mother. The snake is his daimon, Olympias tells him; she has one of her own. Philip enters the bedchamber drunk, naked, one-eyed, horrifying as Polyphemos. The parents rail at each other ('How dare you bring your filthy vermin in my bed'); the child, 'taut with uncomprehended agony', attacks his father ('She hates you! She will marry me!'). Flung out by Philip, he is comforted by the guard who tells him how Herakles dealt with serpents and laboured 'to show he was the best'. He is wounded but the wound begins to heal.

'All Alexander's story testifies to the effect on natural genius of the deep insecurity felt in those tormenting early years.' This observation in *The Nature of Alexander* is the key to Mary Renault's fictional portrait.[12]

> What hidden agonies he endured remained his secret; suppressed perhaps even out of his memory. That he did not emerge a psychopath like Nero is one of history's miracles.[13]

The primal scene in *Fire from Heaven* establishes her vision of Alexander; his boldness and intelligence, the origins of his sense of a destiny to match that of Herakles, the situation of an only son with two wilful quarrelling parents, the comfort an unhappy garrison child can find in the friendship of soldiers. It is based on Plutarch who says that Philip's estrangement from

Olympias began when he found snakes in her bed, 'which more than anything cooled his passion for her'. This is credible. Whatever his personal revulsion – Philip was not squeamish – the Orphic snake-mysteries which the queen brought from Samothrace offended policy. Philip was sensitive to Athenian charges of Macedonian barbarism and concerned that his son be brought up as a modern Greek. Plutarch also says that Olympias was 'a woman of a jealous and implacable temper who set Alexander against his father'. Such a woman, Miss Renault says, must have taken offence early in her marriage. Macedonian kings were polygamous. Philip was notoriously promiscuous; he took several campaign-wives and one of his affairs with young men led to his assassination. Hence the insults flung across Alexander's head in this first episode, and the deeply unsettling home-life which is traced in the rest of the novel.

Alexander's worst battles in *Fire from Heaven* are fought before he grows up. His parents attack each other through him and he cannot mature in his relationship with either without offending the other and so injuring himself. On the day of Demosthenes's embassy, as his mother is fussing over his clothing to prevent him going to join the King, he admits that his father is right to despise Demosthenes. Olympias's fingers mismanage the pin of his cloak, drawing blood: 'the smart of the pin was soon forgotten . . . the other was like a pain he had been born with' (Chapter 3). In a later scene he reviews a campaign with Philip before visiting his mother. She bursts in, full of reproaches, and the first quarrel which follows her intrusion is between father and son. Philip and Alexander are trapped in alternating friendship and hostility because their periods of goodwill tempt Philip to win the boy's first loyalty away from his mother and provoke Olympias to claim it. The possible turns of the screw within such a family circle of love and hatred are universal, and novelists from Henry James to Angus Wilson have explored their ramifications in modern sensibilities. Mary Renault brings the expertise of modern fiction to this situation in an ancient royal household, observing the different conditions for what she rightly takes to be the same kind of unpleasantness. Alexander lives between the separate households of King and Queen; the usual move out of the women's quarters at the age of seven is less than complete because Philip provides a tutor in Leonidas who is severe even by Macedonian standards, while Olympias's rooms offer refuge and comfort. In her Epirote homeland the customs attending women's rule have lingered on; there a boy obeys his mother. Alexander is caught between two sets of cultural expectations about his role as a son. Since the King's approval is the mark of success for a Macedonian heir-apparent and military experience, essential if he is to have the army's support, dependent on it, Alexander is obliged to offend his mother whether he succeeds or fails in pleasing Philip. These niceties, which arise from Plutarch's hints, were beyond his comprehension or Arrian's interest. Mary Renault does them justice, keeping Freud in the back of her mind, ancient custom and religion to the fore.

The Oedipal aspect of Alexander's inner story is complicated by the possibility that Philip is not his true father: like Theseus he may be 'god-got'. The bed-snakes have caused one set of rumours; Olympias's report that she dreamed of lightning when her son was born, another; popular belief holds him to have been fathered by Zeus Ammon, in the form of a serpent or as 'the fire from heaven'. Olympias half-encourages him to think on these lines. His looks do not resemble his father's; as a worshipper of Dionysos she may not have been sure whom she had been with 'in the grove'. The question is introduced in the novel's second episode. Six-year old Alexander has heard in the guardroom that Ptolemy, known as Lagos's son, is his brother. Ptolemy, twelve years older, has to explain; then wonders whether the King's bastard has not a better claim than the Queen's. But bloody succession struggles are usual in Macedon, and Ptolemy is too sensible to want to complicate the next. Seeing the boy upset, he swears blood-brotherhood. 'If I die in a strange land you will give me my rites, and so I will do for you.' The balance of affection and embarrassment is delicately managed, establishing the value of Ptolemy as a lifelong friend who early senses Alexander's superior gifts, and his vulnerability. However Philip's sons came to terms in reality, they cannot have done so more fittingly. The words of the oath touch on our knowledge of their future; Ptolemy will give his brother his rites in Alexandria. This particular awkward moment, of a kind which must have been commonplace in Macedon where the charge of bastardy was a killing matter, is discreetly given its historical dimension.

Alexander's natural genius is illustrated in Plutarch by the richly ironic story of how Persian envoys were received by the young prince and questioned with precocious understanding. The third episode of *Fire from Heaven* enlarges on Plutarch, exploiting the irony. Alexander explains that his father is training the foot-companions in close-and-open order drill. 'They may be better today. They have been working hard at it.'

> The envoys exchanged delighted glances. It was all charming; the pretty grey-eyed prince, the little kingdom, the provincial naivety. 'The King drilled the troops himself.' It was as if the child had boasted that the King had cooked his own dinner . . .
> 'How many men has the Great King in his army?' Both envoys heard this aright; both smiled. The truth could only do good; he could be trusted, no doubt, to remember most of it. 'Beyond number,' said the elder. 'Like the sands of the seas, or the stars on a moonless night.'   (Chapter 1)

They list the forces at Ochos's command while Alexander listens 'like any child hearing marvels'. Then he asks them how long it takes them to assemble. 'There was a sudden pause.' Plutarch records these and related questions and, implausibly though predictably, says that the Persians recognised Alexander's genius. The Renault ambassadors are merely amused. Alexander asks them about the custom of prostration and assures the guests that Philip will not require it. 'The envoys clutched at their gravity. The thought of prostrating themselves before this barbaric chief . . . was too grotesque to offend.' The irony directed against them (Ochos, Arses, Darius, Alexander) is extended here, involving our awareness of how much the Macedonians in Persia were to resent prostrating themselves for Alexander. Few encounters in history convey so vividly mankind's disabling lack of foreknowledge, or how the 'normal' disposition of the world, which separates a Great King from a barbarian chief, conceals possibilities. Mary Renault's grasp of that truth is more convincing than Plutarch's fuss about early witnesses to the rising star. Alexander is convincing too, watching his etiquette, framing his questions and speaking with a child's disconcerting directness. Unlike Plutarch's prodigy, he is a quick-witted boy, eager to learn.

Mary Renault always wrote with relish of the pleasures of youth. She is sharper than her source in seeing through the surviving stories to a credible Alexander. Plutarch explains as 'high spirit' his refusal to run in the Olympics but misses the point she sees, that he knew others would let him win. In the novel Alexander's wits are sharpened as he negotiates a course between his parents and he develops a keen sense of their moods and unspoken thoughts. Watching his father for love-affairs, his mother for court-intrigues to stop them, he gains useful experience in reading people accustomed to guard their minds. Because he is so often glad to get away from his parents he spends spare time among the troops, soon knowing hundreds as friends. From them he learns the trooper's view of war, and acquires early his lifelong skill in winning their affection. That his love of Homer started young is suggested by Plutarch's reference to Lysimachos who styled himself 'Phoinix' to Alexander's Achilles. Plutarch dismisses this as a piece of flattery. In the novel, Alexander makes the Homeric world into an early established part of his imaginative life.

The novel proceeds in a continuous sequence of selected scenes, some based on Plutarch, others invented; it is among the best of recent stories about growing up, so skilful in its interweaving of the themes of Alexander's nature that 'conventional' seems an ungenerous term. The characterisation need not be less true, we are persuaded, because Alexander would not have understood it himself. It is conceived as an interplay of tensions. One is that pointed out by Tarn: the opposing influences of Aristotle and Olympias, 'a philosopher who taught that moderation alone could hold a kingdom together and a woman to whom any sort of moderation was unknown'.[14] Through them came the influences of Athens and of Thrace, of Greece and of barbarism. Aristotle taught the lesson of the ruler who is self-ruled; Olympias of the divine hero who fears nothing. Alexander can be pragmatic; he can be almost insanely reckless. He can be astutely analytical but he trusts his intuitions. He talks philosophy and he sacrifices black goats to Dionysos. He is Spartan in training and yet in some of his feelings, Macedonians think, as soft as a woman. He commands men efficiently when still in his teens, and in the bisexual ethos of Philip's Pella he causes them – *en masse* – to be at least half in love with him. Circumstances make him emotionally guarded but his instinct is to trust; he watches for personal slights but wants to give himself in friendship – as he does to his comrade Hephaistion. When he rejects Aristotle's teaching that barbarians are fit only to be slaves there are many factors at work on his judgement: he has known foreign hostages all his life; he has seen enough barbarism in his own family; Xenophon's *Cyropaedia* shows in a Persian king a hero whom he admires; as he admires the Trojan heroes as well as the Greeks, in Homer. Above all, his nature, educated but not ruled by Aristotle's teaching, disinclines him to believe that virtue proceeds from obedience to a single system. His own strong blend of positive qualities has to co-exist with an inner 'barbarism' of pain and doubt. The mature Alexander contains an unhappy child and a confused adolescent. It could be objected that the author shows too much approval of Alexander's exceptional resilience. A 'modern' Alexander ought perhaps to be destroyed by such an upbringing as his, made hopelessly neurotic by family conflict and alienated by the Aristotelian impact on his Macedonian heritage. The Alexander who faces his kingdom with outward calm at the end of *Fire from Heaven* is inwardly master of himself only by a heroic act of balance. The taming of the horse 'Oxhead' makes an appropriate symbol in this interpretation: Alexander will ride the world and, more daringly perhaps, his own life, against the odds. The ride is such a moment for him as Nikeratos's triumph on the fraying rope at Delphi. His success in such early trials is what comes most vividly from the stories in Plutarch and Arrian. He can seem far removed from us, as when he contemplates the dead on the battlefield at Chaironeia and shrugs off responsibility: 'it is with the gods' (Chapter 7). Perhaps he thought so when Thebes was taken and destroyed by an army under his command – an episode which this novel and its sequel avoid. But the quality shown in other incidents frees him from his background and we respond directly as every age has done. According to Curtius he received a warning on the march in Asia Minor that his doctor had been bribed to poison him. The doctor, a personal friend, had just prepared him a draught. He gave the man the letter to read and drank off the medicine. He lived in that style in Miss Renault's imagination. *Fire from Heaven* shows how he comes to it.

The Persian Boy deals with the last decade of Alexander's life, and it follows the narrative in Arrian's *Campaigns*. Modern historians have concentrated, in the thirty years following Tarn's *Alexander*, on discrediting the sources, especially Arrian, favourable to Alexander.[15] Mary Renault makes a vigorous defence of Arrian's reliability in *The Nature of Alexander*. Arrian states that Ptolemy is to be trusted because 'he was a king himself and falsehood would have been more shameful to him than to anyone else'. Mary Renault comments, in a passage which shows how her good sense can be almost, but not quite, completely convincing:

> Modern sniggers at Arrian's childish snobbery, evoked by these words, are themselves curiously naive. He is not of course attributing to kings a superior sense of honour, but stating the obvious fact that they are vulnerable to public disgrace. Ptolemy was more than a decade older than Alexander, who in turn had had in his army, towards the end of his life, many men at least ten years his junior. In a city like Alexandria, the recitals of the History — the method of publication in the ancient world — would have attracted plenty of alert veterans still in middle life, living on their memories. The founder of a dynasty cannot afford the ridicule of such an audience.[16]

Detractors, she goes on, are annoyed by the fact that the most 'favourable' sources derive from people who actually knew the man. When they say that Ptolemy flattered Alexander in order to enjoy reflected glory, they concede that his reputation twenty years after his death was not that of a corrupted tyrant. Doubts remain, but she has the support of logic, and on such logical grounds she constructs a biography intended to rebut detractors and clear away myths. The Alexander legends, in East and West, have been extensive and fanciful; he fights for Islam and for Christendom, in medieval romances.[17] The view that he was a corrupted tyrant began in Athens where Demosthenes's case against Macedon was improved by the

'Persianising' policy, by the executions of Philotas and his father Parmenion and by the murder of Kleitos. The devotion of nineteenth-century historians to the ideal of Athenian democracy caused George Grote and others to side with Demosthenes. Tarn's position has been widely attacked. F. Schachermeyer's *Alexander der Grosse* (1949) portrays a ruthless megalomaniac, and work in classical journals has tended to incline that way rather than Tarn's.[18] R. D. Milns's *Alexander the Great* (1968), meant for the general reader, claims to be a balanced view but is given to faint praise where not damning bluntly. Mary Renault's novels are combative history, aiming to establish beyond doubt Alexander's true genius and greatness. If our age is inclined to join ancient Athens in hating Alexander's excellence, she hopes to correct the inclination.

The Persian Boy has an ingeniously chosen first-person story-teller in the eunuch Bagoas who, according to Curtius, was a favourite of Darius given to Alexander by the Persian general Nabarzenes. He is mentioned in two other contexts as a member of the royal household, loved by the king and possessing in Curtius's view a sinister influence.[19] Mary Renault does not doubt his worthiness of Alexander's regard. Her Persian boy makes a well-informed narrator; he hears news of the invasion from the inner circles at Darius's court; later as Alexander's personal servant, skilled in eavesdropping, he sees and hears more than anyone else. As a hellenised Asian he watches the interaction of Greece and Persia from a privileged position. Such a love-affair, one reviewer reflected, would not do in modern Hampstead. It does very well here. Alexander is an exceptionally gifted man who has retained in maturity many of the inner drives of early youth; Bagoas is a remarkably gifted youth who has been compelled to exchange childhood, too soon, for the worldliness of a courtier. Neither, for different reasons, has much interest in sexuality, but it is easy to see why they might find each other attractive. Miss Renault's first purpose is to retrieve for history an interesting figure from the past and to do so she has to show his appeal to Alexander. The Western idea of a eunuch is probably the same today as it was in Greece in the fourth century, because equally based on ignorance. The Author's Note to *The Persian Boy* reminds us of the elegance, charm and social acceptability of the great eighteenth-century castrati. Bagoas is a gentleman's son, enslaved and castrated as a child when his father was killed in a *coup d'état*. After two wretched years of prostitution at Susa he is bought and trained for the King's service; beautiful, well-born and quick to learn elaborate ritual, he becomes Darius's favourite and so a person of consequence at court; he is with the last remaining entourage when the King is killed. Nabarzanes offers Alexander not an obscenely simpering minion but a trophy, certainly, and also an accomplished, intelligent and very well-informed Persian courtier, with some knowledge of Greek; he is precious to the royal chroniclers, more handy about the King's tent than the Macedonian squires, and useful as an adviser in the increasingly difficult dealings with the Persian nobility. One can believe that Bagoas would have been a valuable servant. In the novel's interpretation of Alexander, the perverse love-affair is made to seem natural.[20] They share a love of excellence. Bagoas is a skilled dancer, singer, horseman, traveller, Greek scholar and interpreter, Persian folklorist, nurse, valet, spy, poisoner, 'Chief Eunuch of the King's Bedchamber' (itself the height of an ancient profession in Persia), as well as courtier, gossip, dandy, and past-master of the oriental arts of love – these respectfully hinted at, rather than described, by Mary Renault. Alexander, who likes all things good of their kind, admires him and enjoys the Persian's subtle appreciation of his own quality. Bagoas regains his lost youth:

> At sixteen, in Zadrakarta, my youth began. Before, I had passed from childhood into some middle state, where youth was permitted only to my body. Now for seven years of my life it was given me back. All that long wandering has the taste of it.   (Chapter 14)

Once again he celebrates his birthdays (greatly prized, it appears, in ancient Persia); he discovers the pleasures of reading and all the tastes of adventure.

Several of Mary Renault's novels are, among other things, homosexual love-stories. Alexias and Nikeratos refer to their affairs with men as common practice and Theseus only disapproves because he associates it with the old-fashioned matriarchy which he overthrew in Eleusis. Tarn is shocked by the slander that Alexander loved a eunuch and dismisses as absurd the idea that his friendship with Hephaistion included sexual relations.[21] Miss Renault upsets the long tradition (seen in Dryden's 'The lovely Thais by his side'; she was in fact Ptolemy's mistress)[22] in which the world conqueror wins the world's loveliest girl, but she does so in the interest of history. It is now accepted that Alexander's marriages were formal. Her Note to *Fire from Heaven* insists that his contemporaries would not have considered homosexuality a dishonour, and Sir John Dover's *Greek Homosexuality* (1978) confirms this.[23] All the Renault novels emphasise the usefulness of homosexuality in ancient Greek society, as an educational and military bond, a way of humanising bleakly isolated communities of men, on campaign and in cities where women, except for the expensive and probably fastidious hetairai, were neither educated nor accessible outside marriage. Womanising is in many ways more socially disruptive. 'Better a boy than a woman' is Alexander's attitude to Philip's love affairs; his own troops are indignant about his barbarian wife, Roxane; undismayed by his Persian boy. There are passages in all the books where the author's enthusiasm fails to save Greek mores from seeming tiresome; in others they seem more sensible than ours. This is obviously an area in which the truth (long censored) about the distant past can apply to issues not yet resolved in the present day. Mary Renault censures Tarn, in this connection, for having defended Alexander 'where he can scarcely have thought his actions needed extenuation' – another case of 'the fatal commitment which vitiates conscientious fact with anachronistic morality'.[24] John Dover's book ends by chiding 'the modern sentiment . . . "it's impossible to understand how the Greeks could have tolerated homosexuality"'.[25] *The Persian Boy* is meant to promote understanding.

The meeting of East and West which is historically the most interesting aspect of Alexander's conquests is presented in the context of this relationship. Bagoas's attraction is mixed with the appeal Persia has for Alexander; but to Bagoas Alexander is, though beloved, a barbarian to be civilised and assimilated. In the first part of *The Persian Boy* he is seen from Darius's court as an unpredictable outlander. A senior eunuch tells Bagoas how Alexander has captured the royal tent: 'he stared like a peasant . . . however he soon moved in, like a poor man with a legacy'. He also tells the story (from Arrian) of how the Persian Queen Mother was offended by her captor's sending her wool to weave, as one would to a peasant wife, or a queen in Macedon. Later 'I tried to picture this strange and wild barbarian in the palace at Babylon I knew so well' (Chapter 7). Bagoas enters Alexander's service with dismay at the prospect of being barbarised himself. He is shocked by coarse food, public nakedness, pollution of sacred waters, no reverence about the King; 'I looked about for the perfume sprinkler but could not find it' (Chapter 10). Although he later comes to a more just appreciation of the Macedonians, he never likes their customs.

> I had long heard that Queen Olympias had been a turbulent jealous woman, who taught him to hate his father. This, I thought, is what comes of having no one trained to manage their harems properly. I could have sunk with shame.
>
> (Chapter 16)

Bagoas is a hero-worshipper, and even the most fascinated reader will not accept uncritically all his views of Alexander. The narrative itself is a *tour de force* as the work of a cosmopolitan Persian and life-long royal servant who can be witty and cool even about his intensest adolescent passions and who remains dignified about even the most grotesque indignities. But he pays certain tributes unconsciously. His moments of modern-seeming human sympathy come among so much that is alien – though he gives it charm – to us that the moments seem to derive from Alexander's influence. Bagoas will poison an enemy or watch inscrutably as a prisoner is tortured; he can rule a harem and could rule a kingdom if set to it. But we believe him when he admits that the hanging of his father's killer, towards the end of Alexander's reign, gives him less than the proper satisfaction.

> He kicked and writhed, on the high gallows against the wide sky of Pasargadai. I was ashamed to find it distasteful and take so little pleasure in it; it was disloyal to my father, and ungrateful to Alexander. I prayed . . . 'Accept this man through whom you died . . .'   (Chapter 25)

A sensibility is shifting here, and it is plain how the change has started. The Macedonian King of Persia and the Hellenised Persian eunuch make an extraordinary pair. If Mary Renault has retrieved a vestige of the past, here, it is one of the most eccentric friendships in history. She makes it seem worthwhile.

Alexander's 'atrocities' in Persia, observed by a cultured Persian, appear in a different perspective from that of history books, ancient and modern. News of the burning of Persepolis reaches Bagoas when he is still with Darius; it is further evidence of barbarism, in Persian eyes, but even there it is realised that an army cannot be kept indefinitely from looting. (Babylon and Susa, having surrendered, have been spared.) Bagoas learns from Alexander's soldiers their revulsion at the Persians' mutilation of Greek prisoners, and the murder of the wounded at Issos, avenged at Persepolis. Mary Renault assumes, with Arrian, the guilt of the Captain Philotas whom Alexander executed for treason; and Bagoas pleads that this necessitates the subsequent killing of Philotas's father, Parmenion, whose blood-feud would have led to civil war. Alexander's killing of his old friend Kleitos in a drunken after-dinner quarrel was murder: Macedonian kings had no right to kill their subjects. Arrian records and the novel portrays Alexander's remorse. But to Bagoas, who says that Kleitos would have had to beg Darius for the easy death he got, Alexander's spear-throw at the dining-table is merely undignified. A Persian Great King would have motioned with one finger to his guard. Alexander's barbarism, as Bagoas judges it, seems more akin to our own.

Its worst feature, to a Persian, is informality; Bagoas helps persuade his master to require 'the prostration' from Greeks and Macedonians. The more we are tempted to share, in his beguiling narrative, a Persian's view that the ritual bestows dignity on King and courtier, and his contempt for the Greeks who resented it as boors, the more we sense the incompatibility of the Eastern and Western cultures Alexander's policy tried to reconcile. The central scenes of the novel concern the profound conflict of values which prostration represents. In becoming Great King, Alexander has committed himself to an Asian empire which in Greek terms can only be civilised by the use of an un-Greek style of absolute power, and which in its own older and more rigid terms is fully civilised already. Having his own robes cut in a Graeco-Persian compromise Alexander looks poignantly helpless before the historical forces he is trying to turn. Bagoas yearns to see him truly civilised (or thoroughly Persianised), while the Athenians think that he has already become a barbarian. The novel touches here on issues which are left unresolved at Alexander's death. They have not been resolved today, and although the novel never obtrudes a hint of 'parallels' with the modern world, we follow this encounter between civilisations with a sense of how its implications bear outwards through history towards our own time.

The novel's largest questions are posed as in life, ramifying and finally unanswerable. In the weeks before his death Alexander is an almost defeated figure, close to madness after Hephaistion's death, wounded by the Macedonians' recalcitrance at the Indus where they forced him to turn back, and at Opis where they mutinied. But his foremost gift is resilience and there are signs that he has scarcely started work. In the context of the trilogy his death is a great open question, and the great loss to those who have known him is conveyed, without sentimentality, in the last pages of *The Persian Boy* and throughout *Funeral Games*.

The wide range of mostly military and political action taken from Diodorus Siculus (Books XVIII and XIX) requires a constant shift of viewpoint in *Funeral Games* and this is unsettling after the first two novels of the trilogy. Many reviewers complained of disunity.[26] As the scene moves from Babylon to Macedon or to Egypt or to desert or mountain camps, we share the thoughts of Alexander's generals, as they compete for power; of Perdikkas, Ptolemy, Eumenes, Peukestas, and Kassandros; of his wives the Baktrian Roxane and the Persian Stateira; of Bagoas; of Alexander's half-wit brother Philip whom the Macedonians made king and of his enterprising wife Euridike; of Olympias. The only unity comes from the lack of a central figure and the common consciousness of the absence of Alexander.

The transitions of scene and viewpoint can give the impression of a series of fragments from unwritten Renault novels. In the few passages where he reappears it is intriguing to see Bagoas as others see him. To Ptolemy he has been 'simply a tactful and well-mannered concubine' but now is a puzzling and formidable figure; his interest for us, who have known him better, is quickly revived in the new circumstances. When we are briefly allowed access to his point of view it is tempting to think that his story might have made a better novel than the one we have, even at the risk of too much reported off-stage action, and of too prominent a role for an historically very minor figure. Bagoas had a far stronger claim on the novelist in Mary Renault than on the historian. The ambiguities of his social role and his character might have been explored further. But nothing is known about what became of him after Alexander's death; and the historical evidence for the relatively dull captains and kings was too good for her to resist. *Funeral Games* is exceptional because it sometimes makes one regret that Miss Renault was so conscientious in her respect for history; for the earlier Alexander novels history lived up to all her talents. Bagoas's part, and the scenes which show the mourning of Olympias and Sisygambis are as fine as any in her work, but elsewhere we lack the usual sense that she lived imaginatively with her characters. In consequence, much of the brawling and warring among the Macedonians is, by Mary Renault's usual standards, thin. Like *The Bull from the Sea* – and *The Praise Singer* – *Funeral Games* is a very competent performance well within the author's powers. Within the trilogy, however, it acts as a reinforcement of the bleaker aspects of the period.

The story of feuds and civil wars is one of almost unrelieved failure, Ptolemy's Alexandria where Bagoas takes refuge being the only bright exception. Most of the characters are murdered or executed, many of them in spectacularly horrible fashion. 'It has indeed been necessary, for the sake of continuity, to omit several murders of prominent persons', the author notes. There is a spirit of melancholy absent from the earlier novels, and a larger share of attention is given to the victims of war, including the women, and the child Alexander IV. One point is of course that none of Alexander's able and experienced generals could control the empire he had ruled. A connected point in her defence of Alexander is that atrocities were exceptions to his rule, commonplace afterwards. Re-reading the trilogy after *Funeral Games*, one is more aware of how she shows his age, so full of new ideas and new ventures, to have been locked in ancient brutalities. After Philip's capture of the Greek city of Olynthos, in *Fire from Heaven*, he enslaves the citizens.

The boys of Macedon saw the hopeless convoys pass, the children wailing in the dust as they trudged at their mothers' skirts. It brought the millenial message. This is defeat: avoid it.   (Chapter 2)

A civilised city or kingdom is a short-lived triumph over barbarism; its own civilisation is a series of compromises with barbarism and within the most civilised man civilisation is precarious. The Alexander of these novels deserves to be admired by the criteria established in the earlier books. He and his empire are 'nothing much' by the standards the mind can envisage for human affairs; in the setting of the real thing, he represents the best kind of endeavour.

4 Anthony Burgess: *Nothing Like the Sun* and *Napoleon Symphony*

The perspective of Anthony Burgess [John Anthony Burgess Wilson] in his two historical novels is that of a teacher who is also an entertainer. Both roles are natural to Burgess. He is a witty, often somewhat frivolous literary journalist and broadcaster. He has been a schoolmaster, a colonial education officer and a university teacher: there is a pedagogic element in much of his work.[1] His liking for wordplay, for intellectual puzzles and coarse jokes, for pattern rather than plot, and cyphers rather than character, has drawn him to the fashion for 'ludic' blending of fiction with literary and verbal games. The modern novelists he most admires are in the 'ludic' tradition: James Joyce, Ronald Firbank, Flann O'Brien and Vladimir Nabokov. But the aesthetic and sceptical side of Burgess's mind coexists with an appetite for realism, for facts and, above all, for tradition. He conceived *A Clockwork Orange* as 'a work which combined a concern for tradition and a bizarre technique'.[2] As a critic he works within orthodox bounds. Besides his studies of Joyce, he has written a sound book on Shakespeare for the general reader, and a students' history of English Literature.[3] His historical novels are well-researched and accurate in detail, and full of their author's evident wish to communicate his own information and understanding. Burgess's achievement in *Nothing Like the Sun* (1964) and *Napoleon Symphony* (1974) is in having combined his urge to instruct with his instincts for comic sabotage.

Shakespeare and Napoleon present, in many respects, contrasted problems. A novel about Shakespeare offers a challenge to write English worthy of the subject: Shakespearean English, as Burgess proves, is just within the scope of contemporary literary language. To write about Napoleon in English is to misrepresent the subject almost as badly as Shakespeare would be misrepresented in French. Very little is known for sure about Shakespeare's life; we know more about Napoleon than a novelist can hope to accommodate. Burgess writes on the assumption that his readers know the stories and have thought about them already. In each case the fictional and historical problems are 'foregrounded', to use a term common in discussions of ludic literature: the limitations imposed on the writer by his material are made clear to the reader. The perspective, imaginative speculation starting from the evidence but ending in fantasy, is represented as a game. *Napoleon Symphony* attempts what is frankly admitted to be impossible: a verbal equivalent to Beethoven's *Eroica*. *Nothing Like the Sun* poses as a drunken end-of-term substitute for a lecture. In each case we are meant to be conscious of a modern mind playing with what it knows of the past. Although the game is played irreverently, the knowledge is always treated – sometimes almost pedantically – with respect.

The Foreword to the 1982 paperback reprint of *Nothing Like the Sun: A Story of Shakespeare's Lovelife* reflects the two elements of Burgess's talent. He begins by introducing a light-hearted squib but ends by claiming a responsible work of art. Most reviewers, he says, 'failed to see that the story . . . was presented in the form of a drunken lecture given to students in a Malaysian college'. The book's dedication is from 'Mr Burgess' to 'his special students', 'who complained that Shakespeare had nothing to give to the East'. The Foreword continues in the same tone. The lecturer 'seems especially irresponsible' in stating that Shakespeare's tragedies were influenced by syphilis acquired from an East Indian dark lady and that he was cuckolded by his brother Richard (a theory Joyce proposed through Stephen Dedalus in *Ulysses*). We are told that readers have missed the acrostic presence in the text of the name Fatimah and the Arabic word *Fatmah*, 'destiny'.[4] The tone changes towards the end of the Foreword. 'For the rest, the known history of Shakespeare's life has not been tampered with: the exterior biography is probably correct, and the interior or invented biography does not conflict with it.' 'Professor S. Schoenbaum, the expert in Shakespearean biography and author of *Shakespeare's Lives* was good enough to say that it is the only novel about Shakespeare which functions as a work of art.'[5] 'The book is intended to be a presentation of life and real people, who remain very much the same whether in the proto or the deutero-Elizabethan age.' The last three claims are those of a sober lecturer: the novel is true (as far as possible) to biography, to art, and to human nature.

There are so few facts about Shakespeare's life that most educated people know most of what there is to be known. Speculation, even at a scholarly level, has always been somewhat reminiscent of a parlour-game. Schoenbaum's study shows how various and incompatible the sensibly-constructed lives have been, and how absurd the rest. Only a sceptical sense of humour, it seems, can save those who pursue biography in the *Sonnets* from the way that madness lies. We can only guess, and as E. K. Chambers wrote about Shakespeare's early life 'it is no use guessing': 'the last word for a self-respecting scholarship can only be that of nescience'.[6] Schoenbaum ends by doubting whether narrative biography of Shakespeare is possible in our present Socratic state – of knowing, better than past periods, what we do not know. But he then concedes that 'the subject still beckons': 'every age craves its own syntheses', and we know more than our predecessors about the background.[7] An historical novelist who writes about Shakespeare knows that he must invent most of the story and he should make it clear that he is inventing. However brilliant, no account of Shakespeare's daily life is to be taken very seriously as biography. Burgess's approach satisfies Schoenbaum's requirements. His preface offers a bravura end-of-term performance – not a wholly serious part of the course.

The story is interrupted from time to time by reminders of the lecturer with his bottles of *samsu*. 'Another little drop. Delicious. Well, then' begins the sixth chapter of the book's first, Stratford Section (p. 38. Page references are to the 1982 Penguin edition). The 'I' of the Epilogue is ambiguous: 'I am near the end of the wine, sweet lords and lovely ladies' (p. 224); 'Questions? You wish to know how ventriloquial all this is, who is really speaking?' (p. 233). Mr Burgess is speaking for Shakespeare; the reader is not meant, here, to yield to an illusion. Mr Burgess has placed the cryptic signs of his character's 'destiny' in a sonnet of his own composition. 'Fatimah', the golden Firbankian lady, is only a jest. When WS 'dies', breathing 'my Lord', we are asked to applaud the lecturer, not grieve for the Bard. The students who complained that Shakespeare had nothing to give to the East are whimsically answered. His son by Fatimah was sent to her own country: any of the 'special students' the dedication affectionately names, Miss Alabaster or Mr Ahmad bin Harun, may claim descent; frontiers are illusory, and Shakespeare belongs to the world.

'We have but to open a door that any key will fit.' In this spirit, we may say that the lady of the *Sonnets* is a beautiful Malay. We may say that she represents the goddess of his dreams, a creature of desirable dark flesh, and a Muse who will lead him to a vision of evil. From the flesh we might imagine him contracting syphilis; from the Muse a knowledge of metaphysical disease.

> The foul wrong lay then beyond a man's own purposing; there was somewhere, outside time's very beginning, an infinite well of putridity/. . .

So the poxed WS reflects. Burgess reflects, his lecturing voice sounding through Shakespeare's, that this 'is a modern disease'. It is of course a reading of Shakespeare for the 1960s. The uninhibited bisexual eroticism of the WS of the novel is, though not the cause, closely connected with his genius. The same Muse who frees him from Puritan morality shows him the heart of darkness; the mature plays 'show' the evil of the concentration camps, and the possibility of nuclear war.

Any emphatic interpretation of Shakespeare is partial, and there are various objections to this one. 'Lust', to Elizabethans, was only one aspect even of the most amorous relationships, and different from the modern concept of 'sexuality'. Shakespeare's humanism transcends his knowledge of evil and the tragedies have impressed most people with their affirmation that evil can be withstood. There is no reason to agree with Burgess that Shakespeare must have written comedies when he was happy and tragedies when life went wrong.[8] Ivor Brown is one biographer who made that assumption. Finding (though one need not) that the Jacobean Shakespeare is radically different from the Elizabethan, he supposed that the Bard was 'plagued with boils' soon after 1600.[9] 'Burgess is even more ruthless; his 'subjectivism' is equally dubious. But Shakespeare criticism is a debate in which the balance shifts from one period to the next. Burgess is justified in objecting to the prudish respectability so many biographers imposed on the public image of a 'national poet'. Schoenbaum cites a newspaper tribute to C. W. Wallace's research: 'Prof. Wallace's Remarkable Analysis of 3,000,000 Documents which Prove the Immortal Bard Never to Have Been a Roistering, Reckless Profligate'.[10] At a higher level of historical responsibility, E. K. Chambers's sonnet pictures a cleansed Shakespeare who 'caught tragic hints of heaven's dark way with men', as will any thoughtful civil servant, before shaking off misgivings in retirement among 'the little streets of Stratford-town':

> I like to think how Shakespeare pruned his rose,
> And ate his pippin in his orchard close.[11]

It is understandable that Burgess likes to think differently; one extreme tends to provoke the other.

The 'inner, invented biography' of the novel is fantastical and admits to being so. In treating the outer, relatively verifiable, Shakespeare, Burgess can sound very conventional. WS possesses Keats's negative capability. His own rather passive personality is, as many reviewers have pointed out, rather like Enderby's.[12] There is an impressive cast of minor characters who represent major historical figures, but Marlowe, Chapman, Jonson, Kemp, Burbage are only outlines; Burgess has none of the power to create characters with which Mary Renault brings Philip of Macedon to life. But they are accurate sketches, true to what we know of their originals. The exquisite gallants wonder at sweet Master Shakespeare's conceits as Francis Meres's *Palladis Tamia* tells us they did.[13] Fancies are loosed from a firm base of historical responsibility. However far he is willing to let whimsy take him, the lecturer in Burgess wants the facts known.

WS is the son of a Stratford glover whose fortunes are in decline; his mother is an Arden and proud of it; he is the eldest of the children — one sister is known as 'greasy Joan'. At eighteen he marries Anne Hathaway, an older woman; there are three children. He becomes a successful poet and actor-playwright in London, is with the Lord Chamberlain's Men by the late 1590s, already recognised as a poet and rich enough to buy the big house in Stratford at the age of thirty-three. His acquaintances include the Stratfordian Richard Field whose shop in the Blackfriars printed *Venus and Adonis* and *The Rape of Lucrece*, and London theatre people including Philip Henslowe the theatre-owner and diarist. These are facts. Many of the story's assumptions are those of responsible biographers. Will has been at the grammar school under Thomas Jenkins and left early to learn his father's trade; in adolescence he is 'a word-boy' and a reader of Ovid and North. He courts Anne Whateley of Temple Grafton (who may be no more than a clerical error on his marriage licence), but is compelled to marry the elder, shrewish, pregnant Anne of Shottery (as in Ivor Brown). He works briefly as a private tutor, Englishing Plautus for the boys to act, and then as a lawyer's clerk. In London Henry Wriothesley, Earl of Southampton (to whom *Venus* and *Lucrece* are dedicated) becomes the loved boy of the *Sonnets* (and the Mr W. H. to whom they were dedicated in 1616). George Chapman is the *Sonnets*' 'Rival Poet'. None of this can be proved but most of it is, as an outline, orthodox interpretation. John Aubrey believed that 'he had been a schoolmaster in the country'.[14] Burgess's idea of a private tutorship makes sense; the young Shakespeare would have been able and cheap. The Dark Mistress of the *Sonnets* could have been anyone. Burgess's Fatimah (known as 'Lady Negro') is not a new idea. In 1861 a William Jordan suggested that she might have been a negress. In 1933 G. B. Harrison made her a 'notorious Black Woman', *Lucy Negro*, Abbess of Clerkenwell.[15] Burgess reserves the horrors of the pox for his last few pages.

Shakespeare's mind and opinions must be learned, if at all, from the works. Here again Burgess as lecturer wants to convey the conventional outlines. WS grows up impatient with provincial Puritanism ('cheesy Banbury cant'); he is undismayed to hear Florio talk about Montaigne, but too cautious to join the School of Night or risk Marlowe's name for atheism. A Stratford boy, he means to restore the family fortunes (and be, perhaps, 'as great a Stratford's son as Clopton ever was'); the theatre is a better trade than gloving, and he must send money home, but as a gentleman he would sooner be a poet than a playwright. Prentice riots confirm his burgher's love of order. He dreams of giving Hamnet a better start in life, and borrows money from Southampton to buy himself a theatre share. Fascinated by aristocrats, but disapproving, he fears political involvement and warns Southampton against joining the Essex faction. Other passages illustrate his mind and art, especially the bearing of the Globe's motto; '*Totus mundus agit histrionem* . . . The whole world, no, all the world acts a play, is a stage . . .' he tells himself (p. 214). This is Mr Burgess, tipsy at the end of term but still very well informed on his subject, in a sprightly lecturing style.

Elsewhere the author makes specific class-room points. *The Rape of Lucrece* is published and it rapes its readers' senses, 'though many saw in it a sterner moral core, a stiffer and maturer view of virtue (not the seeming virtue of the innocent but the achieved virtue of the experienced) than in the earlier poem' (p. 125). Some cruces are irresistible:

I made Ariadne and Arachne one, a fair heroine become a spider by virtue or vice of her labyrinthine weaving. Ariachne. Some cold man some day, reading, will cure that name.   (p. 228)

This helps to promote the quarto/Folio reading at V. ii. 149 in *Troilus and Cressida*; nobody knows if the coining is Shakespeare's or the printer's; and nobody knows whether Shakespeare could foresee how editors would attempt 'cures'. WS constantly reflects on his art in terms which are conveniently suited to a modern student of the plays. He is sometimes troubled about Greene's charge that he borrowed others' feathers. Are the last words of *King John* filched from a pamphlet (p. 161)? 'A manner of thieving.' He is a patcher, a glover still, 'five feet instead of five fingers' (p. 79). In the early years he envies his rivals. There is real poetry in *Friar Bacon and Friar Bungay*; Greene is closer to Marlowe than WS will ever be; despite 'the filthy lodgings of Greene, the bloodshot staring eyes of Marlowe', they have 'true nobility of soul' (p. 85), thinks WS at the time of writing *King Henry VI*. Sidney's *Defence* is out at last; Sidney is wrong about right tragedies and right comedies. Jonson, a bricklayer who knows Greek, builds good plays, but his humours are not the truth about people. Humours are mixed, in all of us; Jonson's satire is only a part of poetry. All this is routine classroom comment. It is entertainingly presented, and so is the (questionable) view that Shakespeare disliked having to work for the stage; that he loathed the foolery of Kemp, the taste of the groundlings, and the 'word-hungry wind'.

In one of the novel's boldest critical performances the adolescent Shakespeare composes a sonnet while the family bicker around him (pp. 16–22). He has been dreaming of a dark goddess, a mistress and a muse. She promises that he is to be 'possessed of all time's secrets', that his mouth will 'grow golden and utter speech for which the very gods waited and would be silent to hear' (p. 9) – which nicely turns the highest pitch of Romantic bardolatry into a typical versifying youth's daydream about his future genius. Bretchgirdle the parson has lent him books; he reads Ovid in Golding. A sonnet's shape, he knows, must be that 'first made by the Earl of Surrey' to allow for English's poverty of rhymes. Words chime, 'Fair is as fair as fair itself allows'. Paradox gives a structure, 'And hiding in the dark is not less fair'.[16] The clinching couplet is seven times more work than the twelve before; 'And, childish, I am put to school of night/For to seek light beyond the reach of light'. 'It is very poor stuff, but I was only young', he judges later (p. 172). The juggling with light and dark, the hesitant fitting of stopped lines into rhymed quatrains, and the already smooth matching of voice to blank verse show what the juvenilia may have been, and the Shakespeares' quarrels which almost quench the faint dawn of Will's talent are suitably humdrum. Joan whines, 'Will is crazy and lazy'. His father wants his apprentice back, 'Come thy ways, Will'; mother nags about 'idle versifying' and the shame of selling silver, like to end with 'digging hollows in the table'. But she crosses herself when her son reads his lines aloud, and shudders; incantation is magical in Stratford, where old mad Madge is whipped as a witch in the street, in times of drought. Simple-minded brother Gilbert has just seen God 'with's hat on, a-walken down Henley Street'. Brother Dickon 'is all dirt and feared to come home'. WS has no notion yet that the life and language around him are to give his writing more than a sonneteer's facility. The author knows: his sonnet is a thin tissue of artifice compared to the live speech he recreates for the Stratfordians.

Burgess is a committed writer in his concern about language. 'There is too much grey prose about',[17] he has said; and his own work is meant to brighten contemporary English. A novel about Shakespeare offers a wide range of linguistic opportunities and here the past is firmly a part of the present. We know Shakespeare in his language; Elizabethan English is close enough in everything but syntax and spelling for a novelist to borrow. The chief attraction of the period for such a writer as Burgess is the fund of words and idioms waiting to be revived by the historical novelist who can use them and hold attention for the length of a book. The brightest parody quickly cloys. Burgess's Foreword stresses the brevity of a work which required so much effort, implying regret that he dared not try our patience further; no doubt he could have gone to three times the present length (of about ninety thousand words) and no doubt he was right not to. For the stream of Shakespeare's consciousness, he avoids the problem of choosing between cumbersome or anachronistic sentence-structure by imitating his second-favourite author, Joyce:

> Goat. Willow. Widow. Tarquin, superb sun-black southern king, all awry, twisted snake-wise, had goat-like gone to it. So *tragos*, a tragedy. Razor and whetstone. But that was the other Tarquin. WS saw great-bellied slack whiteness in the spring of a southern country, a Lucy lawn peacock ghost-aglimmer, Arden, patrician, screaming. No willow she. But a willow was right for death. He watched the strange back-eddy under the arch. Back to the strait that sent him on so fast. As great a Stratford's son as Clopton ever was? He seemed to himself to be dreaming of dreaming of straining after some dark image just beyond the tail of his spaniel eye.   (p. 4)

This is from the second page of the novel. WS at fourteen is juggling with images: what he has seen at the bedroom door, the lambs for Good Friday dying 'maa aa aa', Tarquin raping Lucrece, Clopton's bridge and Stratford greatness. His sister Anne speaks of 'goat-willow' and the words begin to swarm. Goat gives goatish Tarquin, a patrician rapist known from Ovid: Arden is a patrician name at home; razors and whetstones are for lambs in the market; the other rapist Tarquin was Sextus not Lucius (Lucy?) Superbus, the Italian king; a willow is right for Lucrece's death. The eddy under the arch of Clopton's bridge recalls his thoughts of fame; the spaniel revolves like the eddy, eye chasing tail; whiteness, for lawn-white skin and for ghostly death, contrasts with sun-dark lust and Will's dream of the dark goddess. Commenting on Joyce (or Shakespeare), we might link superb with 'peacock' and peacock with the other 'lawn' seen at patrician houses; 'loose' and 'see' might be linked with 'Lucy'. Burgess means this to be the origin of a passage in *The Rape of Lucrece*:

> As through an arch the violent, roaring tide
> Outruns the eye that doth behold his haste,
> Yet in the eddy boundeth in his pride
> Back to the strait that forc'd him on so fast . . .   (1667–70)

'Planting' lines in this way is easy, a temptation perhaps to be resisted. The Joycean flow of Shakespearean phrases is successful, though, and one reviewer remarked on how well he uses the overlap between Shakespeare and Joyce.[18] 'Water hath a trick of drowning' WS warns his small brother Dickon, 'and, at best, is a wetter':

> 'Wetter water'
> 'Debtor daughter. Ducats suckets . . .'   (p. 4)

Puns are as natural to Burgess as to Joyce or Shakespeare (who presumably must have wearied at times of the play on his given name). Elizabethan vagueness about the form of surnames affords scope for play on them. WS is Shagspere, Chaxper, Jackspaw, and Jakes peer; he is Shake-scene to Greene (as in *A Groatsworth of Wit*),[19] Shakebag or Shakeshaft to Southampton, Jacques Pere to Florio, and to Fatima, of course, he is noble, 'a Sheikh'. These are old quips, probably as old as Shakespeare. Meanings, the characters feel, must lie somewhere in a name: There is Gemp or Camp or Kempe; Chattle or Chettle, and the Godless Merlin or Marlin. Andrew Wise the stationer poses no problem: he is wise in his station. Chapman is a Cheapside name. Fashion in plays, Will thinks, is like fashion in gloves, 'out-kydding Kydd'; he started out in 'kidskin slavery'. Southampton speaks of his own 'burly guardian'. Raleigh is the tobacco man 'Sir Walter Stink'. John Lyly's troupe are Lyly-white boys. Allusions improve on names. As the father of a Judith, WS sees himself as Holofernes, Rabelais's schoolmaster. Machiavel is 'an Italian devil', that is called also Niccolo or Old Nick. Names for plays have to be pushed into shape. A spirit in Spenser is 'the pouke, so Pouke or Puck'. A sense of the magic in names, the power of words, and the power to form words is present here as in Elizabethan word-play. Ships are obvious symbols; the bearers of treasure, they can be prizes too. Southampton is a fine prize, a 'graceful lordship, silver-masted, silk-caparisoned'. Fatimah is a dark little doxy: 'heterodoxy'. Burgess's text catches something of what conceits meant to the people of his period.

Archaism is offensive to some tastes. Reviewers were divided about the success of Burgess's Elizabethan English. Peter Buitenhuis found the writing gave 'a hard and earthy sense of the filth and splendour of Elizabethan London', and 'the flavour of the most English of writers'. 'It has taken a poet to catch a poet.'[20] Warren Miller wondered 'Who would be a fifth rate Nashe when he can be a first-rate Burgess?' and cited Keith Waterhouse's mockery of fake Yorkshire dialect in *Billy Liar* which he thought had 'finished Olde Englande once and for all': 'the mun laik wi't gangling iron'. Burgess is 'neither muckling nor mickling'; Nashe is mixed up with passages closer to Dylan Thomas or Ronald Firbank.[21] Burgess would presumably reply to the last charge that he meant to play Shakespearean notes among those of Joyce and Firbank: that he is not pretending to be WS but a modern lecturer impersonating Shakespeare while inspired by *samsu* and the end of term. Many sections of the narrative are written in relatively grey modern English, relieving the headier passages through what another reviewer called 'the more extreme reaches of language'. Like Firbank and Joyce, Burgess could plead, he writes to brighten the drabness of modern English and a novel beautified with Tudor feathers was appropriate for the quatercentenary. Burgess would no doubt be pleased, as he is by Schoenbaum's praise, to see Buitenhuis's tribute to his realism. The Elizabethan element in the language is meant to be realistic (much of it *is* Elizabethan); this element is one among several but it predominates. Variety of registers helps to mitigate the cloying effect of too much archaism. The danger with country dialects is of burying the sense in lexical slag. Burgess has a good ear for what conveys the right sort of meaning. Waterhouse's 'muckling' and 'mickling' are Jabberwocky, at least outside Yorkshire, but 'you are but country cledge, all' – from a *miles gloriosus* back from the Low Countries – addressed to bumpkins at a Stratford tavern, implies 'stuck in the mud', even if we do not know that 'cledge' meant clay. 'Had I my hanger I would deal thee a great flankard', he threatens WS, and 'flankard' sounds military, its bearing plain.[22] The soldier is cup-shotten. Burgess borrows from Shakespeare – 'He stank of Banbury cheese. He belched forth the soul of an alehouse' – and from Joyce: the other tipplers are peasants, 'their browned pickers a-clutch of their spilliwilly potkins'. WS is soon 'bunched, butched, birched, birled, swirled over and out': he has not yet drunk his sixpence but his sense of language is becoming blurred, the precise term for his feelings hard to find. Some modern slang-words sound Elizabethan. 'I will make his gnashers to be all bloody', says the soldier. This scene (pp. 25–7) of the adolescent Shakespeare's toping is rich, not stale, with period-dialect.

This is fiction by an historian of language who relishes words on the edge of English. Some deserve to have a longer life, such as 'kibey' in 'so cold and kibey a day' (p. 146); kibe is still, just, a chilblain. A glover would still know 'trank', the oblong of skin from which the 'fourchettes' are cut, but gloves mean less to us than to Shakespeare's contemporaries. 'And thereto is signed an adventure', Gilbert tells WS when his contract as a tutor has arrived at home (p. 52). Legal terms are tiresome to the young Shakespeare on first encounter, as they remain in our dealings with law. 'And so to learning the high terms and rites of the law's creaking workings, the quiddits and quillets, statutes, recognizances, double vouchers, conveyances' (p. 68). Burgess's writing is given to quillets. WS is at first put out by this terminology: 'it is all words'; there are signs in the plays that he was impatient with lawyers. The Brownist Banbury cant of the Puritans can still be heard today on a religious fringe which was once central in everyday language; 'God's coming thunderbolt' is still foretold and the low-Protestant note of 'a most potent purge for the bellies and bowels of them that are unrighteous and believe not' (p. 31) is still audible. Kemp's one-word skit on Latin and Latinisers still sounds amusingly unEnglish: 'perpetuabilitatibus'. Pavanes and sarabandes are danced no longer; the words are reminders that not everything Spanish was unwelcome in Elizabethan England. Burgess's pedagogic instinct has ample scope but there is an artist's (and a popular writer's) sense of what will work. His writing avoids the wilful and coy obscurity to be found in Frederick Rolfe's romances of medieval Italy (reissued in the 1960s), for example.[23] His characters often speak plainer than their modern counter-parts. 'The black Machiavel and the boys baked in a pie' sums up *Titus* in one theatre-goer's thumb-sketch (p. 91); 'eggs will not be thrown now as they are 1d', Will notes, as inflation provokes riots (p. 159); 'Will . . . had filled their daughter with kicking feet', protests a Stratford father (p. 11). *Nothing Like the Sun* celebrates not only Shakespeare but the English language at a vigorous time of life. Metaphor was fresh in common speech: 'a pea of truth beneath the mattresses of verbiage' sounds spontaneous and makes three points at once (p. 133); and so was a deft pointedness in common words: 'I would have one pennyworth of the future', WS tells mad Madge, the witch to whom he goes for career guidance (p. 14). Some features of common ordinary usage must have been as tiresome to live with as they sound in the plays: references to 'coney-catchers' and jokes about 'horns' recur in the novel too. It is a playful, enthusiastic and an honest rendering of the language of Shakespeare's time, and a demonstration of how colourful a contemporary style can be.

The way the novel explores the resources of language and demonstrates the author's linguistic skill can be seen as an elaborate game; as such it matches Shakespeare's sense of the games to be played with language, and of the extent to which life is shaped by words. If *Nothing Like the Sun* were a thoroughly ludic novel it would try to persuade us that 'words alone are certain good', that Shakespeare's (verbal) world was as real as Elizabeth's, and that Burgess's Shakespeare is as real as any other. Instead it respects the distinction between word-games and functional writing, between the power to purvey illusion and the power to convey reality, and this distinction is recognised by WS, as it was by Shakespeare. 'With words there was a realm' decides the word-boy, early in the story. The lawyer for whom he clerks tells him that language is a form of power:

'This realm is ruled by words.' WS seemed suddenly to see the light. Words, pretences, fictions. They ruled.   (p. 69)

'Fictions' is anachronistic; 'fiction' was first used in English in 1599; the general plural sense is more recent. But WS never believes that the realm is made of words. We are made to sense how a word may look innocent and contain a horrible bearing on reality: 'what then are these pocks?' young Will, reading, asks his father (p. 222). Elsewhere, Southampton argues that 'treason' and 'folly' are 'but words' (p. 196), the author meaning us to think of 'What is honour? A word.' WS warns him that when he is 'truly grown up' he will see 'where metaphors go wrong' (p. 201) and how the noblest sentences — 'it is for the good of the commonweal' — are distorting mirrors. Words rule, seduce and deceive; there is power in the theatre as in the Law or the Church. But *res* and *verba* are not to be confused; their relationships are to be scrutinised with the greatest possible care. A pea of truth may lurk under mattresses of verbiage. At the height of a performance an actor may speak, aside, one true word to another (p. 155).

Sometimes the reality of a situation resides in the contrast between two registers, as in the London walk in the course of which WS composes the dedication of *Venus and Adonis* to Southampton: 'I know not how I shall offend in dedicating my unpolished lines to your lordship . . .'. The rest of the dedication is counterpointed with more impressions of a London day, a catch in a smoky tavern, pickpurses among the rustics, a limping child with a pig's head, Paul's men, stale herrings, a whining beggar girl, a one-eyed soldier munching bread, skulls on Temple Bar, a brass consort, . . . a drayhorse farting as the poet signs his name. Burgess contrasts the formal deference of the epistle with the squalid relations between poet and patron. It may of course, in reality, have come from the heart. It may have been written by Southampton's secretary, or have been dictated impromptu to the printer. A century later such homage would begin to sound hollow. Today it seems sycophantic. Shakespeare knew that it sounded so to a Hamlet, a Hal, or a Southampton. His lordship's wealth and power, in 1593, are implied in the contrasting details of misfortune in the interpolated London sketch; without the prop of patronage a poet might be a beggar or end up a corpse in the Thames. The fresh sensations of common life are, none the less, reminders of how inadequately rank has ever imposed on life. The coexistence of formal assertiveness and low irrelevance is true to experience of life in any time, and to Shakespeare:

As who should say, I am Sir Oracle
And when I ope my lips, let no dog bark.

If Shakespeare was not present at the execution of Dr Roderigo Lopez he must have heard accounts of it. *Nothing Like the Sun* obliges him to watch, at Southampton's insistence (pp. 126–131): 'Words were safe, words, safer than reality', Will tells himself later when his lordship is risking the Queen's displeasure (p. 204). Many words have grown even 'safer', today, so that we lose their force in Shakespeare. The relationship of language to reality can be seen in the way the life of words can decay in time, so that many common Shakespeare words have stage rather than street connotations: 'sword', 'beggar', 'bear', 'whipping', 'plague', 'treason', 'axe', 'the Tower', 'gentleman', 'Godless', 'pox'. *Nothing Like the Sun* restores the reality they once had and conveys the difference between the age of one Queen Elizabeth and another.

At its most realistic, as in the scene of Lopez's execution, the novel brings Shakespeare as he must have lived closer to us. At its most speculative, in the scenes of 'love-life' especially, and in WS's musings on the nature of evil, it accommodates him to modern thinking, as all treatments of Shakespeare must, and does so in play. The realistic and the ludic are well mixed in this work, which accepts that, in a novel about Shakespeare, truth and invention have to mix, but leaves us in no doubt about which is which. The portrait of the past is very incomplete; that and the writer's bias are gracefully conceded in the title-phrase. Yet the work fully deserves Schoenbaum's conclusion that '*Nothing Like the Sun* is the only novel about Shakespeare acceptable in its own terms as a novel'.

Napoleon Symphony was much more exhaustively discussed by reviewers in 1974 than *Nothing Like the Sun* had been ten years earlier. To read in succession the reviews by Jonathan Raban, R. K. Morris, Graham Fawcett, John Bayley, Roger Sale, Peter Ackroyd and Frank Kermode is equivalent to attending a seminar in which the speakers are sharply divided for and against the novel.[24] Geoffrey Aggeler has given it a chapter of almost unqualified praise in his book on Burgess. Burgess has written a modestly pitched account in his *This Man and Music*

(1982).[25] Opinion divides in accordance with the critics' sympathy for ludic fiction. For Kermode in the *Guardian* it is historical fiction 'a-shimmer': 'very serious comedy . . . with extraordinary resource, variety and pace'; 'games' with Beethoven's Eroica Symphony are artistic; the composer played games himself with the music of Clementi.[26] The reviewer in the *Times Literary Supplement*, who was already well-disposed to Burgess ('his splendid Shakespeare novel'), sees him as a novelist of European stature, a successor to Proust, Joyce and Mann: 'there has been little like it since Joyce'.[27] But Roger Sale calls his piece in the *Hudson Review* 'Fooling Around and Serious Business': 'of course fooling around can be elevated to a principle, proclaimed high art', but in fact Burgess has 'ended up with 363 pages of nonsense'.[28] Jonathan Raban's review article in *Encounter*, 'What Shall We Do About Anthony Burgess?', sums up the mixture, of admiration for technique and exasperation at the method, to be found in several other notices:

> Taken at random, almost any paragraph of this will be brilliantly written: but taken in context, reading the stuff is like being in a battle. One hears a great deal of noise. One doesn't know where one is. One aches for silence and just one clear command from that superior officer, the novelist.[29]

We can in fact find some clues, in a number of games the novel plays: with music, language, history and literature. The verse 'Epistle to the Reader' at the end of the novel helps us to find our bearings. The structure, the author claims there, is taken from Beethoven's third (Eroica) Symphony: 'The *Allegro*: see him live and vigorous,/striding the earth, stern but magnanimous'; the *Marcia funebre*: 'already dead,/The ironic laurels wilting round his head'. Beethoven's *Scherzo* and *Finale* invoke Prometheus; the novel has 'forced mythic and historic into one' so that Napoleon is Promethean in these parts, tormented by a liver complaint on St Helena in the Finale. *This Man and Music* elaborates. A wooden leg, which smoulders while its owner sleeps by the fire in the first scene of the book, is the conductor's baton. The *Allegro* takes the hero from his victories in Italy to his coronation. The *Marcia funebre* 'matches defeat and the mere memory of past triumphs to the funeral tempo'. The

Beethoven *Scherzo* 'resurrects Napoleon as Prometheus': in the novel the Emperor has to sit through a dramatic performance of the myth in which he sees himself satirised. In the novel's Finale where he is 'chained to the rock' of St Helena, Beethoven's Prometheus variations are matched by a series of parodies (or 'pastiches' according to the author). The kind of exegesis which would be required in a study of the relation of text to score is indicated by a sample of the author's account of his own work:

> I felt on safer ground with the finale. Beethoven begins with a rapid grandiosity matched by a rapidity of grandiose reminiscence as N approaches St Helena. 'Egypt 18 Brumaire coup 3 cons 1st con 1st con for life exec of duc denghien Emperor Emperor EMPEROOOOOOOOOR.' His island of exile is named for the Romano-British saint who found the true cross. Christ died, but Christ lives. N is removed from the worldly scene but his charisma cannot be quelled. Christ had INRI on the titulus of his cross. INRI can stand for Imperatorem Napoleonem Regem Interfeciamus. The initials and the whole phrase can be brokenly sung to the theme of Beethoven's variations (which, you will remember, comes straight from his *Prometheus* ballet music).[30]

The music hall and soldier songs, imperial and anti-Gallican verses which occur throughout the novel can also be sung to Beethoven. Geoffrey Aggeler demonstrates some of the correspondences.

> There he lies
> Ensanguinated tyrant
> O bloody bloody tyrant

sing the enemy at the start of Part 2, the *Marcia funebre*; each syllable matches a note in the theme statement. Aggeler finds more, very obscure musical hints which help 'the alert reader' to hear the music.[31] But the novelist intends spontaneous amusement rather than scholarly analysis. The 'Epistle' admits that the task was impossible: it is to be enjoyed as an elaborate joke which the unmusical may disregard.[32]

Jonathan Raban commented on the 'outwardness' of the method; the use of Beethoven imposes design from outside, and so, he says, does 'a ruling metaphor rooted in anthropology'. This is a metaphor of 'head and arms' (*tête d'armes* was among the last intelligible phrases of the dying Napoleon): 'everything that happens in the novel – the whole vainglorious career of moving armies, grumbling civilians, sexual treachery and failure – is a representation of a body politic which is also Napoleon's own, haemorrhoid-ridden, liverish and angry body'.[33] This is, certainly, one way of finding bearings. Images of making love and making war are alternated, counterpointed and fused; wordplay, for example has Napoleon in arms, and Napoleon in Josephine's arms. Military and sexual violence occupy equally extensive sections of the novel; Napoleon's erotic fancies are aggressive; Josephine finds him always in too great a hurry. 'Head' and 'arms' are a frequent pair of ambiguous metaphors. Napoleon is said to have a machine-mind set in an animal-body. As a rationalist he gives France a Code and directs a world-war; as a frenetic sensualist he is constantly cuckolded and cuckolding (Burgess's terms). He is also head of the army and of the state, and also the would-be head of Europe; the masses frighten him unless they are under the discipline of arms. An almost exhaustive account of *Napoleon Symphony* could be made on these lines; they offer one possible clue to a reading.

There are others, also derived from outside the human and dramatic interest of Napoleon's story, usually in coincidences of language. 'Waterloo' is a reminder of how his victories on land were matched by defeats at sea. '-loo' is close to '*l'eau*' and [Sir Hudson]*Lowe*, in charge of St Helena, is even closer. 'Water comes from wells and is ever Welling forth from the natural springs by the very Ton – and, for good measure, may we not add that his own *L'eau* was in orthographic bo-peep hiding in the Loo?' (p. 287. Page references are to the Cape 1974 edition). (The novel is full of such 'literal magic'.) Land is hard and masculine, we are told; the sea, of course, is a woman: Napoleon is always a master of men but is never successful with women or able to appreciate them. Mme de Staël said that he was 'not a man but a system': that he thought women useful only to breed future generations of conscripts; otherwise, they were '*une classe qu'il voudroit supprimer*'.[34] A Jungian might try to connect this imbalance with the fortunes of Napoleon, as 'a man of land' on whom the sea took vengeance. Some novelists would find a mystic correspondence, in the nature of things, or a poetic, symbolic truth. For Burgess it furnishes another system within the verbal structure; it is a fascinating game: it helps a novel to develop like music. Napoleon is haunted by the English (unFrench) *W* in Wellington, Waterloo, Lowe. There is further play with his name: he is 'N'; he is Buonaparte as well as Bonaparte; to his subordinates he is *he* or *lui*. The uses for the New Testament INRI suggested by St Helena have been indicated in the passage of Burgess's commentary quoted above.

Besides the musical and the language games there is the historical game of understanding, or finding out, what each section is about. If many historical novels may be said to labour under a weight of explanation, *Napoleon Symphony* floats free of it, offering little help. Perhaps all successful historical novels encourage the reader to go back to the history books; this novel requires it. Frank Kermode's review admits that he had to reread J. M. Thompson and Felix Markham as a 'necessary propaedeutic'.[35] Mary Renault's novels no doubt offer greater entertainment to those who have read her sources than to those who have not, but she assumed little if any prior knowledge. The opening pages of *Napoleon Symphony* send the non-historian to the history books. Vincent Cronin's *Napoleon* (1971), a recent biography when Burgess was writing, is a useful guide to the novel. For example, the first scene presents the witnesses to Napoleon's first marriage, waiting with Josephine for him to arrive; it assumes that we know, as we do if we have read Cronin, that Barras was a Director who had been Josephine's lover; and that Tallien had freed her from prison when he came to power on the fall of Robespierre. From Cronin, who follows Tallien's memoirs, we know that the triple-plumed Director's hat and the registrar's wooden leg in the fire, in Burgess's picture, are historical details. 'Did not the way to the Alps lie between Josephine's legs?', Barras muses in the novel; we need to know that he is presumed to have made the marriage a condition of Bonaparte's appointment to command the Army of Italy; (although Burgess was probably aware that some scholars discount this gossip, believing Napoleon's invasion-scheme captivated the Directors and won the appointment).[36] Burgess has, presumably, been reading the same sources as Cronin; both choose the liveliest scenes and the best jokes. But the biography explains where the novel alludes. For the *Allegro* section, we need to have read an account of the Italian and Egyptian campaigns; for the *Marcia funebre* and the *Scherzo*, we require the course of events from the coronation as Emperor to the defeat at Waterloo; the *Finale* makes more sense if we are aware of Napoleon's circumstances on St Helena. Familiarity with the novel's cast is wanted too; Talleyrand's remark at dinner that a salt-cellar looks vaguely ecclesiastical alludes not only to the precariousness of Church property under the Directorate but also to his pre-revolutionary status as a bishop. To know of gossip spreaders such as Mme de Staël and of gossip about her is also an asset. Most of the details can easily be traced and conversations are often, in part at least, from sources, even when they appear on first encounter typical of the novelist's own imagination, or wit. 'General Bonaparte has got off the Po' (p. 25) was a witticism of Lieutenant Hippolyte Charles, the lover of Josephine while her husband was in Italy.[37] Napoleon's obscene disparagement of subordinates often seems to be the licence of a modern novelist; in fact there was no need to invent. Most reviewers commented on the homoerotic twinges the young Czar causes Napoleon at Tilsit as a comic invention, but the scene is justified by several of Napoleon's remarks about his own nature.[38]

There is indeed more novelistic material in accounts by Napoleon's contemporaries than a novelist can use. In one scene of the novel the Emperor sends out the servants who have been listening and 'making mental notes for memoirs' (p. 210). Several servants and secretaries published memoirs. Those of his valet Louis Marchand were first published in 1955.[39] Few past lives are known in such detail; a novelist can hardly compete with a biographer because so little scope is left for the kind of imaginative reconstruction without which no Life of Shakespeare is possible. In such a case the modern novelist may reasonably start where biography ends; making the game of recognition part of the ludic approach to a subject which has been realistically treated by historians. Competence in the history is a prerequisite for *Napoleon Symphony*. A tone-deaf reader quickly bored by puns could enjoy the book, but a lover of Beethoven and crosswords would be lost without historical background. It is necessary to enjoy the game. John Bayley knows the history, but objected:

> Mr Burgess's problem, which he cannot be said to have solved, is that his more informed readers cannot really need this kind of thing to imagine themselves into the Napoleonic era, while all the sound knowledge of corps commanders, horse batteries, Continental System, which he strews so prodigally but inconspicuously around, cannot do much to edify his more popular readership.[40]

Evidently he does not find the game amusing, as a scholar's holiday. Bayley has become inclined to judge all literature by the standard of Tolstoy who imagines us back into the Napoleonic era so much more effectively than Burgess. The 'Epistle to the Reader' which ends *Napoleon Symphony* tries to anticipate that comparison.

> No critic would be fool enough to bring
> In Tolstoy guns to blast me into dust.
> This is a comic novel and it must
> Be read as such, as such deemed good or bad
> A thousand versts away from Tolstoygrad.   (p. 348)

His 'more popular readership' may be deterred by so learned a comedy. It may be that the erotic element compensates, there, for the erudition, as in the case of Nabokov's huge popular success; and is excused and camouflaged, for some, by the learning; these questions lead beyond criticism into the sphere of John Sutherland's studies of the common readership.[41]

As a literary historian Burgess contemplates and exhibits his Napoleon in a wide range of pastiches; the novel frequently turns into a literary exercise. Many scenes and changes of scene could be called cinematographic; especially in view of the informal commission apparently arranged by Stanley Kubrick who wanted material for a screen-play. Many other scenes would exasperate a screen-writer, and dismay a budget-conscious producer. The novel was not filmed; it could serve as a demonstration of how far the linguistic and imaginative resources of fiction surpass those of the cinema. There are streams of consciousness, Napoleon's memory replaying his past, which convey the remarkable scale of experience of life in such a career, the world's conquest and the body's defeat, in a way that Mary Renault's techniques do not allow. But these Joycean passages are juxtaposed, with dialogue among officers, politicians, diplomats and girls, who talk about *him*, with proclamations ('Know that we come to free the peoples of the Nile . . .'); with lists of *personnalités*, with historical jottings as though from a student's notepad; with footnotes within the text, with tavern songs and jingles, and convenient verse choruses which summarise the action. There are Popean and later eighteenth-century couplets:

> He conquers first, then seeks to civilise,
> With speed he bids an *Institute* arise.   (p. 50)

There are exultant Byronic stanzas:

> *O shake yourself awake and take your lance,*
> *For Bonaparte has kissed the soil of France.*   (p. 68)

There are new versions of W. S. Gilbert:

> I was made First Consul by my fellow frogs
> And was on my way to Emperor
> (Vive L'Empéreur)
> Of an empire not much bigger than the Isle of Dogs.
> (p. 258)

The political point of view varies with the style. Napoleon may be an 'ensanguinated tyrant' or, as in the first set of verses, a civiliser, responsible for the founding of Egyptology, patron of scholars, artists and scientists. As in the second set, he may be the incarnation of the Revolution for whom all enlightened men (the pseudo-classical note is correct) willingly fight to spread the rights of man (or at least the career-open-to-talent) across Europe. In the eyes of the British jingoist, exuberant after Waterloo, he is a comic ogre. The voices of the French soldiers, who present a recurring commentary from their own point of view (and are compared, by several reviewers to a Chorus), have a similar effect because they talk like Tommies. They are, justly, given the account of the retreat from Moscow.

> The Cossacks are coming, Sergeant Brincat said, and they'll be in here to slice everybody's balls off, you know what they're like, so draw rations and dress up warm and get fell in on the road. Jesus Christ, Grandjean said, isn't that the bleeding army all over? What did I tell you? Matheron said. Didn't I tell you that the first rule of the army is when in doubt fuck everything up?   (p. 189)

Napoleon, here, is the remote general, ignorant of soldiering as his men know it; the 'glory', 'honour' and 'France' of his speeches are vulnerable in this setting. In the scene where he confers with Alexander at Tilsit he is a figure of fun who seems to belong to contemporary comic fiction, as he struggles with the seductive Queen Louise of Prussia for the personal and political loyalty of the Czar. On his return from Elba, he is the hero of France. In the private thoughts of his mother he and his royal brothers are playing a game which is likely to end in tears. In the opinion of the Saxon student who wants to assassinate him, given in one of the novel's serious and extended historical discussions, he is behind the times: an eighteenth-century enlightened despot blind to the Romantic nationalism of the German *Volk*. None of these views receives identifiable endorsement from the novelist. What Napoleon is depends on who judges him and is reflected in the style in which he is presented.

The fact that the novel misrepresents him simply because it is written in a language he never learned, is implicitly acknowledged by the Finale, which is a series of parodies of nineteenth-century English authors: Jane Austen, Scott, Wordsworth, Dickens, Bulwer Lytton, Tennyson and Henry James. Burgess is as skilful a parodist as Beerbohm or Chesterton. His Sergeant Trouncer, a guard on St Helena, can talk with the fantastical fatuity of a Dickens character: '"When I says", said the sergeant, "them boots has marched, I would not have you believe that they has marched of their own accord"', and the listening trooper has a 'sudden very clear picture of a pair of boots vigorously marching across a map of Europe' (p. 298). Eighty lines of plodding *Excursion*-style verse introduce Wordsworth remembering the days 'when France was teaching Brotherhood', but baffled by Burgess's word-play, on 'spade' as (Italian for) sword for example: 'I could not comprehend, as though he thought/Our English spade was an Italian word' (p. 296). 'The prisoner' confronts his jailor 'the British knight' Sir Hud in a pastiche of Scott. Napoleon is imprisoned in the Finale in varieties of literary English which are all equally remote in connotation from the courts of Napoleonic Europe. 'Keep away from tyrants, my dear,' Sir Hud tells Betsy, the pert English miss who likes chatting with the Ogre, 'since good rarely comes from them' (p. 283). England never recognised Napoleon as Emperor or head of state. On St Helena his status was insultingly belittled, perhaps by policy. Vincent Cronin suggests that Napoleon, unable to understand the governor, created and then believed in a fictional version of Lowe. The novel makes artificial fictions of his experiences and ends by a declaration that he is a fiction himself, not only in misconceived English versions but in everything. Dying, Napoleon meets on some astral planet a Jamesian lady, in a James pastiche, who ventures to imply that the most successful heroes are artistic creations, *Don Quixote*, *Don Juan*, and that he 'could have been made . . . in words, you know' (p. 331) – or in music. Napoleon was unworthy of the dedication of Beethoven's symphony: the composer deleted it after the execution of the duc d'Enghien, an action which persuaded him that France had just another tyrant. The symphony rather than Napoleon's achievements, this enigmatic passage seems to say, is what has really survived.

This is close to the ludic novelist's view that one interpretation is as good as another, although it may be more or less amusing. But Burgess reworks the history with complete fidelity to detail; and he does put a case, that a great artist ultimately matters more than any man of action. Pieter Geyl's *Napoleon: For and Against* might be recommended reading after this Burgess performance: it illustrates the manner in which the Napoleonic legend has both influenced the course of events in French history and also been influenced, in the sense of being differently interpreted, by events; Napoleon's stock falling during the Second World War from the parallels with

Hitler. Burgess's Napoleon is true at times to all the interpretations which existed in the Napoleonic period. It is consistent with David Thomson's verdict, in *Europe Since Napoleon* (1957, 1966) that 'the importance . . . [of Goethe and Beethoven] is quite unaffected by their relation to Napoleon', and that 'when the thud and smoke of gunfire had died away, more permanent forces of human destiny [than Napoleon] could be seen'.[42] 'Burgess has given us a Napoleon for our time', says R. K. Morris: 'he is lover, general, doting father, gourmandiser [although he is not, and was not], whoremonger, cuckold, dyspeptic, tyrant, Emperor, genial Mafia cutthroat, martyr, myth . . .'.[43] He is a Napoleon for the more sceptical opinion of our time, founded on the evidence, but unshaped by any convictions except a doubt concerning what a statesman-general ever achieves. Burgess's 'N' is a hero and a clown, as Shakespeare in *Nothing Like the Sun* feels himself to be. The fusion of these roles, both of which were long asserted by propaganda, makes him an appropriate figure in the ludic mode of contemporary fiction.

Present mirth is the first aim of these novels, as good in historical fiction as any other. An intelligent, well-informed, imaginative talent for comedy plays upon two figures who have received more than full measure of solemn treatment from other writers. Burgess can be serious, but not solemn. Some readers, like Geoffrey Aggeler,[44] may respond earnestly to signs of Burgess's interest in opposed metaphysical forces, but more are likely to agree with John Bayley that Burgess does not quite expect us to take his intellectual pretensions in earnest. Burgess relishes ideas but mistrusts them. Discussing poetry with his pupils in *The Clockwork Testament*, Enderby argues that 'the urgencies are not political or racial or social' but 'semantic'.[45] This is true of Burgess's fiction. His historical novels make a claim to literature in their concern with meaning. Bayley is mistaken to ask why *Napoleon Symphony* is needed to help us imagine ourselves into that part of the past. Both novels provoke us to think about how we understand the past, how Shakespeare is known to us in his language and – for the lecturer who claims to know the whole story is drunk – unknown in the facts of his life; how the amply documented life of Napoleon is removed from our understanding by ideological conflicts and even by the English language. These novels show that imagining the past *is* a kind of game, one which the author plays expertly, and with a sure sense of the first rule: that what we know is distinct from what our own time disposes us to invent. Burgess believes in a real Shakespeare and a real Napoleon; he turns his comedy on the limitations of our ability to know them, without losing faith in what can be known.

5   Robert Nye: *Falstaff*

Lucian's jests in the first lines of his *True History*, that he is a more honest liar than other historians because he admits that he is lying, conveys the scepticism which appears again today in the 'ludic' approach to history and fiction. Robert Nye has found the ideal narrator, for an historical novel which owns up to lying, in Shakespeare's Falstaff whose career he enlarged and revised in *Falstaff* (1976). Nye has complained that much modern fiction amounts to 'a grammar of dissent', and has declared his own aim to revive 'good straight nouns like . . . fun, fury, joy'.[1] The bluffness of 'good straight nouns' is misleading. Nye is a novel reviewer for the *Guardian* who knows how the subtlest of dissenting novels works, and *Falstaff* is meant to be seen as an intellectual as well as an intelligent book.[2] But Falstaff suits him as a narrator because he acts as a voice in the cause of 'fun, fury and joy' with almost unlimited heartiness.

Nye calls his hero (except in the title) Sir John Fastolf, equips him with a breezy modern-English prose style, and lets him tell the history of his times in his own way. Here is a sample of one of the most responsible passages:

A very rich Welshman called Owen Glendower had a quarrel with his neighbour, Reggie, Lord Grey of Ruthin, over a field which both of them wanted. For whatever it's worth, I think Glendower had the better claim.

'Truth is various', Fastolf observes later (Chapter LVII). He is a connoisseur of lies and an expert liar. But his summary of Glendower's revolt has a clear relation to the facts. Glendower's private quarrel with Lord Grey of Ruthin led in 1400 to an insurrection which lasted almost a decade. The English Commons requested sanctions against the Welsh in 1402 and in the same year Glendower appealed to Robert III of Scotland

and to Irish chieftains for an alliance against the English. Prince Henry spent many of his adolescent years attempting to subdue the Welsh. Nye's Fastolf scales down these events in the modern-English, plain man's style which Keith Waterhouse might employ in a popular newspaper column, but he does so with the scorn for all affairs of state which belongs to the Falstaff of Shakespeare's plays. The novel's account of English history in the reigns of Henry IV, Henry V and Henry VI (for Fastolf survives Hal) is told with the licence we expect from the hero of Gadshill. There is one sense, however, in which he can claim to be telling the 'true history'.

Nye's opportunity arose from Shakespeare's artistic indifference to historical accuracy. The opening of the novel's subtitle indicates its primary comic ploy: 'Falstaff: being the *Acta domini Johannis Fastolfe, or Life and Valliant Deeds of Sir John Faustoff* . . .'[3] Shakespeare's Falstaff has little or no connection with Sir John Fastolf, who was a fifteenth-century soldier-adventurer. Nye pretends that they are the same man – that Falstaff is an historical figure such as Caesar or Richard III whose recorded remarks might be quoted in the plays. The pretence is supported by the treatment of historical events from the plays, such as the Battle of Shrewsbury, and by detailed accounts of incidents in Falstaff/Fastolf's life which are mentioned there. 'Then was Jack Falstaff, now Sir John, a boy, and page to Thomas Mowbray, Duke of Norfolk,' Shallow remembers; 'The same Sir John, the very same. I see him break Scoggin's head at the court-gate' (*2 Henry IV,* III. ii. 24–29).[4] The service as Mowbray's page and the breaking of Scoggin's head provide two elaborate episodes in the novel.

There is some evidence that if Falstaff owes anything to an historical model it is to Sir John Oldcastle (*c.* 1378–1417), Lord Cobham, who was High Sheriff of Herefordshire and died at the stake as a Wycliffite. Anti-Lollard propaganda misrepresented Oldcastle as a coward and an unsuitable companion of Prince Henry, rightly rejected; to Foxe, he was a martyr. There are Elizabethan references to Falstaff as 'Oldcastle'. Hal calls him 'my old lad of the castle' in *1 Henry IV* (I. ii. 41). In the 1600 quarto of *2 Henry IV* 'Old' appears, uncorrected, at the head of a speech for Falstaff. The epilogue to *2 Henry IV* disclaims a connection: 'Oldcastle died a martyr, and this is not the man'. There are traces of the man, none the less. Oldcastle was a page to Thomas Mowbray, Duke of Norfolk (and so, by coincidence, was Fastolf). It has been suggested that Falstaff's age has its origin in Oldcastle's name and his scriptural tags in thoughts of Lollardism.[5] Obliged to make a change when the Cobhams objected to the plays' libel on their family name, Shakespeare looked for an alternative Sir John from the same period, and finding Fastolf, discreetly adjusted it to Falstaff. Nye insists on the identity of the plays' invented character and the knight whose name was borrowed. 'This *is* the man!' says Nye's Falstaff, in effect; and he obscures the question of spelling with sixty-nine versions (Fallstuff, Fairstolf, Fourestalf . . .), 'all of them right', in the second chapter; and provides an etymology reaching back to the Old Norse *Falstulfr*, 'a pirate prince'.

Sir John Fastolf, who died at a good age in 1459, was a brilliantly successful soldier in the French wars and made his fortune there. He won twenty thousand marks, in ransom, in one day of The Battle of Verneuil in 1424. He was later one of the richest and most powerful men in England.[6] He seems to have had little in common with Falstaff of the Boar's Head, except that he must have been an intelligent rogue. Falstaff would envy such a man the fruits of his career, although not the manner of earning them. Nye gives his Falstaff Fastolf's name, his life-span and his successes, making him much younger when he knows Hal, and sending him to France with the army. Like the real Fastolf he is at Agincourt; he is routed by Joan of Arc; he amasses money; by the 1450s he is the owner of the original Fastolf's castle at Caister in Norfolk, attended, as was that Fastolf, by a secretary called William Worcester and a chaplain called Friar Brackley, among others. His will, like Fastolf's, is contested. Like Fastolf, he is in dispute with the Crown over a 'great bill of claims'. Like Fastolf he is a friend of the Pastons, a patriot and a 'feudalist', with a poor opinion of English foreign and domestic policy. 'No wonder the country is in such a mess', says Nye's Falstaff/Fastolf (Chapter II); the original Fastolf makes the same observation in more laborious English in surviving memoranda.[7]

Since Nye's Fastolf is also Shakespeare's Falstaff this success in life delights him as material for boasting and he is never at a loss to invent more. Set free from the restraints placed on him by the history plays, and given the scope of an undisciplined autobiography – a four hundred and fifty page monologue –

Fastolf/Falstaff takes a kind of revenge, talking away the humiliations he suffers in Shakespeare. Nye is helped by the effect the two Parts of *Henry IV* have produced on so many audiences since Queen Elizabeth I commanded (if she really did) *The Merry Wives of Windsor*: Falstaff seems to be unduly contained and censored there. We can find hints that Shakespeare felt so. 'Play out the play! I have much to say in the behalf of that Falstaff' says Falstaff playing Hal, when interrupted by events in *1 Henry IV* (II. iv. 478). Nye is right to let him play it out in his own terms, as Maurice Morgann was right to defend his courage and military reputation.[8] More than any other character in Shakespeare he seems perennial and universal, a visitor to the plays, somebody we have always known. Arguments about royal responsibility in Tudor England, about Hal's choice of virtue and the pattern of the Morality play, or about seeking the strongest dramatic impact, fail to dispel the sense that his dismissal and off-stage death are evasions: that there was dramatic life in him still, denied because the author's scheme could not accommodate its subversiveness. E. K. Chambers put concisely the view that Falstaff, whether or not wronged by his creator, is an indestructible fact of life: 'in such a figure literature provides a standard to which ever after we refer half-insensibly our judgements not only of art but of humanity'.[9] Peter Conrad, reviewing *Falstaff*, thinks that he is wronged – he 'has always had cause for complaint against Shakespeare' – and sees the novel as a proper revenge.[10] As such, it is made possible by the whirligig of time which has in 1976 placed the Elizabethan characters in a new fifteenth-century role.

Retaining most of Falstaff's part in Shakespeare, Fastolf can improve on it:

'Mr Shallow,' I said, 'I owe you a thousand pounds.' Poor Shallow thought I meant him. I did not.   (Chapter LXXIV)

Shakespeare may have intended the ambiguity; it is there for those who want it. Elsewhere Fastolf exploits the semantic concentration of Shakespeare's images. 'Why, thou globe of sinful continents', says Hal in *2 Henry IV* (II. iv. 283). 'I should say', Fastolf speculates, 'that my soul was about the size of Spain, though in a better spiritual condition'.

It has in its charge and command, this captain soul of mine, great territories of flesh and terrible cohorts of blood. It controls a continent. It rules over and administrates an empire of sense. It is the emperor of my senses, and some of those fellows are arch rebels, I can tell you.   (Chapter XLVI)

He also plunders and tries to improve on other plays than those he might be thought to have a right to quote. Many of the newly invented characters are given Shakespearean names. Fastolf's cook is Macbeth; his pet rat is Desdemona; a sorcerer is Malvolio; an effeminate French count is Cordelia; a list of his girls makes a roll-call of the heroines of the plays. All the characters are liable to talk in quotations. 'Mind you', says Bardolph, 'there are more things in heaven and earth than are dreamed of in your philosophy' (Chapter LXXIX). It is a facile humour, already overworked, perhaps, in Shaw's *The Dark Lady of the Sonnets*. But the outrageous nature of the thefts is true to the character's effrontery, and his Saturnalian pleasure in reversed roles. It recalls his lament for Hal's bad influence on his own life, and his telling the Lord Chief Justice that Mistress Quickly is 'a poor mad soul' who 'says up and down the town that her eldest son is like you' (*2 Henry IV*, II. i. 102). Where there is a need to modernise or to modify borrowings, Fastolf's ready excuses can again seem to turn the tables on Shakespeare. Pistol's actual words have not been recorded because he 'always bored and irritated me'.

Where Fastolf's career diverges from Falstaff's, Shakespeare is shown to be 'wrong'. There was a rumour of his death, he explains, on the eve of the French expedition, but he was merely dead drunk – and pleased afterwards to let his creditors think him dead. Historians will, no doubt, set all to rights.

Fastolf's secretary Scrope complains that his master is 'King Liar' (Chapter LXXVIII), never to be believed, and this is the source of much of the comedy. While other historical novelists minimise or disguise the anachronistic nature of the genre, Nye revels in it. Fastolf retains the anachronisms Shakespeare gives Falstaff, drinking throughout his fourteenth and fifteenth-century adventures the 'sack' which was not known in England until the sixteenth; it is nothing to his knowledge of plays not yet written. When the first 'given' is conceded, that

Fastolf/Falstaff belongs to 1400 and to 1600, confusion of periods turns to comedy. Fastolf talks of potatoes, Greensleeves, and typography. He appears to know Rabelais, whose sixteenth-century literary devices he uses himself. But he can also quote T. S. Eliot when he chooses: 'here I am, an old man in a dry month' (Chapter XXXVIII)). His castle of Caister ('an Englishman's castle is his home') is, he suggests, made of words and these can be medieval Latin or just modern English. 'Who is speaking, and from what perspective?' is a difficult question to answer. It is not exactly Shakespeare's Falstaff, nor his supposed 'true original'. Drinking sack, or making a distinctly Protestant joke about the spiritual state of Spain, he is the first; ruling over Caister in the mid-fifteenth century he is the second. He is the Falstaff who speaks from a kind of literary limbo (perhaps Arthur's bosom) which is timeless. He is the Falstaff we imagine behind the play's portrayal: the embodiment of the standard to which, as Chambers said, we can refer our judgements of art and humanity. The proper critical corrective to 'naive' essays on such topics as the childhoods of Shakespeare's heroines, for example, which insists that a character is no more than one set of speeches in relation to others, or any one theatre performance, will not prevent our private imaginative excursions on Falstaff's or Hamlet's behalf, and Nye addresses us through the Falstaff we might imagine for ourselves. His point of view shifts therefore, from the time of his 'setting' to the time of his creation, and on to our own. If the book achieves any degree of literary and historical truth, the truth is mixed with the misleading in more complicated ways than in most historical novels.

In his last confession to Friar Brackley, which occupies the ninety-ninth chapter, Fastolf admits that his memoirs are;

lies about my whole life. But try & explain: some *true* lies?

In one of his many earlier speculations on the nature of truth, in which he seems to have read Jung, his words imply that the truth in his lies is to be found in the mythic quality which Shakespeare created and which Nye conveys in *Falstaff*:

I like the philosophy of Democritus best of all. That laughing doctor, that dear droll of Abdera, he taught that Truth lies at the bottom of a well. A well of what? Of memory perhaps. Not just *my* memory, mark you, or *your* memory. A common memory of more-than-us.   (Chapter XXXVIII)

Shakespeare's conception of Falstaff began with an assembly of old and culturally widespread figures from literature, legend and popular lore: the Vice, the comic devil, the Lord of Misrule, the *miles gloriosus*, the licensed Fool who can be wittier and wiser than his betters, the drunkard who can, for all his fantasy, speak truths, the old man who will not come to terms with his age. From these, and from the poetry of his (prose) language, is created an original character with the power and range of connotations we associate with myth. As myth he belongs to the 'common memory'. He is descended from Dionysos and Priapus; he is distantly akin to Trimalchio and Oblomov. But he charms because the godlike scale of his attributes is mostly in his imagination. He appeals most in Shakespeare by the force with which he can project his visions of himself, transforming a tavern to a throne-room or a battlefield to a tavern. It is because his imagination acts unsettlingly on life, because he lives, like Quixote, in disregard of reality, that the 'rejection' at the end of *2 Henry IV* is called for, and is resented. We are unwilling to banish the Falstaffian in ourselves, and (as with Quixote) we feel that there is good in the lies, of a different order from that of cold reality. The truth Falstaff represents has to be found in the ambiguous nature of his banishment, the rights and wrongs of which cannot be resolved.

Nye works on this common ground. Fastolf's 'Apology' is a tissue of lies. Some are alluring; all are vigorous and persuasive. We are allowed to enjoy them but made to see what they are; and we are left to wonder about their value. We are also kept in mind of Nye's literary fraud, to be enjoyed and recognised as no more than a 'web' of his words. Since the book borrows from and partly incorporates a great work of literature we are reminded that Shakespeare too is illusion. His Sir John Falstaff is not the Sir John Fastolf who was known to Henry V, and the history in the plays is as inaccurate as the history in the novel. A strictly 'ludic' novel, however, in Roland Barthes's sense of the term, would expose the cultural and literary myths, convincing us that literature reflects social and human nature only because everything we can know is made of words. Nye employs the right methods for such a task but he does not pursue it. He encourages us to believe in the true humanity of Shakespeare's character as it is seen today, a humanity we share with Shakespeare – which for Roland Barthes was a myth. 'Translated' into modern English, into modern fiction, and into an historical setting which claims to be more realistic than Shakespeare's, Fastolf remains Falstaff, glorious and pathetic, and meant to be heartening.

The use of English, which puts Fastolf and his world in a contemporary perspective makes the book a success, as J. I. M. Stewart observed in a generous review in the *Times Literary Supplement*: 'Mr Nye gets away with his project – triumphantly, it must be roundly said – because he is a minor lord of language himself'.[11] Stewart identified traces of Joyce, and rightly said that Nye's prose is best when least derivative. Then it is good enough to seem at home with its borrowings from Shakespeare. There are few attempts at a substitute for late Middle English and these are derided by Falstaff himself. The novel's first page shows a sureness of rhythm and management of a long sentence, fluctuating in tone, which puts a distance between the narrator and the time and place to which he is supposed to belong. Fastolf is talking aloud and, in character, acting and showing off before his scribe, Worcester; but at the same time he is addressing us. A sharply modern idiom establishes a direct, 'matey' relationship with the reader. The Constableships and Grand Butlerdoms of the period will be viewed from a caustic distance where we can feel at home, it is implied, however unfamiliar we are with the fifteenth century.

Fastolf's memoirs can be wittily and coarsely erotic; pedantically, whimsically, and intelligently erudite; boorishly facetious and delicately lyrical. He discourses on farts, and on angels – on whom he quotes Aquinas the doctor of angels (noting that Poins thought Aquinas was a mineral water). He quotes Isidore, ridicules Gower, retells fabliaux and farces; he finds war grotesquely comic, and unheroically dreadful; he uses language to scandalise his chaplain, and to evoke the poetry of childhood (his kite was 'a plug plugged into the sky' in Chapter IV). Although he constantly echoes Shakespeare and Rabelais, and sometimes later writers – Sterne, Carroll, Joyce, Dylan Thomas – he sounds, throughout his wide range of registers and tones of voice, a Falstaff who has learned modern English. Fifteenth-century affairs are presented for our inspection, in our own idioms, by a narrator whose habits of mind are, none the less, those of his own time. He is essentialist, conscious of mysteries behind the commonplace, and respectful of 'authorities' although not solemnly so. It is as though a late-medieval knight has visited the present day and absorbed, superficially, a body of modern literature; has been delighted to find a brilliant travesty of his life in Shakespeare; and in setting out to write memoirs for us to read has retained his original culture intact.

In the twenty-fourth chapter, for example, 'About St George's Day and flagellants and the earthly paradise', his style alternates nimble chattiness and scholastic precision. For part of the chapter he sounds like a well-read, whimsical present-day undergraduate, amused by the quaintness of his period but close enough to it to borrow its presuppositions:

He did not kill a dragon, that I grant you, if by dragon you mean one of those monstrous snakes, *dracontes* to the Greeks, which used to lurk in the Alps and come swoughing down the sky every now and then to eat diamonds and belch fire. As I say, it depends what you mean by dragons. The devil, St Augustine tells us, *leo et draco est; leo propter impetum, draco propter insidias*. George certainly resisted the persecution of Christians which was all the rage under the Emperor Diocletian, who invented farthings.

The speaker might be a quarter of Fastolf's age, and talking in a student pub; in 'depends what you mean' the seminar phrase is freshened by 'dragons', and there is a juvenile relish in the thought of them 'swoughing down the sky'. Facetiousness excuses the show of information, while the swift flow of the sentences reveals eagerness and the last irrelevance the irresistible pressure of new knowledge. A Falstaff alive today might seek out just such company, and hold his own there (although Shakespeare apparently concealed the extent of the knight's antiquarian curiosity and love of recondite detail). This relaxed university-tavern perspective on history obtains in a substantial part of the novel.

The last section of this chapter records a discussion held with Friar Brackely concerning the earthly Paradise and here the modern English is much closer to a version of medieval speculation. How may we know of it? 'Ha, yes. Basilius, in his *Hexameron*, also Isidorus, *Eth. lib. quartodecimo*, and Josephus, in his first book, say that waters falling from the hill of Paradise constitute a great pond, and out of that pond – as from a well – the four rivers spring . . .'. This language is plain in order to be methodical. The interpolation 'as from a well' suggests a scrap of Latin recalled from Friar Brackley's discourse which must be preserved to keep the exact text of the authority. Details *count* here; the earthly paradise is a subject for science. The ancient fame of it is another proof, Fastolf reflects; 'fame that is false would not have lasted so long'. Paradise cannot be in the moon for there it would 'bereave the light'; and if it were in the sky and 'quite divorced from every land', how could the four rivers flow in 'lands that men have lived in?' Careful wording adjusts logic from premises we cannot share, while Fastolf talks to himself. Baffled by the problem, he consoles himself with what is known of paradise; now his style softens and catches a note to be heard in medieval lyrics.

> As John Damascene says, that place has mirth and fair weather, apples and laughter, for it is the fount of all fairness.

Nye the poet links Fastolf and Paradise through the thought of apples and the Fall: 'And I am Fall stuff'. The style changes again when grave reflections are eased by burnt brandy and a game with his pet rat Desdemona (who has 'eyes like intelligent bonfires'). There is news of civil wars. His secretaries scratch.

> The country's going to the dogs.
> You can't get secretaries without
> fleas anywhere.
>   St George save England!
>   (He'll bloody need to.)

Medieval hagiography is seen through a Fastolf with whom we can readily identify; his account of St George is one of the styles in which we talk about the past. Medieval knowledge of heaven is seen through a character removed from our theologies and set in his place in history; he is a son of the (Catholic) Church, as not of course in Shakespeare. In the last lines the modern note of his scepticism about public affairs and impatience with them chimes with the attitude of the character in the plays when disturbed by the prospect of civil wars. His final thought is one that occurs in every century. As our own attitudes mingle with alien assumptions in this imaginary Falstaff, the language varies in style and tone as the perspective changes. His versatility, incredible outside the rules of Nye's game, is acceptable because the linguistic game is played so well.

These illustrations from Chapter XXIV do not exhaust its scope of topics and styles. The first four paragraphs touch on the question of the 'verisimilitude' of the memoirs and reveal a modern critical sense which is present in many of the narrator's asides about his own 'status' in the narrative. William Worcester has been sent away on a mission to Wales and the circle of secretaries is reduced.

> The reader has seen and heard him go. By his absence we are true, being diminished.

The novel constantly calls attention in ways like this to its own artifice: to its 'fiction' in the sense in which Fastolf might have used the word: 'feigning' or making belief. While Mary Renault asks that we suspend disbelief in a modern English novel as the medium for an ancient Greek, Nye encourages us to notice the use he makes of conventions. Unlike the Renault Greeks whom we are to accept on their own terms or not at all, Fastolf is both an irresistible and a very unreliable narrator.

Even without the anachronisms (Shakespeare included), his story would be far beyond belief; his exploits, in bedchambers and battlefields, and at table are 'Rabelaisian', except that there are no rules by which to judge the varying degrees of exaggeration. Fastolf is like any raconteur who improves a good story except that his improvements are totally lacking in discretion.

> Fact? My belly gives me licence to give imaginative body to what is essentially sparse, even skeletal material: memories, biographies, jokes, histories, conversations, letters, images, fragments.   (Chapter XXXII)

'Imaginative body' means more than day-dream and cleverly articulated fantasy. He is like a man talking to himself, old, tipsy, and egotistical, but certainly imaginative. Being fully conscious of his powers, he is, perhaps, an artist; and as we become familiar with his art, the surrealism of the stories only confirms the reality of the teller. 'The sea fight at Slugs', and the Battle of the Herrings (one of the 'seven great and decisive battles in the history of the world') are beyond belief, but that confirms our expectations of Falstaff ('We shall have more anon').

The anachronisms are meant to undermine this reality in the character. 'I begin to sound like something made up by a poet', he notes; 'better shut up' (Chapter XXXIII). Such allusions to his literary origin exclude him from Nye's joke with the reader, but his hold on Nye's imagination is stronger than that of the 'ludic' points about illusion and 'fictiveness'. When, occasionally, Fastolf is given modernist critical talk, it seems a mistake. In the passage which follows his remark about 'imaginative body', justified in scale by the size of his belly, he says that the book is his 'pattern' and that the reader is free to impose whatever other patterns he wants upon it, since there is 'an infinite series of possibilities' of interpretation. The first idea is Falstaffian; the second sounds like Roland Barthes, or Nye after reading Barthes.[12] Such points are so fashionable that the reader is almost certainly familiar with them already; they do not engage our attention as much as the recreation of Falstaff, which is something new. And since they come within the scheme of the fantasy – Fastolf can speak in any twentieth-century vein he likes – they tend to become absorbed in the rest of his nonsense, without diminishing him.

Fastolf's presence turns theory comic and he takes charge of the issue raised by his own reality or unreality, involving that too in the comedy. He can always dismiss the question by talking and overwhelming the reader with his own personality, but even when he is ousted from the narrative and argued out of existence he seems to count for more than the voice of reason which supplants his. His plan is to dictate the hundred chapters (although he writes some himself) on a hundred days, interrupted by bouts of drinking and wenching, to his secretaries. The secretaries are thin men who deserve to be mocked; as he bullies and humiliates them, they are obliged to write down his insults, and the process of composition is made another tavern game. Bringing the narration (rather than the writing) into the story enhances its claim to be real, as Fastolf points out in his comments on Worcester's mission to Wales. We see the lord of Caister swaggering before his underlings, provoked by their literal-mindedness into ever more outrageous improvements on his true career, whatever that has been. But the thinnest, most recalcitrant of the secretaries, a much abused stepson called Stephen Scrope, rebels and takes over seven of the chapters in order to 'tell the truth' about Fastolf. A dialogue develops between them about what Fastolf *is*: the incarnation of Englishness, a banquet, the round table, Fastolf maintains; the devil, 'King Liar', says Scrope.

All the rational objections which a reader might bring to Nye's fabrication are angrily conveyed in Scrope's intrusive notes.

> Scrope writes this
> N.B.: Not him saying 'Scrope writes this'.
>
> . . . . . .
> I do not write lies.
> I do not write Fastolf.
>
> . . . . . .
> It is time for the Truth!   (Chapter LXXVIII)

He struggles to explain himself, denouncing Fastolf's anachronisms. There are no such things in this world as potatoes and sack! How can a man spend his whole life consuming a drink which does not exist? We are obliged in these passages to reflect on the novel as a post-modernist *fabulation*, or literary game, in which invented characters are made to detect the invention and assert their reality, as vainly, it is implied, as we assert ours. Scrope's claim to belong to the fifteenth century is, we are to see, more real than Fastolf's; he is properly ignorant of potatoes. But he, too, as he innocently says at one point, is in 'a work of fiction' (Chapter LXXXVIII) – by which he means magic. The novel might have ended with something like Thackeray's transformation of the characters to puppets, to be returned to their box, and a firm insistence that this fifteenth century is a puppet-theatre of the mind, as it is. That is only a small part of the effect Nye produces.

The fifteenth century offers Scrope one explanation for such total bafflement. Fastolf, who was already old in the reign of Henry V, and then known as Falstaff, must be the devil, the father of lies, or at least a devil. Augustine taught that the human senses may be played upon by spirits, as Fastolf reminds us. Worcester, Friar Brackley and the others must be ghosts. Caister must be a devilish illusion: 'Cobweb Castle' (Chapter LXXVIII). The reflections on fictiveness which arise in these interpolations are quickly absorbed. They are less interesting in relation to the novel than the question of Fastolf's spiritual condition (which is touched on lightly in the scene in *Henry V* where his death is reported). The title of the first chapter where Scrope intervenes is 'How Sir John Fastolf went on a pilgrimage to the Holy Land' (Chapter LXXVIII); the title of the next is 'How Sir John Fastolf went as a nun to a nunnery' (Chapter LXXXI). Fastolf's blend of piety and unholy riot is seen in relation to its fifteenth-century context.

He is approaching the end of his hundred days and the end of his life. As he makes his will, which Scrope falsifies, and his last confession, which Scrope disbelieves, he arrives at his own formulation of the truth about himself. Prayers are to be offered in perpetuity, according to the will, for the souls of Bardolph, Nym, Pistol, Shallow, Mistress Quickly, Doll Tearsheet, 'Robin my page', and Henry V; among others. In the last confession to Friar Brackley Fastolf admits that the memoirs are mostly lies, although there have been some 'true lies'. The last chapter is told by Scrope who has hastened Fastolf's death, and who taunts him as he dies babbling of green fields. Scrope is given the words of the Hostess speech in *Henry V* (II. iii. 9–27) mixed with his own, so that Fastolf becomes Falstaff and disappears into Shakespeare's text where he belongs, except for a last borrowed tag, 'Remember me'. Whether he deserves to have completed his 'long march to heaven' is a question which is more likely to make us reread the novel than any of the issues of fictiveness now laid to rest. In rereading, a fifteenth-century Fastolf can appear more distinctly, still a very elaborate joke derived from Shakespeare and still an impressive recreation of Shakespeare's Falstaff, but also a character who can be seen against a fifteenth-century background.

In that setting he is Nye's character whose Shakespearean properties coexist with all that the novelist has extrapolated from them. Although the multifarious episodes from childhood on may be (and in many cases must be) lies, there is an inner life, of the kind implied by Shakespeare, which gives an extra interest, there, to his talk of repentance and reforming.[13] Nye tries to show this in relation to medieval life. In this perspective we must see him as a character, not necessarily less comic, who believes in his spirituality and who has to come to terms with religion and the Church.

Late-medieval attitudes to the blatant shortcomings of the Church are too well known from Langland and Chaucer to offer new material to an historical novelist. The young Fastolf's education and intelligence make him doubt the worth of his Uncle Hugh's collection of relics: the sweat of St Michael the Archangel, holy hay from the manger, the finger of St Thomas Didymus (Chapter XIX). The spirit in which he counts himself a Christian (and no Lollard) is distinct from the fantasising relish with which he presents himself as a soldier, a hero, a giant, a tireless lover. He believes that he is a true although not a good Christian, yet he brings from his role as Shakespeare's Falstaff most of the seven deadly sins and a pagan satisfaction in the enjoyment of them. His life and fantasy-life in the novel are as complete a defiance of what the Church taught as his role in the plays is an affront to Tudor Puritanism. Here, as in Shakespeare, he is a sinful glorification of the body and the senses, and here the pagan features of his role are emphasised and extended. They appeal to Fastolf's own imagination. He begins the story with the Priapic giant of Cerne Abbas. 'Wiclif' has preached against it as the devil's work, building a pulpit 'on the giant's stalk, for the purpose of delivering a sermon against it': 'Gentlemen of Dorset . . . I stand here on the worst part of our human nature.' A fig tree, according to Fastolf, is grown to cover the offending ten yards of the giant and under this tree he was conceived. As page to Mowbray he is dressed up as a girl at the whim of the Duchess of Norfolk and spends three years of his youth living among women; in this, he observes, he resembles Achilles. In the 'Battle of Slugs', fought at sea when he is fourteen, he prevails over the French by pouring hogsheads of sack on them from the rigging, where he appears as an elf, or 'puck', or a combination of Bacchus and Cupid (Chapter XV). Classical paganism blends in Fastolf's imagination with the old, preChristian England of which he likes to think himself the champion. His fondness for green fields is tied to his appreciation of May Day, both in a rather Romantically expressed pastoral manner:

> *Forth goeth all the court, both most and least, to fetch the flowers fresh.* That's The Clerk of Works. Nice. That's May Day as it should be . . .
>   May Day: Aphrodite born from a foam of may.
>
> (Chapter XXXIII)

'Apprenticed monk' at the age of fifteen, Fastolf pines, for once (in Chapter XVII); monasticism denies the natural man whom he represents throughout the book. Although the medieval Catholic church was more tolerant of such pagan practice as Maying than the Puritans were to be, it was wary of heretical dangers in an appeal to nature, and Fastolf makes this appeal at every opportunity.

'I am a man made of stars and mud, like the rest of us' (Chapter XLVI) is orthodox, but he exults in his muddy as fully as in his starry nature, and more readily. He defends 'the flesh' facetiously: 'if heaven is unendurable bliss infinitely prolonged then we had better start learning how to endure it' (Chapter LXXXVII). He finds comfort in the indulgent aspect of the Church: 'Oh, Mother Church takes care of all her sons, including hogs and cormorants'. Saint Boniface has instituted a special indulgence to those who drink his health or that of any Pope: Fastolf celebrates his Day with 'my great sequence of Toasts to the Bishops of Rome' and earns thirty-eight indulgences (Chapter XLV). He asserts the virtues which can accompany self-indulgence against the vices the puritan risks, generosity, conviviality, tolerance, against their opposites. The devil he sees as 'thin-bellied', and men such as Scrope can be devilish in their meanness of character and mind. His vitality, imagination and above all laughter are more pleasing to God than the devil. He can be cruel, but he admits that cruelty is sinful; he can be compassionate, and he wins his knighthood for an act of mercy (in Chapter LXXXIX). He claims, too, the virtue of honesty, admitting himself a coward and blaming the hypocrisy of 'honour' for the curse of the wars in which his rascality has been a minor matter; his later relatively sombre accounts of the wars in France lend this view some support. His lechery, real or imagined, has to be confessed in the ninety-ninth chapter as mortal sin, but it has all been conducted in a confident obedience to Fastolf's rules of life. Halfway through the novel (in Chapter XXXVIII) he counsels his niece and mistress Miranda on the forgiveness of sins. There will be joy even in Purgatory, he says. Sins are only human nature and Christ has atoned for them. It is 'a tall story' but 'God is a tall story' and 'we are a tall story too'. He quotes Tertullian's *'certum est quia impossibile'* and pleads on his own behalf that he has a passion for 'the wisdom of foolishness'. Most of the rest of the chapter describes his subsequent sport with Miranda. Friar Brackley is said to correct Fastolf's wilder notions. From his point of view, there is presumably more folly than wisdom in the speciousness of this scene.

The real Brackley was apparently more interested in politics than theology.[14] But the novel's friar might maintain to himself or to God that Fastolf is a huge sample of all that is baptised but incompletely tamed by Christianity in medieval England. (In medieval literature, The Wife of Bath is another.) The eighth chapter of J. Huizinga's *The Waning of the Middle Ages*, 'Love Formalised', provides reminders of how thoroughly mixed pagan and Christian conceptions remained in medieval culture. 'The brutality and the licence of the lower classes was always fervently but never very efficiently, repressed by the Church', Huizinga wrote there, and 'the sexual life of the higher classes remained surprisingly rude.'[15] He provided ample illustration. There were 'two layers of civilisation superimposed, coexisting though contradictory', and these can be seen in 'courtly' and 'primitive' verse.[16] In Charles d'Orléans he found 'erotic poetry [striving] . . . to recover that primitive connexion with sacred matters of which the Christian religion had bereft it'.[17] Discussing Jean de Meun and the second part of the *Roman de la Rose*, Huizinga's argument recalls that more heretical, and modern, ideas than Fastolf's were current at the beginning of the fifteenth century. 'It is impossible to imagine a more deliberate defiance of the Christian ideal' than Jean de Meun in the *Roman de la Rose*.[18] Sexuality is defended, there, by Venus, Nature and Genius.

Chastity is condemned as Nature's enemy, unacceptable to God. 'The intimate circle of Jean de Meun's admirers . . . is identical with that of the first French humanists'.[19] Despite attacks, the most effective by Jean Gerson of the University of Paris, this work was profoundly influential and tags from it became common sayings. Attempts were made to 'moralise' or reclaim it for orthodox Christianity, by finding religious meanings in its allegories.[20] The cultured Brackley, knowing of Jean de Meun, will perhaps think Fastolf an innocent, and a relatively docile child of the Church.

Fastolf's reading seems to have been conventional and there is no reason to suppose him influenced by the later part of the *Roman de la Rose*. He is, rather, a spokesman for the 'primitive' elements in medieval life which his intelligence and smatterings of learning can articulate. Like the common soldiers who are unaffected by honour, and the taverners whose licence is inefficiently repressed by the Church, he remains firmly within organised religion but equally firmly recalcitrant.

As a character in a sort of historical novel he can be called realistic in representing a rebarbative humanity which the Christian religion has always had to contend with. In a later age of faith than that which Nye portrays, Shakespeare's Falstaff was able to still the theatre's groundlings, according to a contemporary report, as no other stage character could.[21] One reason for Falstaff's power is that he represents the human, more than the devilish, component in the Church's stage figure of the Vice. Another is the imaginative life which Shakespeare bestows. The chief reality in Nye's book is that of Falstaff's imagination which remains even when we have seen the illusion of an historical Falstaff ridiculed away. Nye's achievement is more difficult to assess because its centre of interest is not his property; Fastolf could not have been conceived without Falstaff. Since Falstaff is present at the back of the reader's mind, several features of *Falstaff* look very flimsy. The erotic fantasies are written with the right deft gusto but they are too many and too long, of little literary and no historical interest. The Rabelaisian lists (of Popes, giants, banquet-courses) are appropriate, in that Falstaff would like Rabelais and in that we think of him as Rabelaisian. The typographical oddities and the diagrams which fashionably decorate many of the pages can be defended too: Falstaff would scrawl graffiti. But these devices quickly come to seem doodling on Nye's part. As a wit, as a poet, and as an historical novelist, he has achieved far more than that.

In the foreground of the novel is one of the grandest of literary characters, 'dismantled' in the ludic manner: it is good to see how well he survives the process, how easily imagination can get the better of theoretical manipulation. The background is the historical period from which he was borrowed for Shakespeare's purposes sketchily but vividly shown. The book is a celebration of Falstaff and a reflection on his origin in Fastolf, and in the religion of Fastolf's time. As a hero for today Falstaff might have been seen as the champion of modern 'permissiveness'; this novel often implies that he would think poorly of the later twentieth century (he makes caustic comments on 'modernism' observing that it was an exhausted movement in the sixth century –in Chapter XXXVII). He is, rather, the champion of imagination, 'ludic' in the most positive sense. Games and laughter, he maintains, take place in all healthy minds and his is superbly healthy, although not clean. 'O the laughter of God is endless', he says (Chapter XXIII); 'a soul that could not laugh would be a dead soul, a stick, a devil' (Chapter XXXVIII). Because he maintains that there is truth behind laughter he speaks for his own age and for what survives from it in ours. Modern theories which count him no more than illusion, he would say, belong to thin men.

6   J. G. Farrell: Empire Trilogy

Mary Renault reminds us of an historian interpreting facts and bringing the past to life for present readers on the basis of the evidence. Burgess and Nye put us in mind of literary critics for whom facts about the past are seen in relation to the literature, language and legends which have survived. J. G. Farrell resembles a philosopher for whom facts are curious in themselves. Margaret Drabble's essay on his work comments on the abundance of ideas which obsess the characters and of things which beset them.[1] It is the most pervasive characteristic of these novels. Facts for Farrell are made of ideas and of things; he holds up these specimens of the past for inspection, with a kind of wonderment. Objects give reality to facts. A hotel is in charred ruins today because it was burned down in the Troubles of 1921. There are funeral-wells at Lucknow because of the Mutiny. Ideas helped to make the facts, and offered explanation at the time. Farrell has ideas of his own, although he is not doctrinaire. His ruling idea is that man is caught between the irresistible temptations of thought and the recalcitrant nature of the physical world about him. He set his best novels at three points in the hundred years before he began to write and he argued that this distancing gave a freedom to his vision of life. Life, he thought, 'basically does not change very much'.

This recent past was very real to Farrell. He set out the facts from his research, he let the ideas of the period loose in his characters, and he surrounded them – indeed, bombarded them – with its physical substance. The books deal with three of the most disastrous episodes in the course of the British Empire: in *Troubles* (1970), Ireland between 1919 and 1921; in *The Siege of Krishnapur* (1973), the Indian Mutiny; and in *The Singapore Grip* (1978), the Japanese Invasion of 1942. The people of these stories are in historic difficulties ('Difficulties' was a working title for the Mutiny novel)[2] which they find hard to interpret, while struggling in mental and physical turmoil. We are meant, although without much fuss on the author's part, to find that a metaphor of our own condition. In the following passage he used this term in the course of remarks about *Troubles* recorded in 1972.

> It is a common misconception that when the historians have finished with an historical incident there remains nothing but a patch of feathers and a pair of feet; in fact, the most important things, for the very reason that they are trivial, are unsuitable for digestion by historians, who are only able to nourish themselves on the signing of treaties, battle-strategies, the formation of Shadow Cabinets and so forth. These matters are quite alien to the life most people lead, which consists of catching colds, falling in love, or falling off bicycles. It is this *real* life which is the novelist's concern (though, needless to say, realism is not the only way to represent it). One of the things I have tried to do in *Troubles* is to show people 'undergoing' history, to use an expression of Sartre's. The Irish troubles of 1919–1921 were chosen partly because they appeared to be safely lodged in the past; most of the book was written before the current Irish difficulties broke out, giving it an unintended topicality. What I wanted to do was to use this period of the past as a metaphor for today, because I believe that however much the superficial detail and customs of life may change over the years, basically life itself does not change very much. Indeed all literature that survives must depend on this assumption. Another reason why I preferred to use the past is that, as a rule, people have already made up their minds about the present. About the past they are more susceptible to clarity of vision.[3]

We are more likely to see what is absurd in a Victorian phrenologist's attempts to reduce human nature to a convenient system (in the portrayal of the Magistrate in *The Siege of Krishnapur*) Farrell's last point says, than to see the same essential absurdity in the post-Freudian psychiatrist – if we believe in psychiatry. We are more likely to sympathise with the man blinded by Victorian science – if we disbelieve. And we may be led to see the phrenologist's predicament as a metaphor for that of the psychiatrist. As for *real* life, if we look at a war-artist's record of such a scene as the relief of Krishnapur, we assume as historians that those present were filled with personal and patriotic elation at the return of Imperial order. In Farrell's '*real* life' his phrenologist, 'the Magistrate', takes advantage of the moment to place his hand on the neck, publicly inviolable in normal circumstances, of Lucy – a fallen woman and an ideal phrenological test case. He finds to his 'dismay and incredulity' that her organ of amativeness is by no means as developed as her character and career require. Slapped by Lucy, and caught in the act by a passing subaltern, the Magistrate is scientifically and socially mortified at the very moment when history expects him to exult. This is how an individual may undergo history, 'falling off his bicycle', in the *real* life the novelist observes. Farrell's talent was for comedy and his first instinct was to show the disparity between everyday life and history. In the midst of the Troubles, the Mutiny, or the invasion of Singapore, he shows moments of history which are lifelike in seeming so unhistoric to those involved. 'Undergoing history' suggests human helplessness and Farrell's work makes this seem to be in the nature of things. He shows how the scale of most lives differs from the scale on which we conceive history. This can help dispel present prejudice; the novels combat prejudice too, by showing ironically how passionately wrong ideas, and ideas open to question, are held by his people of the past. Given that life is always 'essentially the same', this makes a metaphor of the past, always comic and sometimes shocking.

This particular blend of humour and pathos, of the bizarre and the horrific, has been traced to a wide enough variety of sources to establish its originality. John Spurling's essay detects Stendhal, Conrad, Mann, Malcolm Lowry and P. G. Wodehouse.[4] It is true that one chapter of a Farrell novel can bring Stendhal and Wodehouse to mind. Evelyn Waugh and Anthony Powell are also sometimes audible in the background of Farrell's writing, although it is less barbed and less mannered than either. He sounds most like himself. In *The Siege of Krishnapur* the poet Fleury, loading a gun, seems to discover a truth; that 'nobody is *superior* to anyone else, he only may be better at doing a specific thing'.

Doubtless, Coleridge or Keats or Lamartine would have been as clumsy with the sponge as he was himself . . . but wait, had not Lamartine been a military man? With French poets you could never tell. He stepped back, his ears ringing as the cannon crashed again. He could not remember.

(Chapter 10)

It would be tedious to try to add to John Spurling's sound observations on how Farrell absorbed other modern writers or to relate this moment of ill-advised absorption to a long, rich tradition of comic writing. It is a clue, however, to what is most characteristic in these novels and to the way in which the past is made a metaphor for the present. It is Farrellian in making the real world, which perhaps includes both the fact of Lamartine as a military poet, and the cannon, threaten to obstruct the free flow of ideas.[5] Farrell gave such intellectual characters as Fleury his own love of ideas; it may be that his physical disability (after polio) sharpened his sense of the intractable nature of things and of the facts with which we report on them. Ideas are increasingly abundant in the 'Empire' sequence. The novels present worlds crowded with things and facts which counter the characters' speculations. The intellectual life of the recent history with which they deal overlaps, of course, with ours which so much derives from the hundred years they cover. The period is so well documented that a researcher is liable to be overwhelmed with facts, and things in which the past survives are known to all of us. The three Imperial failures in Ireland, India and Singapore are conscientiously treated as historical episodes. The novelist is most interested in showing them as examples of theory in conflict with contingency, of ideas at odds with hard fact.

Puzzling over the character of his fiancée, 'the Major' in *Troubles* ponders the 'precise and factual letters' which she wrote to him while he was at the front. The letters are no help, although they were 'filled . . . with an invincible reality as hard as granite'. On the day the Mutiny breaks out in Krishnapur Fleury is engaged in a long and fruitless lecture, aimed at the Maharajah's unappreciative son Hari, on the futility of materialism. There are various ironies at work as he talks of the holiness of the heart and the uselessness of modern inventions. He is speaking to the only Indian in Krishnapur who, because he has accepted European ideas about material progress, does not at this moment intend to do Fleury to death and drive the British out of India. He is soon in the exigencies of the siege, to be inventing new weapons himself, and slaughtering Indians on behalf of material progress, among other causes. But the most telling irony is that while he speaks he is in the grip of metal clamps attached to his head so that Hari can take his picture with the latest daguerreotype machine: 'he was seething with excitement and would have sprung to his feet, gesticulating, had not his head been firmly wedged in the iron ring.' (Chapter 5). The world of objects imposes a more subtle restraint on intellectual passions later in the book when the Collector of Krishnapur is reduced to sitting on an oak throne which has a missing front leg. Since the Collector cannot express strong opinions without leaning forward to emphasise them the chair teaches him to see 'several sides to every question': 'It had once even gone so far as to empty him onto the floor for voicing an intolerant opinion on the Jesuits'. The chair's influence becomes permanent, acting on the Collector even when he leaves it.

> 'Without love everything is a desert. Even Justice, Science and Respectability.' The Collector was careful to embrace this conviction in a moderate manner, lest he be tipped out of the chair in which he was no longer sitting.   (Chapter 31)

Margaret Drabble's essay is partly an attempt to rescue him from the charge that he makes history appear comic but meaningless. She rightly identifies the ruling spirit in the books, which is honest bafflement.

> There are few writers who have made such pervasive use of the emotion of bewilderment. Confused, puzzled, surprised, doubtful, uncertain, hesitating, depressed – these are words that appear with haunting regularity. The typical Farrell man is baffled by politics, by economics, by history itself, which cannot be made to fit his preconceived notions. His response is at first eager, vulnerable, naive. Yet he is honourably and honestly, if a little hopelessly, engaged in an attempt to understand, to fit the incomprehensible parts together.[6]

The typical Farrell man fails, and the reader's wish to fit the parts together receives little help from the author. The Major's belief in the civilising power of the British Empire is, Margaret Drabble notes, 'a view clearly not shared by the author'.[7] That is clearly so, although the Major and many of the other characters who represent Britishness remain civilising powers themselves, on a small scale. Why the British Empire fails is still an open question at the end of *The Singapore Grip*, when the nature and extent of its failure have been thoroughly surveyed. By the time he wrote this, Farrell had come to think that most of the clues were to be found in economics. When he was awarded the Booker Prize for *The Siege of Krishnapur* he spoke scathingly of Booker McConnell's treatment of Third World employees.[8] His sympathy is obvious in the books, for the Irish poor, for the Asians of Singapore, and for the Indians although they are seen through cool and amused British eyes in *The Siege of Krishnapur*. The sympathy is unmixed with sentimentality, and it does not simplify Farrell's thinking or distort his portrayal of characters in possession of wealth and power. Margaret Drabble ends her essay in well-intentioned confusion about Farrell as a political writer.

> Finally, it seems to me that his last three finished novels are at heart political, and that his own attitude is neither as detached nor as neutral as it may at first glance appear. All the distancing is directed towards one end – the revelation of the absurdity and injustice of things as they are, and the need for radical change. How much faith he had in the possibility of change is another matter . . . Farrell combined a sense of the pointless absurdity of man with a real and increasing compassion for characters caught up in decay and confusion, so that, though they may be the puppets of history, they are not merely puppets. Kindness, gentleness, concern for others – these are enduring values in which British gentlemen like the Major do not hold a monopoly (witness Matthew's delight in *The Singapore Grip* at finding a non-European doctor, a 'lonely philanthropist', devoting all his spare time and money to the inmates of a dying-house). There is hope for the future . . .[9]

This begins with a bold statement about politics and 'radical change' and ends with the author's respect for the 'lonely' good man amidst the chaos, who may be British or Chinese. Hope today is no more or less than when Raffles first visited Singapore, on this basis, which is all Farrell offers. Will any new undertaking with ambitions on the scale of the Empire's do better? The question is bewildering.

Whereas Burgess and Nye, ludic historical novelists, reveal the problematic nature of fiction, Farrell reveals the problematic nature of historical interpretation. He accepts the older conventions of modern prose narrative and believes they reflect what we normally experience. Each novel is a story which proceeds from a start to a finish in an orderly manner. The characters are presented as they conceive themselves and see one another. Farrell is a realist. The masonry of the Majestic Hotel in *Troubles*, the furniture of the Residency at Krishnapur, and the rubber in the godowns at Singapore are real and their reality is accessible to common sense. Farrell is sceptical about general ideas, suspecting the false comfort they can offer us, and our reluctance to keep testing them against real life. It is an understandable, although a disastrous reluctance, because Farrell's real world is not kind to theory. It is not totally perplexing. A good deal of liberal opinion is obviously endorsed by the author. But in *The Siege of Krishnapur* points are made, in favour of female emancipation for example, which seem almost trite; and Farrell's imagination tends to be engaged on the 'wrong' side; he is better at imagining the Collector's view of women, attracted but patronising, than at imagining the suppressed personalities of the Victorian ladies, and more interested in what most fully occupies his imagination. But he does not indulge the fixed ideas of his characters, even when he sympathises; if he had chosen to put a feminist into *The Siege of Krishnapur*, the novel would probably have started to find facts which fail to fit.

A definition of the perspective in these novels was offered in her review by Elizabeth Bowen. Saying that the book 'is not a "period piece"', she went on:

> it is yesterday reflected in today's consciousness. The ironies, the disparities, the dismay, the sense of unavailingness are contemporary.[10]

It would be more completely accurate to say that doubts, detected in the periods in which the three novels are set are adjusted to contemporary consciousness. As for the period of *Troubles*, one can find something of this consciousness, for example, in the writings of AE (George William Russell); although he was, in spite of it, an optimist about the hope of uniting Ireland, he was as sensitive as the narrator of *Troubles* to the absurd and destructive divisions which events were making worse in the years after 1916.[11] *Troubles* lets us hear the fanatical voices of those years. The narrative voice which records them is more quietly aware of irony and unavailingness than would have been possible or acceptable at the time. Although Irish history began to renew the old voices while *Troubles* was still in the press, the intention was to show the perplexities of half a century ago as a metaphor for those of the time of writing. Its distance, now, has an unintended irony but the method works, here as in the two sequels. Modern history is baffling, at Krishnapur and at Singapore and although we know more about how, we are little wiser about why things happen as they did. Only human worth, in the Major or the Chinese doctor Margaret Drabble mentions, can finally be set above the granite hardness of fact. Each novel portrays characters who are trapped, because each novel is the story of a siege. In the first, a community of British residents is isolated in a vast decaying hotel in the Irish countryside. Krishnapur is a remote station cut off from the British world once the Mutiny starts. Singapore is gradually encircled by the Japanese. When we look for metaphor, the first is plain to see. British civilisation is besieged in the modern world; and we may remember the phrase from Vauban used in *The Siege of Krishnapur*: '*place assiégée, place prise!*' – although the novel proves that wrong for once. Siege-mentality in each book offers a metaphor for modern British thinking: it is not insisted on, but once noticed is full of implications which we may take if we choose. A siege can bring out the best and the worst in those who undergo it. It does concentrate attention on physical realities.

The point of observation in *Troubles* is inside the Majestic Hotel at Kilnalough during the residence of Major Brendan Archer (always known as 'the Major') between 1919 and 1921; for most of the story the point of view in the third person narration is his. In the summer of 1919 he leaves the army, after a period of convalescence following shell-shock in the trenches, and goes to Ireland for the first time to seek out Angela Spencer, whose father owns the Majestic. She is an Anglo-Irish girl he once met briefly on leave; she has corresponded with him ever since and they rather vaguely appear to be engaged. Although Angela declines and dies early in the story, the Major is drawn into the life of her family, the hotel, and its neighbourhood. Angela's brother Ripon upsets their father, Edward Spencer, by marrying a Catholic heiress. Edward comes to depend on the Major to help preserve the hotel, although relations between them become strained when both are in love with Sarah, another Catholic girl. A cheerful note is provided by Angela's teenage sisters, twins who involve the Major in their pranks. Sinn Fein militants (Shinners) are a constant menace but the darkest shadow is cast by the presence of Auxiliaries who make themselves a nuisance at the hotel and at the golf club. The story reaches a climax on the night of the Ball which has been arranged in the hope of reviving the hotel's former glory. The result is a disaster, partly because of the indiscretion of Edward and Sarah, partly because of the Auxis' loutish behaviour. A dénouement quickly develops. Sarah runs away with the leader of the Auxiliaries, the hotel guests are driven away by the news that the Republic is to be recognised and British troops withdrawn. Only then does a Sinn Feiner appear, to be shot dead by Edward for trying to blow up Queen Victoria's statue. When a Black and Tan arrives he is drowned by Sinn Feiners, who would have drowned the Major too but for the timely arrival of some last-ditch old lady residents. While they are rescuing the Major the hotel butler sets fire to the Majestic which burns to the ground.

There are key incidents in Farrell which are minor in themselves but very memorable and very concentrated in effect. It would be hard to forget the moment at which the great metallic letter 'M' becomes detached from the rest of the name on the hotel's facade and falls on a terrace-table where an old lady is about to take afternoon tea. She is unhurt but indignant. To Edward's relief it transpires that she has not identified the source of the large 'sea-gull shaped piece of metal' which has dropped from the sky, and that she is annoyed only at the destruction of her tea, having spent much of the afternoon searching the hotel's interminable corridors for a servant to take her order. Edward orders fresh tea to be brought. Henceforth the hotel proclaims itself 'AJESTIC'. Edward soon stops worrying but the Major, who worries about everything at Kilnalough, thinks that the hotel may be on the point of collapse.

Majestic and graced by Victoria's statue, the hotel symbolises the British connection of the Anglo-Irish ascendancy rather than the Anglo-Irish themselves – a varied, complex society. The house 'was still standing', we are told in the first paragraph of the novel, 'in those days'. Once, yachts would have been beached there; an annual regatta was held in July. Today there are charred remains. By the time the place burned down it was 'in such a state of disrepair that it hardly mattered'. From the Major's first surprised encounter the state of disrepair of the Majestic and its occupants is almost lovingly explored. If a large, crumbling Irish house and household appears at first as part of a whimsical literary convention, as Bernard Bergonzi noted, Farrell sets about asserting its reality with enthusiastic conviction.[12] The gateposts, askew although still mounted by their stone crowns, retain the 'skeletons' of great iron hinges which once supported gates. The house is perhaps held together, perhaps in the last stages of being broken asunder, by its ivy and tropical vegetation, covered with dust, like everything else inside the house. Only a few of the three hundred rooms are occupied, by aged guests who can no longer pay their bills. As the Major explores the building, fascinated and appalled, Farrell charts and details a vast, intricate ruin, whose furnishings and equipment recall its former luxury, and testify to the stamina of those who still live in the wreckage. The room the Major chooses has a fine view of terraces leading down to the sea, but a faintly unpleasant smell; in a bedside cupboard he finds a sheep's head smothered in maggots; these sheep-heads, Edward explains, unembarrassed, are what they feed to the dogs. So intensely lived in, once, and now so abandoned, the house asserts itself against its remaining occupants, in various ways. Its size makes human relations difficult. The Major spends hours vainly searching for his fiancée, and does not learn that she has been dying from leukaemia until he attends her funeral. Edward and the rich Catholic miller Mr Noonan, whose daughter Ripon marries, fail to meet after wandering the corridors, always on different floors. At one point Edward attacks the encroaching foliage with a kitchen knife but its hold on the fabric is irresistible. The upper rooms are dangerously infested with cats, whose raids into the uninhabited regions can result in horrible outbursts of violence. Animal life abounds; there are piglets, peacocks, sparrows, owls, rats and mice, all vulnerable; the cats fight back with weird tenacity against all attempts to exterminate them until their flaming finish. The fall of the initial 'M' seems both a surrender and a spiteful act of violence on the part of the house.

It falls in December 1920. November 1920, F. S. L. Lyons writes, was 'by any reckoning the worst month of the entire Anglo-Irish war'.[13] The atrocities committed by Irish and British forces, often against non-combatant civilians, reached proportions in Dublin and Cork which justify the term 'war', although the character of the attacks and 'reprisals' hardly seemed to people like the Major to deserve that term. Farrell amply documents the shootings and other 'punishments' with news excerpts and gossip, and uses newspaper quotations to recall the violence taking place in other parts of the world, in Russia, in Chicago, in India. The Major who has witnessed a killing and counter-killing in a Dublin street feels that journalism reduces the reality of such events, shielding the reader with a screen of 'history'. The novel shields the reader from the full horror of the small troubles. 'Shinners' are discreetly plundering the Majestic, but it is not until Edward shoots the young man who comes to dynamite the Queen's statue that the events which have often seemed to the Major to resemble comic opera turn to bloodshed. Early skirmishes are grotesque or comic illustrations of the lack of understanding between people such as Edward and members of Sinn Fein. This delay allows Farrell to create his siege-mentality within the hotel – a mixture of habitual fear prompted by rumours and a sense of the unreality of violence reported in the newspapers. The decay of the house and the physical struggles with its fabric and its animal life convey the tensions and the hatreds within British Ireland. The British house in which Edward and his guests shelter is out of order and the falling 'M' should recall to them as it does to the reader that danger is as likely to come from 'their' side as from the 'enemy' outside. What falls, though, is neither a symbol nor, once detached, a letter, but a murderous piece of metal which narrowly misses. The victim's lack of surprise or curiosity about its provenance is funny, but also grimly appropriate. By December 1920 people were so accustomed to random, incomprehensible attacks from nowhere that they were, like the Major a year earlier, shell-shocked.

It is partly through Edward and partly through the hotel that Farrell sets the Ireland of 1919–21 against its background of past troubles extending back centuries, and in living memory as far back as the famine. Shabby and precarious as it has become, the Majestic never lets us forget that it has deserved its name. It is still a rich source of accidentally-strewn subsistence for the very poor of the district who come to rifle its dustbins. It is freighted with hunting and sporting equipment, from the best shops, reminders of how English prosperity had affected those in Ireland who had enough money to buy English goods— an alien influence which was especially resented by the Gaelic-Catholic element in the independence movement. Edward is living, like his old lady guests, and his daughter Angela in her last days, on memories of his past in India and in an earlier Ireland. That his son, who has not fought in the Great War, abandons him, sharing none of his basic faiths, indicates (as perhaps does the hint of self-mockery in his eyes) that he knows his fiercely unquestioningly pro-British cause is finished. He is not likely to give in. His broken nose is a souvenir from Trinity, where he boxed against a heavier Gaelic-speaking adversary who repeatedly knocked him down, while he showed British pluck by repeatedly getting up again until felled by a lucky blow. Although not much disturbed by the fallen 'M', he is irritated by the disfigurement of the proud name. If half the house should fall down, the Major reflects, Edward would console himself with the thought of a hundred and fifty rooms still standing, far more than he could hope to fill. Edward's pride, in his hopeless son for example, is touching; the erratic vigour with which he prosecutes the hopeless defence of his interests can be impressive. The Ball deserved to be a success. He is at times more than slightly mad, but he has a touch of the dignity that lingers about the Majestic; and he has a decency, rather lacking in Ripon and completely absent in the Auxiliaries, which finds a warm response in the Major. It would be impossible for him to think of asking the old ladies to pay their bills. Like the house he was solidly built; but as with the house, his position is now indefensible.

It is ironically amusing that Edward is quite unaware of any connection between the state of his house and his own situation. But in reading we are only partially aware of symbolism. The Majestic is a real house, not a 'symbolic system' as it would be in a novel by L. P. Hartley or William Golding. We are constantly reminded of its reality, and the title often seems to apply more immediately to the house than to the political and military affairs in the country. Edward remains optimistic, the Major doubtful, as curious cracking sounds are heard in the brick-work, or a black hole appears in the slates of the roof of the servants' wing, or bulges of new vegetation grow in the walls. The Majestic is in the foreground of our attention. As Edward rails against Catholicism, or Irish Nationalism, or 'traitors' in general, asserting the stock of slogans which serve him for ideas, these interpretations of the greater troubles seem simply irrelevant. Sarah's equally stale and repetitive views on Ireland – Ireland might as well be invaded by Germans as governed by stiff, ignorant British gentlemen of the Major's kind – are their counterpart. Ideas in this novel are reiterated, not developed. More thoughtful, better informed views which might have been used – those of AE, of Yeats or of G. B. Shaw – are left out. De Valera, who is mentioned in the novel, is a figure who seems very remote from the Majestic – but remote too, Farrell might have said, from the experience of most people in Ireland then. The most high-minded discussion takes place when a group of English undergraduates visits the hotel; they are on a vacation study-tour and are sure of getting 'to the bottom of the Irish question'. At dinner they infuriate Edward with their pacifist and democratic opinions; in the rage which follows he kills the Sinn Feiner. That the undergraduates are right that Britain must respect the results of the elections, which have given Sinn Fein a sweeping majority, seems less important than their superficiality. They are so sure of their ideas (all secondhand from the Oxford Union) that they cannot see where they are. They play croquet and rag in the corridors while the post-war Majestic creaks emptily about them. The revolvers set out at dinner are a joke to them – except to the one older sudent who was in the War.

The war is the great fact behind the situation which the Major is unwilling to discuss; it still gives him nightmares. The war has left objects, some cherished by Edward who has a volume of photographs of fallen heroes. (Their fading faces are beginning to look indistinguishable.) The term 'hero' is part of Edward's mental equipment but it means little to the Major. The 'Auxis' are returned heroes, 'the men from the trenches'; the Major suspects that nothing in Ireland is very meaningful to them. The ex-soldier among the undergraduates is dazed by their talk, in which he concurs; but he sits handling the revolver as a familiar thing amidst unfamiliar ideas.

The first two pages of the novel describe the Major's state of mind after hospital. His aunt invites friends to tea to cheer him up. At first he is excessively cheerful, leaping about with cakes and sandwiches. After a time he vanishes and the aunt finds him sitting in a deserted drawing-room with bitterness in his face. Later he returns, cheerful again. When some young ladies are invited he dismays everyone by staring at their heads and limbs. He is thinking, we are told, 'how firm and solid they look, but how easily they come away from the body'. The realities the Major has known make ideas about the war unhelpful.

As a character he is simply composed of the qualities we should expect in the most attractive but unexceptional kind of young officer of the First World War, disciplined in himself, politely tolerant to others. Farrell makes him a remarkably attractive character. John Spurling thinks him 'one of the most sympathetic characters in fiction . . . a Quixote without being a fool, a Galahad without being a prig'; and that praise is not absurd.[14] Always surprised but never flummoxed, often vexed or hurt but always moderate, his partly shell-shocked bewilderment at the Troubles makes an ideal sensibility (given Farrell's uncommitted purposes) in which to record them. He is — gentlemanliness apart — a good as well as a likeable man, something notoriously hard to achieve in literature; and he is entitled, we should feel, to his outburst of injustice when it comes. He has been appalled by Edward's killing of the saboteur; sitting with the priest, listening to one patriot condemning the murder of another, he is suddenly appalled by the man's hatred joined to the sign of his Catholicism, the crucifix on the wall. Edward, he tells the priest, in a surge of anger, was right. This is the only such outburst in three hundred and fifty pages. Soon afterwards, just before the very end, he is, as 'punishment', buried up to the neck in the beach to wait for the tide to come in, and still bewildered.

The Major's role as the sensibility in which events are registered (his role as British representative is obvious) can be seen to justify the feature of the novel which has caused most annoyance. Instead of working the background of Irish and British atrocities into the story, as talk, or ignoring it, Farrell inserts newspaper paragraphs, unrelated to the surrounding text; these cover Irish and foreign news. Bernard Bergonzi, who admires the novel, hints at a disapproval of this inartistic solution which is more strongly expressed by other critics.[15]

> A global context is established by the intermittent quotation of newspaper reports showing what was happening in the rest of the world; Bolshevism in Russia; D'Annunzio entering Fiume; race riots in Chicago; massacre at Amritsar. It is an effective if unsubtle way of emphasising the novel's historicity.[16]

The unsubtlety, in this subtle book, is consciously perpetrated. It would have been in the *Irish Times* that the Major learned of the wider troubles. Newspapers *are* unsubtly insistent and disconcerting in their obtrusion of facts on our attention. The Major, who can cope with things at the Majestic, is at a loss with these reports. The news does not seem to fit into experience and the newspapers seem to jettison horrific events into 'history'. Looking back at the Major we can sympathise with this helplessness – we are invited to make more of these fossils of fact than he could when they were alive. Was Bolshevism connected with the Irish independence movement, however indirectly? That was an awkward question for the Irish leaders between 1916 and 1921.[17] The novel leaves us to contemplate the fact that the uprisings coincided, as though to say 'that is history'. It is concerned with the *'real life'* going on at the time as those who lived it underwent history.

Troubles is not a study of the Troubles which would make a useful introduction for a student of history. We need, at least, to have read F. S. L. Lyons first.[18] *The Siege of Krishnapur* is more ambitious in the scale on which it transforms fact into fiction.

The fictional siege in the novel has been created from accounts of what happened in various parts of India; it tries to show the Mutiny in little, and it could serve as an introduction to the history. Farrell has taken Herbert Butterfield's idea, that the modern historian's final statement may be a piece of detailed research rather than a firm generalisation, and inverted it for his own purpose.[19] He has explored the general history of the Indian Mutiny in order to construct his own particular case; he uses this to illustrate general truths about the British in India and about human behaviour. Farrell's 'Afterword' tells us that the novel has borrowed from diaries, letters and memoirs as well as from history books.[20] The novelist remains, of course, free to invent. There are signs that he has been less exact than we should expect of an historian. He mentions as one of his sources ('among the writers I have cannibalised') 'F. C. Sherer' who is presumably J. W. Sherer, author of *Daily Life during the Indian Mutiny* (1898), or F. C. Maude, author of *Memoirs of the Mutiny* (1894) whose two volumes incorporate Sherer's narrative. In the text of the novel there is a reference to 'the rebel who had just shot the adjutant' (Chapter 2), and who was subsequently overpowered by the moral presence of General Hearsey. In fact the rebel had shot the adjutant's horse and then wounded the adjutant with a sword.[21] Of course the young man Fleury who remembers this incident when he meets the general may be held responsible for a small error. Such details do not detract from Farrell's intention to be loyal to the sources.

It is hard to keep the Mutiny in one perspective. When we read detailed accounts by survivors it is cataclysmic. To the British residents who endured the major sieges at Cawnpore and Lucknow the order of things must have seemed to be changing. As happens in the novel, people went mad at Cawnpore, and the ladies who had been so carefully protected from all forms of Indian unpleasantness were suddenly immersed in it. Other scenes in Farrell are copied from what happened at Lucknow where the European population took its stand in the Residency, attending regular church-services, but hoarding food, auctioning property, and dining on sparrows, like the people of Krishnapur. The siege of Cawnpore ended in the massacre of men, women and children.[22] The slaughter of (often) innocent Indians which followed the suppression of the uprising (and which is not within the scope of the novel) must have been worsened by the sense in those who had seen it that their basic beliefs had been injured or destroyed. But when we look at the Mutiny in the context of the whole history of British India it seems almost a minor matter. It was confined to Bengal. The other regions under the Company's control remained loyal, and even in Oudh where the fighting was worst many Hindoos and Muslims took the British side.[23] Normal life soon resumed, after the reprisals. The displacement of the Company and the assumption of direct colonial rule which the Mutiny hastened would have soon taken place anyway. Farrell does not attempt the larger perspective. His point of view is that of his characters who are fighting for their lives, for all their worldly goods, and for all they have believed; in all these respects he imagines it as a shattering experience.

The novel might be read together with such a work of detailed research as J. A. B. Palmer's *The Mutiny Outbreak at Meerut in 1857* (1966). Palmer begins with background information. 'Chapatis', 'Greased Cartridges' and 'The Presidency Division [of the army], February to May' are the titles of his first three chapters. He proceeds to a minute analysis of the cantonment at Meerut in the late spring of 1857, and then to a day-by-day reconstruction of what happened. His last chapter of 'Conclusions' offers some general reflections, including a comparison of crowd-behaviour in the Mutiny and in the French Revolution. Farrell's Krishnapur is introduced with a series of portraits of the chief European personnel and civilian visitors present when the uprising occurs, and with essential historical background. Mr Hopkins the Collector discovers the famous, enigmatic chapatis, which remain mysterious today. We learn that a Collector is the East India Company official in charge of a region. (It is the post which Jos Sedley, rather implausibly, holds in *Vanity Fair*.) The Collector, the Magistrate, the civilian and military doctors and the Padre are the principal people at Krishnapur, as at Meerut.[24] The Collector is at odds with the officers of the (Company) army stationed nearby at 'Captainganj', because he takes seriously the risk that the greased cartridges, which offend Indian taboos, will provoke an uprising. The army are against showing weakness by taking any unusual precautions. The Collector orders mud walls.[25] We hear of General Hearsey's speech to the native troops at Barrackpore, promising freedom of religious belief.[26]

In Chapter 4 of the novel, news comes of the Mutiny at Meerut, five hundred miles away. General Jackson visits Krishnapur to arrange a cricket match and explain that there is no need to worry about Meerut. Soon afterwards Krishnapur is under siege.

Its defence occupies the bulk of the novel. The conflict is conducted with heroism and resourcefulness of the kinds to be found throughout Mutiny memoirs and in evidence for courts of inquiry. 'Every Englishman', orates the Padre at one subaltern's funeral, 'will relate with admiration what George Foxlett Cutter did at the siege of Krishnapur!' (Chapter 18). In real life, Lieutenant George Forrest of Ordnance was such a man as Cutter (an expert in mines); Forrest was awarded the V.C. after exploding the magazine at Delhi.[27] In the novel as in history daring and endurance are shown by soldiers and civilians, men and women, suffering from wounds, bereavement, disease (Krishnapur undergoes a cholera epidemic), and near-starvation. The Collector is especially impressive, despite nerves, depression, illness and intellectual turmoil, in almost demoralising circumstances, in his stubborn adherence to 'duty' which is, finally for him, the only sure guide.[28] By the end of the story a remnant of the defenders is still holding the Banqueting Hall, and preparing to blow themselves up rather than surrender. The relief force think it depressing to see Englishmen who have got themselves into such a state. Exciting and moving, the novel is also psychologically interesting as a portrait of people accustomed to 'respectability' and ordered lives finding themselves in squalor and under fire. C. S. Forester could not have derived more human interest from the techniques of the defence. Farrell sees all the human interest and also the potential for comedy. His sense of humour at the expense of his Victorians coexists very happily with his power to sympathise with them. A tea-party where all present are filthy and totally exhausted and only hot water is served in the cups, conducted none the less with propriety, is both funny to him, and serious in the Victorian view (repeatedly expressed by the Collector) that if the social rules do not matter, nothing does. The rumour that young ladies have been dragged naked through the streets of Delhi *is* more dismaying than the bloodiest atrocities.

The Siege of Krishnapur is open to a charge of unfairness to the

Indians. It offers no support for the view common among Indian writers that it was a nationalist rebellion.[29] There is only one episode in which we meet Indian characters apart from glimpses of servants and soldiers: the visit to the Maharajah's palace in Chapter 5. The Maharajah is asleep, with servants in attendance to shift the cushions beneath him. We are told that he is averse to the British presence and to Progress. His progressive son Hari reflects bitterly:

> He did not want progress . . . he wanted money, jewels and naked girls, or rather, since he already had all of these things, he wanted more of them. Hari, like any reasonable person, found these desires (money, jewels, naked girls) incomprehensible. His father was prepared to connive at the destruction of the fount of knowledge . . . the knowledge that had produced Shakespeare and would soon have railway trains galloping across the Indian continent!   (Chapter 9)

This is perhaps a necessary reminder of the irrelevance of most of the Rajahs and of rulers such as King of Delhi.[30] But the Anglo-Indian clash of cultures in Hari, who has grown up in the palace with English tutors, seems only sadly familiar. His merging of imperfectly mastered upper-class English with Indian habits of mind (still common in India) is a good piece of mimicry, but the subject is too soft for satirical bite. Hari and his father are set-pieces; and the occasional moments at which an English character senses the mystery of Hind (' "it is the name of God, Sahib," said Ram respectfully . . . an expression of tender devotion coming over his lined face'; 'What a lot of Indian life was unavailable to the Englishman' – Chapter 30) are realistic but irritatingly trite; and oddly untouched, here where it is wanted, by any sense of humour. Farrell's imagination works only with his British characters. It would have been better to have left Indians, except as belligerents, out of the story altogether.

He is most interested in the impact on British mentality. Approximately half the novel's space is given to an intellectual comedy in which the main characters are given roles, rather like those of figures in a Peacock novel. The Collector is an enthusiast for Progress whose whole mind and soul have been possessed by the glories of the Great Exhibition, which he visited on leave (in 1851). Opposing him is the cynical Magistrate whose *idée fixe* is the truth of phrenology. The poet Fleury is a Romantic Young Gentleman in the process of transforming himself into a 'broad shouldered', practical Tennysonian man, because he thinks this more likely, in the late 1850s, to be attractive to girls. The Padre is a Fundamentalist, low in Church and brow, who is obsessed with the 'argument for religion from design in Nature'. The two doctors belong to opposed schools of medical thought. Dr Dunstable dies in an effort to prove himself right about the treatment of cholera. The Collector gradually loses his convictions; and Fleury changes his. Like people in Peacock, although so far from convivial conditions, these people talk with an urgent, obsessed need to prove themselves right and they thrive on opposition. Compulsive speechifying was a feature of mid-Victorian England in which Farrell delights. By setting his characters talking throughout a siege in the Indian Mutiny he discovers a fund of comic effects at the same time that he explores the theoretical background to his topic. Some of the ideas paraded seem ludicrously Victorian; others can seem insights ahead of their time. These may have seemed true to the author, but the novel does not often vouch for them. The characters are at least slightly absurd as thinkers, however they appear as Victorian thinkers.

Two conceptions of the Mutiny can be seen behind the arguments. The first was summarised by Percival Spear who wrote in *India* (1961) that it was a 'last passionate protest against the relentless penetration of the West . . . the swan-song of the old India'.[31] That view is confirmed throughout his study of Meerut by J. A. B. Palmer, and Spear's words are quoted as the conclusion to Christopher Hibbert's book.[32] It was believed in the Company by all who assumed that the cartridges with forbidden animal fats were the real cause (and not just the pretext) — as now seems most probable. Others at the time thought that the rebellion was a divine punishment inflicted on the errant British. In the words of Sir Herbert Edwardes, the reason was 'that the English had ignored the teachings of the Bible and Christianity, that the people of India had been provided with the material benefits of civilisation at the expense of the spiritual benefits of Christianity'.[33] There is a paradox here; 'penetration' by the West was seen by Indians, by

Hindoos especially, as a threat to their religion and, through their religious beliefs, to caste-status. It can easily be argued that English missionaries had been too active in the decade before the Mutiny. General Hearsey chose to soothe the troops at Barrackpore by promising that they would not be forcibly 'converted' to Christianity. There is also the obvious conceptual conflict, as in so much Victorian argument, between the rational and the religious views of the world.

Mr Hopkins, the Collector, believes himself a man of reason, and is sure of his role in India as an agent of civilisation.

> '*Humani generis progressus* . . . I quote the official catalogue of the Exhibition,' came the Collector's voice . . . 'The progress of the human race, resulting from the labour of all men, ought to be the final object of the exertion of each individual.'   (Chapter 3)

He likes to think of the Exhibition 'as a collective prayer of all the civilised nations', and he exults in the power of invention which was displayed there, and which the Company will bring, with the railways, to India. The Magistrate is a disillusioned Radical, once a supporter of Chartists, and now cynical about everything except phrenology, and inclined to snipe at the Collector's official Victorian optimism. As the siege progresses the Collector's confidence wanes; he comes to doubt Progress and the civilising mission of the Company: 'the fiction of happy natives being led forward along the road to civilisation could no longer be sustained' (Chapter 21). After the siege, when he returns to England, he adopts a pleasant but useless Nabob's life as a gourmet clubman, a sad contrast to the days when he believed. The lesson the Magistrate had tried to teach him, that the British were wasting their time in India, has unmanned a genuinely 'manly' character. If the Magistrate has won free from many Victorian illusions at an earlier stage than the Collector, it is because he is convinced that human behaviour is determined by the inner and outer structure of the cranium. The Mutiny and everything else, he thinks, could be explained if one could study all the heads involved; 'more than ever he longed to grasp the Collector's skull and make some exact measurements of it' (Chapter 7). The Magistrate is certainly not meant as a shrewd critic of imperialism. In contrast to his phrenological hobby-horse, the Collector's mania for the Exhibition seems warmly humane, however misguided.

The notion of God's wrath visited on British India occurs to the Padre at Krishnapur and impels him to wage a private doctrinal war against Fleury. The Reverend Hampton, who has been a rowing-man at Oxford, is neither well-informed nor theologically subtle. He puzzles over the problem of why God did not cause the Bible to be written in English, but otherwise is untroubled by doubts. He is a scientific fundamentalist. It may be that Farrell noticed a footnote in Chapter 19 of John Fowles's *The French Lieutenant's Woman*, which observes that '*Omphalos: an attempt to untie the geological knot* is now forgotten; which is a pity, as it is one of the most curious – and unintentionally comic – books of the whole era.'[34] Philip Gosse (Edmund's father) was a biologist who, alarmed by the findings of Lyell's *Principles of Geology* (1830–33), argued that God made the fossils and extinct species on the sixth day of the Creation. Gosse's work is at least a reminder of how desperately the Victorian Church was driven to defend the literal reading of Genesis against Darwin. *The Origin of Species* was to appear two years after the Mutiny, in 1859; its imminent publication is an irony underlying the Padre's speeches on the miracles of nature which modern science has revealed, and a source of small jests. The Padre exhorts Fleury:

> 'Everything, from fish's eye, to caterpillar's food, to bird's wing and gizzard, bears manifest evidence of the Supreme Design. What other explanation can you find for them in your darkness?'
>
> Fleury stared at the Padre, too harrowed and exhausted to speak. Could it not be, he wondered vaguely, trembling on the brink of an idea that would have made him famous, that somehow or other fish design their own eyes? But no, that was, of course, quite impossible.   (Chapter 12)

Fleury shares Keats's preference for a life of feelings rather than ideas, and influenced by Matthew Arnold, he despises materialism. Civilisation must be 'something more than the fashions and customs of one country imported into another . . . it must be *a superior view of* mankind'. Nineteenth-century British culture is *morally* superior, he thinks. When he says that

God is to be found in our hearts rather than in a Grand Design, the Padre suspects him of having been contaminated by the theological avant-garde in Germany. Fleury's presence at Krishnapur, he suspects, has caused God to allow the Mutiny, and he pursues Fleury through the worst moments of battle pleading with him to consider the bent teeth of the Indian hog, and the stomach of the camel. Still sponging the cannon, Fleury politely and firmly defends his theological position.

Incongruous juxtaposition of talk and action can bring ideas back to life in a novel, and show how it is that they exist not in the abstract but in the setting of personality, shaped by circumstances. The Collector abandons his ideas in the course of the siege and ends defeated at least in principles. Fleury has developed his hostility to materialism in the affluent leisure enjoyed by the son of a Director of the Company. Recruited into a military squad he is gradually enthralled by practical gunnery and by cavalry problems; despite his principles he invents a 'cavalry eradicator'. One result of the siege is that he and the Collector exchange their attitudes to culture. 'All civilisation is bad', Fleury explains to the Collector, in Chapter 13; 'it mars the noble and natural instincts of the heart.' 'I have seldom heard such gibberish', says the Collector. In the final chapter they meet in Pall Mall, years after the Mutiny, and the Collector remarks that 'Culture is a sham'. Culture and ideas, Fleury tells him, are essential to our progress. 'No one can say that ideas are a sham'; he is unaware, now, that he used to say so. The novel does not try to persuade us that ideas are a sham, but it demonstrates that our convictions are based on the shifting grounds of our natures; and it does this more effectively because the Victorian setting puts us at a distance where we can be relatively detached. The debate about cholera which is publicly staged between Dr Dunstable and Dr McNab has been settled today. For the besieged, threatened by an epidemic, the solution lies as much in the personalities of the two doctors as in their arguments, and even when Dunstable has died sooner than submit to McNab's (correct) treatment, doubt remains in their minds because Dunstable was the more respectable physician, and plainly sure of himself. Ideas long discredited matter intensely to these Victorians, but they are illusive, and easily contaminated by taboos and superstitious, ghostly ideas about 'respectability' among the British, or about caste among the Indians, proper dress or proper diet. New ideas clash with old on both sides of the battle line. As in *Troubles* the perspective casts a sad reflection on human ability to use ideas and not be used by them. We can think ourselves wiser than the Collector, superior for example to his fixed view that women are 'like children' whom 'we shall always have to look after' but we are not encouraged to think that in general we judge more efficiently.

The Mutiny offered Farrell an opportunity to set Victorian ideas in a pleasingly unsettled condition. It was an even better opportunity to depict the paraphernalia of the age. We can see his relish for Indian Victoriana in his descriptions of the museums he visited, in his 'Indian Diary'. As the siege progresses objects are put to strange uses; they splinter and shatter; they are broken up and hurled at the enemy; such action gives the reality of 1857 to objects which now lie under glass in Delhi and Lucknow.

As in *Troubles*, objects have various meanings, and reality of their own. The chapatis first appear at Krishnapur in the Collector's despatch-box. His major-domo is taken aback.

> He stared at the purple despatch-box for some moments before picking the chapatis out of it respectfully, as if the box had a personal dignity of its own that might be offended.
>
> (Chapter 1)

This is the traditional 'anthropomorphic' device so frequent in Dickens. Here it neatly conveys the affront to British official-dom and to the Company regulations with which Collectors civilised India (everything in its place) which the undignified chapatis represent. The simile is amusing because purple despatch-boxes *have* a dignity of their own, and no right to it. Few peoples have ever loved and valued things so much as the Victorians — if we leave aside the question of their taste; things are to be stripped of all dignity and deprived of all other appeal in the course of the novel, or, from our point of view, their inanimate qualities are to be reasserted against the values the Victorians bestowed on them.

As with the box-full of chapatis, British and Indian things jostle and then clash. When Fleury visits the Maharajah in Chapter 5 there is a profusion of this effect.

Near a fireplace of marble inlaid with garnets, lapis lazuli and agate, the Maharajah's son sat on a chair constructed entirely of antlers, eating a boiled egg and reading *Blackwood's Magazine*.

The chair made of antlers is noted in the 'Indian Diary', seen in the palace at Benares. ('My Rajah might be sitting in the midst of all this gloomily eating a boiled egg and reading *Blackwood's*' he wrote there.)[35] Most of the bric-a-brac in the fictional palace originated in Benares.[36] Farrell is equally thorough with the way his palace daguerreotype works. Fleury's unpacking at Krishnapur is observed in detail: Brown Windsor soap, Seidlitz powders, a tin footbath, bound volumes of *Bell's life*, boots in trees and a wash-stand which turns into a writing-table in emergencies. His books are stored on a table whose feet are placed in saucers of water, to protect them against white ants. Britain in India is surely rendered in the everyday things we see.

A great many other samples of modern arts and sciences have been brought to Krishnapur by the Collector who bought the materials for a private museum when he was at the Exhibition. Where Collectors of earlier periods kept tigers and mistresses 'and heaven knows what else', Mr Hopkins has electro-plated copies of works of art. 'Could anyone doubt . . . that this was an invention which would rapidly make mankind sensitive to Beauty?' Yes: the Magistrate has scoffed at the Collector's suggestion that one day every working man will drink from a Cellini cup. There are many other inventions and the catalogue of the Exhibition supplies further evidence of Progress. Possessions, Mr Hopkins reflects, 'are surely a *physical* high-water mark of the moral tide which has been flooding' (Chapter 9).

The objects which manifest civilisation are also useful in defending it. Two enormous marble heads depicting Plato and Socrates shelter the gunners on the ramparts; the shock caused by the sight of them later turns an enemy charge. More has to be sacrificed when the mud walls begin to melt in the rains. Not only the Collector's museum of inventions but all possessions, 'even the gorse-bruiser', are sent to shore up the walls. This is obviously a symbolic stripping of Collector and community, as rowing oars, fish knives, instructional books, and samplers sink into the mud. But even such a symbolic object as the Collector's favourite bas-relief which shows how *The Spirit of Science Conquers Ignorance and Prejudice* (Ignorance disembowelled and Prejudice 'enmeshed in its own toils') remains a solid thing. It is easy to share Farrell's satisfaction in the thought of it, shipped from England, proudly shown off at the Residency, and finally fired in marble chips from the six-pounder.

The last vestiges of the Exhibition are used as ammunition at the end of the story. For this purpose the heads are severed from the electro-metal figures of the distinguished men of letters. Shortly before the relief of Krishnapur the Collector broods on their effectiveness as improvised missiles.

> And of the heads, perhaps not surprisingly, the most effective of all had been Shakespeare's; it had scythed its way through a whole astonished platoon of sepoys advancing in single file through the jungle. The Collector suspected that the Bard's success in this respect might have a great deal to do with the ballistic advantages stemming from his baldness. The head of Keats, for example, wildly festooned with metal locks which it had proved impossible to file smooth had flown very erratically indeed, killing only a fat moneylender and a camel standing at some distance from the field of action.

The performance of Voltaire is even less satisfactory – his head becomes jammed in the gun, 'rather surprisingly, the Collector thought, a narrow, lozenge shaped head like that'. Other metal objects such as clocks and hair brushes are found to be useless as ammunition, but a store of saints, Virgins and 'heavy metal beads' is found among the effects of the dead Father O'Hara. The Padre is consulted before these are fired and he gives his approval, advising that 'they or any other such Popish or Tractarian objects would very likely wreak terrible havoc' (Chapter 31). They do little damage in fact.

John Spurling finds a 'pure surrealism' in 'Farrell's mature comedy'.[37] The passage about the heads is rather a blend of fancy and realism. The whole platoon and the camel are the touches of exaggeration which make for a good anecdote, and 'astonished' of the sepoys (a word Farrell found hard to resist) creates the momentary effect of a cartoon, perhaps by Bill Tidy. The Waugh-like detachment which dismisses the money-lender with the camel is not realism, but part of the joke of comparing Keats and Shakespeare in a new light. So is the literary poise of the sentences, which belongs more to Farrell than to the Collector. The character is too tired to be amused – almost at the limit of his resources he sees everything ballistically, and 'perhaps not surprisingly' is true to the quirkish behaviour of an exhausted mind; the author obviously relishes his finely tuned piece of whimsy. The glimpse of the defenders working with a file on Keats's head is realistic; they have been fighting for three months and can now hope to be relieved any day. At Lucknow the women's unmentionables were used as wadding for the guns.[38] These grotesque intrusions of everyday objects into battle conditions were characteristic of the Mutiny; private homes suddenly became fortresses. Any cruelty in the passage is not callousness about the comical fate of the Indians but a reflection on how the Mutiny reminded the Victorian English that their attempt to impose culture, technology and religion on India always rested on force. The comic suggestion that the hurtling poets and saints are somehow connected with what they have represented only serves to emphasise, if we dwell on this passage, that the impersonality of objects is proof against the meanings we invest in them. It is a passage to dwell on because it is, almost, Farrell's last word on the Mutiny.

The last words of *The Siege of Krishnapur* raise a question which becomes more insistent in *The Singapore Grip*: 'perhaps, by the very end of [the Collector's] life in 1880, he had come to believe that a people, a nation, does not create itself according to its own best ideas, but is shaped by other forces of which it has little knowledge'. *The Singapore Grip* makes a more ambitious attempt to discover these forces. This novel, which is half the length again of its predecessors (approaching a quarter of a million words) incorporates a formidable body of history: of the development of Singapore Island, of the growth of the rubber industry, of the progress of the Japanese war in the East in 1941 and 1942, seen against the background of world events. The distance between the story and the story teller is only forty years; Farrell was a child of seven when Singapore fell; this book belongs to the borderline group of novels, where the author has written about a period he has discussed with those who lived through it. But the world changes quickly nowadays and between 1940 and 1978 the British Empire, Farrell's great Argument, came to an end. The surrender of Singapore, which Churchill insisted must be fought to the last possible line of defence, although the Island was plainly indefensible, can well be seen as a crucial defeat and a turning point.[39] So J. M. Pluvier writes that 'whatever the ultimate outcome of the Pacific War, 15 February 1942 [the day of the surrender] was the end of the British Empire; it was also the end of European colonialism in Asia'; this overstatement makes a valid point.[40] Singapore's defeat was more than a setback to the Empire. In trying to show the 'forces' which first created and later destroyed the British presence there Farrell undertook a new kind of task. Once again he shows a group of characters undergoing history, but he also contemplates the history itself by making their chief spokesman far more historically conscious than Edward and the Major in *Troubles*, or the Collector and Fleury in *The Siege of Krishnapur*. The novel is full of interpretation and polemic, including a prolonged satire on capitalism, but the only 'message' we are left with is that men create enterprises larger than they can manage or understand. Farrell's view of life is as vivid as before. His characters are free-thinkers bound to the awkward reality of things. We encompass the history of the world in our arguments, and we fall off bicycles at the same time. In *The Singapore Grip* we confront the rise and fall of the British Empire in the East. The history is vigorously debated among the more intelligent characters as they struggle with the physical collapse of their immediate surroundings. As in the earlier novels we see them as figures who are mostly helpless, often absurd, but sometimes unpredictably impressive. If Farrell had a formula to offer the present time, it was quite traditional: we shall fail too, but we had better keep trying.

Singapore was built from nothing in about a century. It is an example of the most business-like imperialism; things here were very efficiently ordered. The novel begins by contrasting the city when the family of Blacketts are living there in 1940 (in 1937 for a few pages) with the Island Sir Thomas Stamford Raffles purchased 'one morning early in the nineteenth century' [1819]. The first page presents one of Farrell's cartoon-like images of Raffles amid the 'prodigious quantity of rats and centipedes' who apparently then had the Island virtually to themselves.

> As he stood there on that lonely beach and gazed up at the flag with rats and centipedes seething and tumbling over his shoes did Raffles foresee the prosperity which lay ahead for Singapore? Undoubtedly he did.

In 1937 an imposing British city stands above a tawdry but energetic underworld in which Tamils, Malays and Chinese pursue their affairs. We look first at the elegant suburb of Tanglin where the Blacketts occupy a large house and grounds. Walter Blackett's godowns of rubber are as yet unthreatened; his business interests extend throughout the East and across the world. Houses such as his are constantly menaced by tropical nature, and the opening pages survey, with Farrell's usual satisfaction in contemplating decay, the vegetable, insect and animal life which surreptitiously infiltrates and subverts everything manmade. But the Blackett wealth affords a display of the material prosperity which is soon to be ravaged by war. Subtle hints of danger are often comically insinuated. In the first major episode, a Blackett garden party is accidentally ruined in a number of ways. Walter's son Monty causes embarrassment by introducing a yogi who amuses the guests by eating things, a box of tintacks, a China tea-cup, and the head of a live snake. Walter is gravely shocked. He tells his wife that the yogi has left 'full of China':

> 'You mean, full of China tea?'
> 'No, not really, no I don't,' replied Walter in an edgy sort of tone.

The yogi has been disrespectful not just of property (and seemliness) we feel, but of the order of things on which Walter Blackett relies. That is not how Singapore was built!

Like Edward and the Collector, Walter represents a class, and a phase of history. He is the Capitalist, the trader, Raffles's successor. The novel provides copious evidence of the mischief brought about in the name of trade and Walter is the ablest villain. But he is extremely likeable as a rogue. John Spurling comments on the honesty which made Walter so 'sympathetic'. In a strictly conducted novel-with-a-thesis only 'authorially approved of characters' (as Spurling says) are allowed such 'scope for seeing the action in his own terms'.[41] Farrell's inclination to 'expose' and condemn Walter is thwarted by his interest in the character's inner life, and also by his respect for energy and practical intelligence. Spurling adds, as though to console us for the sympathy Walter misappropriates, that the grown-up Blackett children Monty and Joan are 'a stinging indictment of gilded self-interest'. They may be so for a reader who is looking for indictment of Singapore's ruling class, but Farrell's contempt is aimed at their stupidity – something he finds offensive anywhere. Walter stands for 'gilded self-interest' and he finds his children disappointing. He envies an American associate who has managed to 'engender' five sons, all business men, who help him pursue family interests far more efficiently than Joan or Monty help the Blackett cause. Walter, moreover, quite sincerely believes – blind to all evidence to the contrary – that his private good and public advantage are the same wherever business operates freely. Farrell is intrigued and amused by this mentality, and he sympathises with the character although not with the ideas.

He needed to give Walter considerable scope in order to accommodate the history of big business in Singapore. At the garden party (held in September 1940) Walter expounds his version to a reporter interested in the forthcoming jubilee celebrations of the house of Blackett and Webb; there is to be a carnival. Back in the 1890s old Mr Webb was a mere merchant, trading in rice, tea, copra, spices, opium and of course coolies shipped as deck cargo. Walter proceeds to explain how 'early snags' (as the reporter jots) were overcome as Indian money-lenders ensnared over-prosperous peasants in debt, forcing down prices for raw materials. The Major, who reappears as a secondary character in this novel, and is listening now, is horrified; but the Major does not understand business. Walter concedes the misfortunes which incidentally befell the peasants of Burma and Malaya as Blackett and Webb rose in the world; the village system was ruined. He explains as an exciting game, needing daring and shrewdness, the efforts of the rubber-merchants to outwit the producers and consumers abroad, multiplying profit. Walter is interrupted (although his frank account of half a century of unscrupulous profiteering is continued in later chapters) by the collapse of old Mr Webb. Brooding on market-fluctuations, and the new risk of strikes promoted by possibly Communist labour-organisations, Walter wanders through the abandoned dining-room where a set of 'effigies in cake' represents Churchill, Chiang Kai-shek, Mr Webb and Walter himself. As he broods, Farrell fills pages with information about the rubber industry as it courses through the shameless mind of the rubber-king. Since something is needed to relieve the tendency in such sections for the novel to turn into a treatise, he causes Walter, who has been deprived of dinner, to break off the ears from the cake which represents his partner and 'crunch them in his strong yellow teeth'. The point is made that 'eat or be eaten' is the rule of the rubber world. But we are presumably familiar with the objections to laisser-faire capitalism which underlie Farrell's presentation of Walter's apology. The Major's innocent astonishment and indignation only serve to absorb the intended strictures. What holds our interest is the detailed grasp Walter shows of how to manipulate the market and the power that the idea of 'business' has to exclude all other considerations from his mind. It is the strong flow of his thoughts which makes him reluctant to summon a 'boy' to bring food; Webb's ears are a convenient snack. He is preoccupied not only by thoughts of Communist and business rivals but also by his children. Joan has just flung a glass of wine in the face of a respectable young man. She ought to be married, to the sort of husband who would strengthen the firm. We know too much about Walter to dislike him, however limited we judge his sense of his responsibilities in Asia. We know, for example, that he never swims in public because he is embarrassed by the ridge of bristle which runs down his spine. If Farrell had meant to use the resources of a novelist to discredit capitalism he should not have made us so intimate with his capitalist.

If Walter is in the grip of incorrect ideas he is impressive in the resolution with which he manages the world, trying to enforce them. In a later scene (in Chapter 45) which is meant to ridicule his early-Victorian notions of trade as a force for progress, the comedy again loses sight of its target. By now the Japanese army battling down the Malay peninsula has reached the Slim River (about halfway) and Singapore is under bomb attack. Walter none the less means to stage his carnival to celebrate 'fifty-years of Blackett and Webb'. The Major dutifully attends the dress-rehearsal in a devil-costume, with horns and a toasting fork to represent 'Inflation' – one of the figures who are to harass Britannia and 'Prosperity'. Monty is to play 'Crippling Overheads'. Walter's younger daughter Kate bears a cornucopia from which motor-tyres, sou'westers and other rubber products spill. A Chinese St George is slaying a much-enlarged hook-worm. An octopus extends arms coloured brown, yellow and pink in tribute to the various races who collaborate in the work of achieving prosperity and spreading it to the eight corners of the world. As the bombs fall the Major doubts if this is really the time for celebration. The objects acquire grotesque features of their own. The liquid gold which pours from a symbolic rubber tree 'looks as if it's . . . well . . .', as the Major says. 'Once we get this jubilee parade on the road', proclaims a Blackett spokesman, 'it should make it clear to everyone what they will have to lose by exchanging us for the Japanese'. But there is a crazy *joie de vivre* in all this which contrasts with Farrell's pictures of Japanese soldiers on the march. Singapore is probably lost already, given the sinking of the British warships *Prince of Wales* and *Repulse*, the state of unreadiness, and the general military incompetence. The most indomitable – although totally unpatriotic – spirit in evidence is Walter's; when he boards the boat which takes him off at the end of the novel, with the Japanese in possession of the city, much of it bombed or burned, he at least does not seem to have been defeated by history. In a few years time he will be doing business with Tokyo.

Opposed to Walter in the novel's central debate is Matthew Webb, old Mr Webb's heir, a man almost totally ruled by ideas. He has – to Walter's alarm – been 'progressively' educated. He has worked, vainly, for years on behalf of the League of Nations. He comes talking onto the stage of Blackett-Singapore, and the hundred-page account of his first encounters with the city (in Part 2) is a comic tour de force in which talk prevails over physical realities. Matthew is, predictably, baffled by the socio-economic questions raised by the life around him. He agrees with Marxist analysis sufficiently to reject Walter's creed of business, but he thinks that 'in practice Communism would be scarcely any better than Capitalism, and perhaps even worse' (Chapter 22). He talks on these lines to the American officer Ehrendorf while Ehrendorf contemplates Joan's bottom and Monty arranges a visit to Fortress Singapore, a show in which an Irish girl is fired from a cannon against the 'treacherous aggressor' (whom she misses). He argues on, about how Singapore's relaxed social mingling of races was absent from the League in Geneva, throughout a visit to a night-club, and, made even more fluent by beer, he discusses the pre-war failures of the League at the brothel to which Monty takes his party next, oblivious to his surroundings. He continues to argue for the rest of the book 'that there *was* such a thing as shared humanity, and that with one or two minor adjustments different nations and communities could live in harmony with each other, concerning themselves with each other's welfare' (Chapter 43).

Matthew and Walter are nicely contrasted: the unscrupulous but ever-successful business-man and the ineffectual idealist who is honest enough to admit that he has always failed, so far. Where Walter has a firm grasp on the real world about him, Matthew is only rather dimly aware of it. The habit of dining alone with a book has made him hazardous in company, liable to let slip a grilled fish or a bundle of spaghetti. On his first evening he fells Mrs Blackett with a careless gesture.

> Matthew watched her from a distance, discomfited and surprised; it had not seemed to him that he had struck her very hard. The impression left on his knuckles by the blow was already fading but he was pretty certain that it had never amounted to a good, solid punch, the sort that one might have expected would drop one's hostess to her knees.
> (Chapter 16)

Walter would have little time for such a young man, had Matthew not come to Singapore as old Webb's heir, and still unmarried. Matthew is frequently left guessing, as he is here, about dealings with the immediate physical world. He is in his element among theories, and it is only in his implacable determination that reality will conform to what reason and humanity lead one to believe, that he resembles Walter, implacably determined that business must go on, although Singapore is in flames.

Other ideas are put forward. Ehrendorf, rejected by Joan,

formulates Ehrendorf's Second Law which holds good for the situation in Singapore.

> In human affairs things tend to go wrong. Things are slightly worse at any given moment than at any preceding moment.
>   (Chapter 37)

The cynical French official Dupigny, an old friend of the Major, argues on Hobbesian lines that people are motivated only by self-interest, and therefore naturally rob and rape their neighbours once law breaks down in an emergency. John Spurling thinks that Farrell decided that the British Empire came to be destroyed because 'competition is built into human beings, from their mating habits to their recreations, to their personal and national relationships, to their religious and political creeds', and that he saw no possible change through socialism or anything else.[42] *The Singapore Grip* is a melancholy as well as a very funny novel. An unusually bedraggled dog attached to the Major, the latest in a long line of Farrell animals, is known as 'the Human Condition'. The Major is always meaning to have it 'put down', but it escapes, despite him, on the last ship out of Singapore.

Because so much space is given to political, social and economic argument, it is natural to look for 'the author's solution'; but that is unrewarding. It is an essential point of Farrell's comedy that definite answers in the realm of meaning are almost impossibly elusive. A characteristic form of humour reflects how hard it is to know what others are thinking. After some disparaging dinner-time remarks about Geneva, Walter wonders what Dupigny's expression means; he is rolling his eyes in horror, but this may be the effect of vinegar fumes rising from the fish. Thoughts, ideas and knowledge itself are impure. Matthew has been warned to beware of 'the Singapore grip', and he is forever trying to discover what it is. It may be what Dupigny calls *la grippe de Singapore* or a type of despatch case, or the hand clasp by which members of a clandestine, possibly Communist, Chinese secret society recognise one another, or a technique known to taxi-girls: 'you wantchee try Singapore glip!' (Chapter 25). The British grip is slipping and that of Japan is about to take hold of Singapore, while both nations are in the grip of forces they do not understand.

The physical city of mansions and Chinatown, infiltrated by

the jungle, is levelled by the bombs and the fires they start. The Major's work as a firefighter, in which he is aided by Dupigny and Matthew, seems more worthwhile than the larger issues, although only a temporary expedient. The Major's quiet, patient, ever polite application to immediate tasks, as free from self-interest as one can be, is an answer to Dupigny's cynicism as Dupigny cynically knows. The novel is sceptical but healthily so. Farrell's people are ludicrous, always arguing and always fumbling with things. General Wavell, the Supreme Commander Far East, (one of a number of Generals whom Farrell observes caustically) is to leave before the capitulation, by flying-boat. He falls while trying to board his motor-boat and lies on the rocks with an injured leg, thinking 'Singapore is done for' (Chapter 66). But people are not completely at the mercy of things. Matthew, the Major and Dupigny survive, despite fearsome difficulties, and are last seen in a Prisoner-of-War camp.

> Matthew found that his world had suddenly shrunk. Accustomed to speculate grandly about the state and fate of nations he now found that his thoughts were limited to the smallest of matters . . . a glass of water, a pencil, a handful of rice.   (Chapter 74)

Seen in these simple counterparts, of intellectual aspiration and physical dependency, human life is always essentially the same. Out of this conception of life, Farrell built three imaginative reconstructions of critical episodes in recent history, showing an increasing wish to document and explain, and a steady insistence that historical explanation is both necessary and unobtainable. In each case he showed this in terms of the period he had chosen, reviving in fiction the ideas of the past and arousing his own kind of thoughtful laughter. He might be called an historical novelist of ideas except that the ideas are always seen in relation to the things of the past, which have a stronger claim in the last resort. 'Faction' is an unsatisfactory term, and Farrell accomplished more in his last book than the blending of a story and documentary. He gave that term a new value with a form of fiction which looks at historical facts through human situations, with scepticism and a mild wonder.

7 John Fowles's *The French Lieutenant's Woman* and William Golding's *Rites of Passage*

Fowles's *The French Lieutenant's Woman* (1969) is fashionably 'troubled' by theoretical questions of form and status in contemporary fiction; Golding's *Rites of Passage* (1980) is not troubled at all. Fowles's book illustrates several modes available to a modern writer: it is an imaginative creation of the past adopting the sight lines of characters of its period; it is an exercise in critical theory, challenging the realistic conventions of its story; and it is a documentary which, like *The Singapore Grip*, could be used in a history class. Golding's novel is a well-made work whose form is subject to the author's imagination and to nothing else.

Both novels subject a nineteenth-century setting to modern scrutiny, Fowles's explicitly, Golding's implicitly. J. W. Burrow mentions *The French Lieutenant's Woman* in the Postscript to *A Liberal Descent*, his study of 'Whig' historians of the nineteenth-century, in the course of reflections on the present state of the Whig view. He attributes the decline – as he thinks – of historical fiction to the weakening of belief in progress, which has weakened the appeal of stories. All stories, he says, tend to be Whiggish because they *progress* towards a fulfilment of expectations: everything told contributes to the ending; the present makes sense of the past.[1] We might object to Burrow that there are stories with endings so surprising that we have to reinterpret everything; but the new interpretation will retain a Whiggishness. Roland Barthes's objections to narrative included a distaste for the order it imposes – an objection, basically, to literature. Dr Burrow thinks that narrative is inevitable:

Yet we tell historical stories, as we employ general concepts, because we must; a condition of permanent obstructive adherence to the particular, however salutary as a challenge, becomes tediously unhelpful. In this plight we may think of the greatest achievements in story-telling; the nineteenth-century novel, in the hands of George Eliot or Tolstoy, with its multiple perspectives which are nevertheless placed and controlled within the architecture of the plot and the moral vision of the author; the analogy of course, if we think of the subsequent history of the novel, also suggests the less appealing prospect of a modernist playfulness in the plotting of historical works.[2]

Burrow's footnote refers us to *The French Lieutenant's Woman*. The purpose of this chapter is to argue that the subsequent history of the novel has not brought us to 'modernist playfulness' as the only option, however sceptical we have become about 'Whig' progress.

The French Lieutenant's Woman has been exhaustively discussed in reviews and critical studies since its publication in 1969. It was greeted as the novel of the decade. Bernard Bergonzi who had attacked Fowles's *The Magus* (1966), in *The Situation of The Novel*, as the work of a pretentious meddler, welcomed this new book as 'a remarkable recreation of the sense of life of the Victorian novel [which keeps] a full consciousness of the problematic nature of fictional form in our time'.[3] Bergonzi is pleased to have the old pleasures of the novel and the new earnestness about theory at the same time. Fowles had written a Victorian love-story framed – or rather frequently interrupted – by an essay about Victorian mores and an essay about fictional convention. Where the novel succeeds it fulfils Avrom Fleishman's expectation that the historical novel would 'join the experimental movement' but it also shows the limits to which such a development can go.

The first twelve chapters set the scene and begin the story at Lyme Regis in 1867 where Charles Smithson, a gentleman engaged to a young lady, Ernestina, is attracted by the romantic figure of Sarah, the French Lieutenant's (abandoned) woman, who stands alone on the Cobb staring out to sea. The style mimics mid-Victorian fiction without falling into parody of any particular author, although often echoing Hardy, sometimes

Trollope or Wilkie Collins. But the first page tells us that the point of view belongs to 1967. A principle of contrast is established in the early chapters; the narrator is close to his characters of 1867, and remote, as though, as one reviewer said, he were a hundred and fifty years old. Sometimes he is demurely Victorian (perhaps Trollope): 'of the three young women who pass through these pages Mary was, in my opinion, by far the prettiest' (Chapter 11). At other times hindsight gives him a more godlike perspective than any pre-Jamesian narrator possessed: 'Charles did not know it, but in those brief poised seconds above the waiting sea in that luminous evening silence broken only by the waves' quiet wash, the whole Victorian Age was lost' (Chapter 10). By the end of Chapter 12 we are at home with a predictably Victorian set of circumstances controlled in the telling by a point of view which both reflects and transcends that of the characters. The result is pleasing and rather flattering to the reader who enjoys the story and looks down on the characters too: 'needless to say Charles knew nothing of the bereaved German Jew quietly working, as it so happened, that very afternoon in the British Museum library' (Chapter 3). The last words of Chapter 12 tease with a consciously-period note:

Who is Sarah?
Out of what shadows does she come?

The first words of Chapter 13 call a halt.

I do not know. This story I am telling is all imagination. These characters I create never existed outside my own mind. If I have pretended until now to know my characters' minds and innermost thoughts, it is because I am writing in (just as I have assumed some of the vocabulary and 'voice' of) a convention universally accepted at the time of my story: that the novelist stands next to God. He may not know all, yet he tries to pretend that he does. But I live in the age of Alain Robbe-Grillet and Roland Barthes; if this is a novel it cannot be a novel in the modern sense of the word.

The rest of the chapter discusses the terms on which the novel is written, introducing ideas which were then familiar in France from Roland Barthes and the *nouveaux romanciers* Robbe-Grillet and Michel Butor, but less well-known in England despite the work of such anti-novelists as B. S. Johnson and Christine Brooke-Rose. In one of Barthes's favourite images, Fowles 'points to his mask'.

The narrative is interrupted again at the end of Chapter 44 and the start of Chapter 45. At this stage of the plot Charles is obliged to choose between Ernestina and Sarah. Chapter 44 offers the respectable solution: Charles is married to Tina; they are given seven children and all the plums of a happy ending in Trollope. But this turns out to be a daydream of Charles's; we are reminded of how we all fictionalise our lives. In his real life he goes to bed with Sarah, but 'loses' her through a Hardyesque misunderstanding and spends the rest of the novel roaming the world while his lawyer tries to trace her. 'The novelist' appears in some scenes watching over Charles and brooding about how to settle his affair; he decides that two 'endings' are needed to establish objectivity. Charles finds Sarah who is now living with the Rossettis in Cheyne Walk. The first ending reunites them. The novelist/narrator, present in the background suitably clad as a raffish impresario, turns back his watch a quarter of an hour and reruns the scene. Charles leaves in dismay at Sarah's unseemly independence. These interventions show Fowles wanting to confer independence on the creatures of his imagination and also drawn towards Barthes's sheer impatience with story-telling. No novelist can 'escape the charge of omniscience' by any device in James or in later fiction. To be godlike today means granting an existential freedom to the characters, by abdicating power over them – hence the two endings. Their reality is not 'less real' than our own, because we fictionalise our lives (as Michel Butor said).[4]

In a set of 'Notes' composed when he was working on *The French Lieutenant's Woman* and published separately, Fowles tells us that he did not think of it as an historical novel, 'a genre in which I have very little interest'. The same notes reveal his care in researching the 1860s and his pleasure in imagining the past. He began with the mental image of a woman staring from an ancient quay. Talking about this he shows a faith in imagination which disappears when touched by French reasoning.

The woman had no face, no particular degree of sexuality. But she was Victorian; and since I always saw her in the same static long shot, with her back turned, she represented a reproach on the Victorian Age. An outcast. I didn't know her crime, but I wished to protect her. That is, I began to fall in love with her . . .

But wanting to write a book, however ardently, is not enough. Even to say, 'I want to be possessed by my own creations' is not enough; all natural or born writers are possessed, and in the old magical sense, by their own imaginations long before they even begin to think of writing. This fluke genesis must break all the rules, must sound at best childlike, at worst childish. I suppose the orthodox method is to work out what one wants to say and what one has experience of, and then to correlate the two.[5]

There is no irony in this and it sounds as naive as the interpolated thoughts about fiction derived from French intellectuals. The best objection to the allegedly 'existential' truth of the double-ending was made by Christopher Ricks in a review entitled 'The Unignorable Real'. Fiction, as he said there, has to be coercive.

> For there would not be, in life, two possibilities but virtually an infinity of them. To reduce this infinity to two alternatives is no less manipulatory and coercive – though because of its quasi-abnegation it is more congenial to modern taste – than was the Victorian reduction of this infinity to one eventuality.[6]

The modernist playfulness is tiresome, at least on a second reading, because Fowles is a better story-teller than a literary theorist. He should have trusted to his 'fluke-genesis', and to the juxtaposition of past and present mentalities which creates an absorbing and thought-provoking perspective whenever the novel is left to its own proceedings.

Fowles is at his best in observing similarities within differences. Charles is a geologist and Darwinist who has 'fixed his heart' on petrified sea-urchins. In Chapter 8 he explores the Lyme beaches for specimens and the narrator watches him, explaining him to us as he picks his way among the boulders on a warm day, laden with heavy clothing, shod in stout nailed boots, carrying an ashplant and a rucksack with all the latest equipment. The Victorians were so methodical, we are told – as we see in Baedeker's advice to travellers – because of a sense of 'duty' which has almost vanished today. Charles is a dutiful amateur, inclined to dilettantism; he knows that the Linnaean *scala naturae* is 'rubbish', but he does not really understand Darwin. We need not feel superior, the narrator warns, because his curiosity is in earnest and – unless research-scientists – we are complacent about scientific truth. In a later chapter he discovers that the local doctor is another 'passionate' Darwinian; like members of a secret society they celebrate, with whisky and cigars, their esoteric knowledge which in time will change the ignorant world, unheeding outside. Darwin's challenge to any mid-Victorian intellectual's composure is felt (Chapter 25) when Charles contemplates the fossil-record of a 'micro-catastrophe of ninety million years ago'.

In a vivid insight, a flash of black lightning, he saw that all life was parallel: that evolution was not vertical, ascending to perfection, but horizontal. Time was the great fallacy; existence was without history, was always now, was always this being caught in the same fiendish machine. All those painted screens erected by man to shut out reality – history, religion, duty, social position, all were illusions, mere opium fantasies.

Several of the Victorian-style chapter-head epithets are from passages of *In Memoriam* where Tennyson contemplates the belittlement of human history in the perspective of geological time: 'There where the long street roars hath been/The stillness of the central sea'. Fowles recognises his own doubts in Charles's, here, and has no need to patronise from hindsight. In the most satisfying parts of the novel we see how far and how near the Victorians are from us.

Das Kapital (1867) was dedicated to Darwin. Fowles likes to remind us that Marx was lurking behind the reassuring facades of Charles's world. Marx is quoted in the chapter-headings about as often as Tennyson or Clough. Could Charles have been told what would come of Marx's writings 'he would not have believed it'; but he cannot see the Darwinian implications of his own position. He is a perfect specimen of a highly developed species which is already being replaced in the rapid evolution of nineteenth-century society. Ernestina's tycoon father offers him a chance to survive by adapting when he offers a business-partnership, but Charles is too much a gentleman for that. It is his valet Sam who pursues the new opportunities in trade: 'if new species can come into being, old species very often have to make way for them' (Chapter 8).

This is a 'Whig' interpretation, and Fowles's view of the nineteenth century often highlights the progress which has improved English conditions in the last hundred years. He anticipates our nostalgia for the comforts of life in Society by dwelling on the horrors of mass-poverty and the abuse of social privilege – in the religiose but unholy Mrs Poulteney to whom Sarah is for an unhappy time 'companion', for example. He checks his disposition to self-congratulation on progress by recalling what has been lost, especially in the satisfactions of community life. Sarah represents a modern emancipation.

> When one was skating over so much thin ice – ubiquitous economic oppression, terror of sexuality, the flood of mechanistic science – the ability to close one's eyes to one's own absurd stiffness was essential. Very few Victorians chose to close their eyes to such cryptic colouration [Darwin's phrase for the chameleon's adaptability]; but there was that in Sarah's look which did. Though direct, it was a timid look. Yet behind it lay a very modern phrase: Come clean, Charles, come clean.   (Chapter 18)

Such authenticity is a virtue for us, as duty was then. Flexibility and mobility are our social advantages; stability and security were theirs. A Dorset ploughman was bringing up eleven children in 1867 'in a poverty too bitter to describe'; his cottage is owned in 1967 by a fashionable London architect who loves it – 'so picturesquely rural' (Chapter 19). In another passage, there is regret for 'our ancestors' isolation [which] like the greater space they enjoyed . . . can only be envied' (Chapter 17). These are conventional points and the characters who illustrate them are conventionally conceived. The statistical and other documentary evidence which clusters in some parts of the book only gives us detailed confirmation of what we knew already, that London was full of prostitutes and that Victorian kitchens were very unhealthy. Fowles is less adventurous in the actual practice of fiction than J. G. Farrell. But he has looked back at the life behind the figure he saw in his mind's eye on the Cobb at Lyme and provided an imaginative, thoughtful and humane view of it from the vantage-point of 1969.

A paper on the novel by Sheldon Rothblatt sums up what is traditional in its perspective.

> Fowles has done something that is close to what the practising historian does or wants to do and in fact has always done, whether monk, positivist or Hegelian: compared past and present in order to understand one by the other . . . [so that] one of Fowles's aims is to explain why his characters are Victorian and why we are not [and] by showing us what we are not, he has helped us to see ourselves as we are.[7]

That is so. But Rothblatt's essay is most interesting because it is full of good sense mixed with an enthusiasm for the experimental aspects of *The French Lieutenant's Woman* which conflicts with everything he says he believes as an historian. His views are an example of the force of Avrom Fleishman's conviction that the 'experimental' modernist movement is all that counts in modern literature, and of the weakness of its reasoning, at least where historiography is concerned.

Rothblatt assumes that modern literature must discard all previous modes of presentation if it is to be true to modern experience. He regrets that historians have 'remained loyal to the academic writing traditions of the late nineteenth century' so that there is now 'an estranging distance between history and literature'. A large part of the introduction to his essay is an explanation of why historians have not been able to join the literary avant-garde: 'one of the programmatic characteristics of the avant-garde has been a rather violent and quite conscientious repudiation of the past in all its institutional forms and values' he says, and he cites Renato Poggioli's *Theory of the Avant-Garde* (1968).

> Dress, manners, conventions of social behaviour; the language of everyday life, the thoughts of everyday life, are subjected to the scorn of the *déracinés*. Out of this terrifying

scorn, with its strong components of nihilism, fright and dream fantasy, has come a perception of human relationships which we call absurd. It is an attitude that the world, physical or social, makes no sense whatsoever, in fact can make no sense, that basic human desires and essential psychological drives cannot be accommodated in any social arrangement, and that communication is a fiction, superficial at best. This prevalent and extensive interpretation of the possibilities of human achievement has had a profound influence on the practice of modern art . . . The importance of sequence, imitation and the careful relation of parts to each other has been vehemently denied.[8]

He rightly concludes that such a view of the world is useless in the practice of history: 'absurd history is a contradiction in terms'. Although the historian may have a sense of the absurd 'he makes certain that mystery stays the subject and not the product of his research'. History in consequence has become separated from the 'mainstream of artistic and literary activity in our time'.[9]

Given his premises there seems no solution. If they were right, it could only be hoped that the mainstream of literature would become less nihilistic in time; and historians in the meanwhile would have to be old-fashioned in their procedures. Rothblatt acknowledges other gulfs set between literature of the Absurd and orthodox history. Truth in the empirical historian's sense is not a criterion for writers of the Absurd. While the historian is a teacher who communicates what he knows of the past for the benefit of the present, the avant-garde is contemptuous of the public; 'if the world is absurd, why bother to communicate?' But some accommodation of the historian's goal to the literary methods of the Absurd must be attempted, and hence Rothblatt's admiration for *The French Lieutenant's Woman*, which he thinks serves as a model since it is true to the past and at least experimental, if only modestly so. Rothblatt does not say how far experiment might go. The thought of social life in the Lyme Regis of 1867 treated by William Burroughs makes Fowles's polite reservations about mimesis seem reassuring. 'To what extent am I being panicked into avant-gardism?' Fowles asks himself in his 'Notes'.[10] Sheldon Rothblatt has been panicked into confusion.

He says that the novel is 'by no means original [by which he means in this context 'experimental'] in every respect', but he does not show that it is experimental and historically truthful at the same time, rather than by turns.[11] He is panicked into pleading that historians and historical novelists join in the one movement among creative writers which has no respect for his subject. It seems unlikely that any writer with a genuine interest in present perspective on the past will follow the experimental features of *The French Lieutenant's Woman* to their logical conclusions.

John Bayley has attacked *The French Lieutenant's Woman* and all such novels which he says are true only to their own autonomy. He regrets that 'the modern novelist is usually self-conscious, and conscious of the game that he is playing with his narrative, in ways which would have amazed Dickens', so that 'the fact in fiction has no status in itself'.

> . . . the sin of semiotics is to attempt to destroy our sense of truth in fiction. There must be in it, as Marianne Moore said of poems, 'a place for the genuine', 'imaginary gardens with real toads in them'. Fiction must lose its nerve if those toads are signs like the story, and as subject to the story-teller's whim.[12]

The real distinction for a story, he concludes, is 'the difference between what is true in it and what is made up'. 'What is true', here, appeals to every kind of verification outside the novel: to historical fact, and to truths about life (Marianne Moore's toads). The claims may, presumably, conflict. A novelist, or playwright, might alter historical fact in the interest of truth to human nature – or he might be careless in ways that do not affect a deeper kind of truth. But they belong together, in Bayley's argument against 'the critical philosophy of today [where] the novelist owns truth and nature as much as he owns his fictions'. Fiction must defer to truth. *The French Lieutenant's Woman* may be accurate in its facts about prostitution in the 1860s and the date of *Origin of Species*, but its two endings are a failure to face the question of how such a man and woman would have decided their future in such circumstances in that period. If the reader is indifferent, then the characterisation is lacking in truth.

William Golding's novels satisfy Bayley's criterion in their approach: they are inventions which explore truths, and Golding, like Bayley, writes the word without inverted commas. His novels have attracted readers and critics by offering a vision of life, of human nature, of good and evil. The title of *Darkness Visible* (1979) suggests the author's special subject. 'Human beings do have a strand of real malignancy', he said in an interview; 'we ignore it at our peril . . . there is active human evil'.[13] His early books were inspired by a sense of the 'folly of the naive, liberal, almost Rousseauesque view of man as being capable of perfection'; and his later novels, *Darkness Visible* and *Rites of Passage* (1981) are equally traditional in their view of man as a creature capable of 'love and self-sacrifice', by a kind of grace, but maligned by nature. Many of the novels offer pictures of innocence, Simon in *Lord of the Flies* (1954), the Neanderthal people in *The Inheritors* (1956), Mattie in *Darkness Visible*, which is, traditionally, seen as a liability. T. S. Eliot told him that good people are harder to 'do' in literature than bad, something he already knew.[14] Human goodness is precarious and often suspect in Golding, but sometimes truly impressive. His novels can impress even when they are difficult and unpleasant because they are free from cynicism.

Concerned with the state and nature of man, Golding has looked for settings, stories and characters outside the common social life of the present day: boys on an island or a dead soul on a Hebridean rock. Where he has dealt with contemporary England, as in *Darkness Visible*, he has often dealt with abnormal states of mind and fringe communities. *The Pyramid* (1967) is an exception. *The Inheritors* and *The Spire* (1964) are set back in time, and so is 'The Scorpion God' – the only one of the three long, long stories with historical settings in *The Scorpion God* (1971) which is equal in quality to the novels.[15] But the historical dimension in *The Inheritors* and *The Spire* is of secondary interest. *The Inheritors* is perhaps a 'prehistoric novel'. The truth that is sought concerns human nature which, fully emerged in *homosapiens*, is horribly familiar but of no 'period' interest. In *The Spire* medieval life is the background for a symbolic, psychological, spiritual study of pride in Dean Jocelin who builds the spire of Salisbury Cathedral as an act of faith. Avrom Fleishman, keen to secure them for the genre, discusses both as historical novels; but they have been exhaustively analysed and praised in other critical studies which hardly mention their historical interest. *The Spire* is an account of an historical event, full of detail about medieval building techniques, but it could be said to be historical in a negative sense since its remote setting makes it easier to exclude all but a few elements of social background. It is as a man rather than a medieval man that we attend to Dean Jocelin.[16] In *Rites of Passage* there is a much more full portrayal of the society within which the characters are seen, and this is honestly done without making use of the past for present purposes. But the past for Golding is still a source of isolated settings in which to observe the permanent condition of man. *Rites of Passage* is an invented tale which aims to tell the truth.

It is unashamed invention. Fowles tells himself not to pretend that he lives in the nineteenth century. Golding's sight lines belong to the second decade of the nineteenth century and the effects, which are calculated for our benefit, are managed with an art which is concealed. The story is in the form of a journal addressed to a noble godfather by a young man sailing from England to Australia. The idea is that his lordship may 'live vicariously', and perhaps forget the pangs of gout. 'Honoured godfather', the first chapter begins:

> With those words I begin the journal I engage myself to keep for you – no words could be more suitable.
> Very well then. The place: on board the ship at last. The year: you know it.

The gap between what we know and what the godfather knows, between the narrator's expected reader and ourselves, is the basic 'pretence'. The godson, Edmund Talbot, has been coached by his godfather in the arts of an eighteenth-century gentleman. He is to study to flatter well, and he flatters his tutor subtly. He is to keep a well-judged distance from the various layers of his social inferiors, guarding himself against flattery from them. He is to exploit the privileges of his rank, using the fact that he is going south to join the Governor's 'entourage' to make the most of the power of patronage. In the scene which makes the first turning point of the novel's very simple plot, Talbot's assumption of his reader's approval is gently used against him.

The 'wooden world' of the decrepit ship of the line, turned now to general purposes and on her last voyage, has dismayed Talbot into giving a vivid impression of stench, sea-sickness and confinement. His quarters are insufferable, the other passengers low. Failing to read the captain's Standing Orders which forbid civilians the quarterdeck, he presents himself to the despotic Captain Anderson who first rails him, then moderates his tone when informed who the intruder is. The description of his transformation is meant to amuse.

> [The situation] made me laugh in what must have seemed an unmannerly fashion but the fellow deserved the rebuke even if it was accidental. It stopped his blusters and heightened his colour, but gave me the opportunity of producing your name and that of His Excellency your brother, much as one might prevent the nearer approach of a highwayman by quickly presenting a brace of pistols. Our captain squinted first – you will forgive the figure – down your lordship's muzzle, decided you were loaded, cast a fearful eye at the ambassador in my other hand and reined back with his yellow teeth showing! I have seldom seen a face at once so daunted and so atrabilious . . . if today when the French clock in the Arras room chimed at ten and our ship's bell here was struck four times – at that time, I say, if your lordship experienced a sudden access of well-being and a warming satisfaction, I cannot swear that it may not have been some distant notion of what silver-mounted and murdering piece of ordnance a noble name was proving to be among persons of a lesser station.   (pp. 30–1)

This is a highly mannered performance; the godfather is no simpleton, but an expert on Racine. The image of the highwayman is there for the sake of 'down your lordship's muzzle', and 'persons of a lesser station' is half in quotation marks. The literary flavours shelter the gentlemen from the vulgarity of snobbishness (the fact existed then although not the word) but allow a residue of self-satisfaction improved by the implied cultural exclusion of 'the fellow' from their sense of humour. Talbot's posing at posing is exactly right for the period, when aristocratic disdain was becoming slightly self-conscious. Observing Talbot in the context of his period we remember that a naval officer's career was subject to aristocratic caprice. Talbot's disdain for the captain would have been shown as vulgarity in Jane Austen, and we can see it as such from our knowledge of her. Today it seems snobbish in a blunter fashion, in our society which rejects, as hers did not, the idea of station.

Talbot is contrasted with the tragi-comic figure of the Reverend Robert James Colley, at the other extreme of gentility from Talbot's eminence, with something of the simplicity of fable. Golding's art often works upwards, through fable. Talbot is handsome, tall, smart, cultivated and subtle, socially relaxed, and well-connected. Colley is none of these things. Talbot's mistake in affronting the captain is repeated, as we should expect in a fable, by the shambling Colley who is swiftly punished for it. Officers and crew are encouraged to goad the parson and to humiliate him in the rites of passage when the ship crosses the line. When Colley goes 'forrard' to rebuke the men they make him ludicrously drunk: he subsequently dies of shame. A righteous ship's officer, Mr Summers, points out to Talbot that he is partly to blame for having provoked Anderson. There are other indications that at some stage of its growth in Golding's mind the book was a fable. Summers is upright and refined although he has risen from the ranks, or 'come aft through the hawsehole'. Another officer, born a gentleman, is a cad. A fable is one of the plainest forms of literary invention and, plainly read, the novel is a story with a blunt modern meaning – that 'station' does not count.

It is more than that from the outset. The novel teems with events and characters which the journal presents in terms of farce. Talbot is seduced by a tart. There is a Jacobin agent on whom Talbot is meant to be discreetly spying, in the interests of government. There is a drunken painter of naval battles who provides an excellent comic scene at the captain's table. The captain himself is mostly a figure of fun – even more a parson-hater than old-navy captains are supposed to have been. These people and their doings have close counterparts, in the social life of a decade or so later, in the early short tales of Dickens and Thackeray. They are caricatures, but they are not kept to the background. Colley's death is almost forgotten in the performance of the drunken painter, The snobbishness of the era is almost lost to view because of Golding's relish for its vitality. It is awesome to think of this lower-middle class Regency crowd arriving in Sydney. There is a continual comedy of language provided by Talbot's (and Golding's) enjoyment of Tarpaulin, the 'tarry' dialect of the ship.

> 'Mr Summers! Will you have the pintles out of her?' Summers said nothing but the thudding ceased. Captain Anderson's tone sank to a grumble. 'The pintles are loose as a pensioner's teeth.' Summers nodded in reply. 'I know it, Sir. But until she's rehung – 'The sooner we're off the wind the better. God curse that drunken superintendent!' He stared moodily down at the union flag, then up at the sails which, as if willing to debate with him, boomed back. They could have done no better than the preceding dialogue. Was it not superb?   (p. 261)

This sample of Tarpaulin – the best in the book – occurs in the middle of Colley's funeral. Comic invention is always liable to upset the 'meaning' of the element of fable, and endorse a remark of Talbot's:

> Life is a formless business, Summers. Literature is much amiss in forcing a form on it.   (p. 265)

This is one of many meanings the characters find in their experience. Ideas abound in their talk. But they do not coalesce; they tend to cancel out. Summers responds to Talbot's 'life is formless' that birth and death are both common among the emigrants on board. The ideas and moods contribute to the picture of the period. Talbot is late Augustan, touched by Romanticism; Colley is popular Romantic. Everyone seems to have read 'Mr Coleridge's poem' and knows 'Alone, alone . . . ', but the rationalist emigrant is resolved to shoot an albatross with a blunderbuss to refute superstition. Golding's instinct for symbolism is given to his major characters, in this novel. The 'wooden world' is a microcosm to Talbot, who broods in – for him – rather banal terms on its 'politics'. It is an image of the soul's plight to Colley, in terms that might be found in a pious but reasonably up-to-date *Monthly Magazine* article. The journey is not a symbol but an occasion for people to think in symbols. Invention creates a crowded lively illusion of life in *Rites of Passage* but it is, though not as formless, as contradictory as life.

Golding achieves accuracy in all this, hitting off the tones and attitudes we hear in the literature of the time, in Byron and Creevey, in Peacock and Leigh Hunt, in Theodore Hook and Pierce Egan. Golding is a naval man. He is probably right about the spars and rigging, the tarry language, the troubles of midshipmen and ageing lieutenants. He seems to accord with C. S. Forester who is certainly right. Golding minimises the spectacular cruelty of life in ships of this time in order to enhance the effect of the scene where Colley is subjected to the rites of passage. In this scene we reach Golding's apprehension of a truth about human life.

The novel is a study in contrast between its two principal passengers, each of whom is seen from the other's point of view since Talbot finds, and copies for his godfather, Colley's long letter home to his sister. We first see Colley through Talbot's irreligious and contemptuous eyes, a shabby-obsequious creature to be avoided, and of course we see the observer in the observation. They are archetypes, the favourite and the butt, nobleman and clown, opposites in social position and in natural gifts. Although Talbot is not the Christian gentleman and ideal Friend Colley imagines, he is able to overcome revulsion enough to intrigue on Colley's behalf when reminded of the duties which ought to go with privilege; and he is moved, as a man of sensibility as well as sense, when he reads Colley's letter, to feel some remorse (soon, naturally, overcome). He finds Colley a poor creature, and so may we. If such a man could have appeared in the Austen world, she would have kept him a minor figure, lampooned for errors in sense and manners, not unlike Mr Collins. Colley is a sycophant, reminding his sister 'not to omit to show any little attention that may be possible in that quarter' (p. 187) when he mentions 'Manston Place', the big house at home. His opinions, which include disapproval of rum for the lower orders, are his bishop's. When he feels an insult to his 'cloth', he protests that he has been received, *twice*, at the bishop's table. Jane Austen would have made him a buffoon and would have modified some of his traits in respect for the cloth and fictional seemliness. The sort of buffoonery whch destroys him is quite outside her world. Although dazzled by the lovely though painted beauty whose favours

Talbot briefly gains, his daydreams dwell on the handsome topsail-man Billy Rogers with whom he is to commit when drunk, as Talbot later discovers, a sexual rite which Talbot calls 'a ridiculous, schoolboy trick' (p. 277), judging him a 'poor fool'.

He is less than a holy fool, and his innocence is mixed with the tiresomeness of an educated simpleton. But he has innocence. Golding is sure enough of his ability to convey it that he deprives his character of every form of dignity. Colley is not spiritually dignified. His devotions are sincere but do not seem true. They are emotional in a man with little emotional maturity, and intellectual in a man with no mental power, except rote memory. His letter inadvertently guys his shallowness. Here he has just noticed that his appearance, for most of the voyage, has badly needed tidying up:

> It was with confusion and shame that I remembered the words addressed to me individually at my ordination – words I must ever hold sacred because of the occasion and the saintly divine who spake them – 'Avoid scrupulosity, Colley, and always present a decent appearance . . .'   (p. 226)

He is not morally impressive either. He does achieve a basic dignity because he is harmless – although a social and perhaps religious menace – in intention, and because he is a victim. Dicken's remark in *Oliver Twist* (Chapter 10) that 'there is a passion *for hunting something* deeply implanted in the human breast' is very strongly felt in Golding. Colley's helplessness makes him a natural victim.

> I heard what the poor victims of the French Terror must have heard in their last moments and oh! – it is crueller than death, it must be – it must be so, nothing, *nothing* that men can do to each other can be compared with that snarling, lustful, storming appetite . . .   (p. 238)

At the second 'nothing', Colley suddenly sounds like Golding (as does Talbot in the novel's last lines on the same theme). It may be an artistic weakness that the author's sense of truth overpowers the character's tone, but the weakness is a small one. In *Lord of the Flies* Golding contrived horrific circumstances to convey what he says here in the context of Colley's shampooing at King Neptune's court in the rites of passage. The historical setting is so fully realised that we accept the horrifying humilation, in 'disrespect-for-cloth' mixed with mob-violence, which belongs to the period. This episode transcends that, observing a universal evil. Golding has said that he believes in God but in little else.[17] There is no Christian consolation in *Rites of Passage*, only an assertion of what is wrong.

Rites of Passage is the product of a very different conception of modern literature from that of John Fowles's

> I do not know. This story I am telling is all imagination . . . .
> But I live in the age of Alain Robbe-Grillet . . .

Golding is much more sure of himself. He does not misrepresent what he shows of the past for the sake of a study in class. Colley and Talbot are enmeshed in social dealings which are astringently but fairly observed, and there is considerable interest and entertainment in the verve with which they are brought alive. But the real purpose assumes that one age is much like another, in the essentials. There is no reason to believe that Golding's sort of fiction need come to an end.

8 Conclusion

These novelists, I have maintained, achieve a fair balance between truth to the past and interest in the present time. They do not appropriate the past, making it serve present causes, nor do they treat it as alien or unknowable; their work accords the past a place as a living 'part of the human environment', in Mary Renault's phrase, not to be ignored and not to be ruthlessly occupied and redeveloped. Unsurprisingly, they write in modes which are rooted in traditional literature, although not in tired forms 'doled out' by former practice; that term of Fleishman's might apply to Hugh Walpole. Also unsurprisingly, they are humanists; they believe in an essential human nature to be discovered within the features of any particular culture. They see a continuity with the past, in history, in literature, and in 'real people, who remain much the same', as Burgess says, and life which 'itself does not change very much', as Farrell says.[1] This is a coherent position, and one which is under attack. To show the continuity, while acknowledging the extent to which life has changed, is itself a creative practice at the present time.

When Avrom Fleishman proposes that the historical novel join 'the experimental movement of the modern novel', he does not consider the implications for the imaginative union with the past life which he finds in the tradition. Thomas Pynchon represents that movement now. Frank Kermode remarks that Mallarmé wrote 'at the end of the great age of the book', and adds that 'Pynchon's joke (about the battleships) belongs to another age, which we have still hardly come to terms with'.[2] In order to find value in the novelists I have discussed it is necessary to discount the widely prevailing view that our age is completely divorced from its predecessors. In this view, which Fleishman traces to Conrad's *The Inheritors*, 'history may be said to have ended';[3] human nature has changed or is changing; literature and historiography belong

177

to a dying world. It is the view most honestly expressed in 'the scorn of the *déracinés*' admired by Professor Rothblatt (and quoted in the last chapter).

A far more temperate and urbane version of the West's deracination appears in a lecture given at Cambridge almost thirty years ago when C. S. Lewis inaugurated the Chair of Medieval and Renaissance English Literature in 1954. His title, from Isidore of Seville, was '*De descriptione temporum*', and he argued that a more momentous change had occurred in his lifetime than that which divides Antiquity from the Dark Ages or the Middle Ages from the Renaissance. Ancient culture, especially Latin possessed by all educated men until the nineteenth century, had died; literature, in the work of T. S. Eliot and David Jones, had altered more drastically than ever before; religious belief had ceased to dominate culture. The ideal of governments had changed from stability to dynamic transformation. Technology had profoundly affected everybody. Medieval and Renaissance literatures were therefore part of a continuum joining Homer to the nineteenth century, and from that civilisation his audience were excluded. Lewis himself was a 'dinosaur', a last sample of 'Old Western Man', still able to 'read as a native texts which you [the undergraduates of 1954] must read as foreigners'.[4] J. H. Plumb's *Death of the Past* is based on the same conviction, although he welcomes as emancipation what Lewis regrets.

If Lewis was right, then the historical novelist's position today would be so different from that of Scott that it would be meaningless to speak of 'tradition' within the genre. According to Lewis, Scott wrote from within a culture ('something which had already begun when the *Iliad* was composed and was still almost unimpaired when Waterloo was fought') which we observe as aliens.[5] His conclusion means that the nature of historical imagination must have changed altogether, or been lost; and the task of recreating and interpreting the past for contemporary minds must belong to a different order of literary effort, perhaps impossible.

He is exaggerating a strong case. Part of the interest which Mary Renault's readers share with J. G. Farrell's is how *different* life and sight lines were in the fourth century B.C. or a hundred years ago. Perspective foreshortens, as Lewis says himself; 'the distance between the telegraph post I am touching and the next telegaph post looks longer that the sum of the distances between all the other posts.'[6] Most generations have thought themselves changed out of recognition from 'the old Age', and several generations have thought themselves close to the end of the world. But few have had the scope or detail of Lewis's knowledge of the past, and what he argues everyone today has at least dimly apprehended. The recent history of war strengthens his case.

But Lewis misrepresents by overstating throughout, so that his overall conclusion is wrong.

> We have lived to see the second death of ancient learning. In our time something which was once the possession of all educated men has shrunk to being the technical accomplishment of a few specialists.[7]

> Of course the un-christening of Europe in our time is not quite complete; neither was her christening in the Dark Ages . . . Christians and Pagans had much more in common with each other than either has with a post-Christian . . .
> . . . The post-Christian is cut off from the Christian past and therefore doubly from the Pagan past.[8]

> Our rulers have become like schoolmasters. . . .[9]

Mary Renault did not write against such a background. The ousting of classics from classroom pre-eminence is not equivalent to 'the second death of ancient learning'. Lewis is thinking of dons; almost all knew Latin and Greek in 1900 as did schoolmasters, clergymen and other professional men who might have been dons if they had chosen; many of the same kind of people in 1954 came from the 'modern' or 'science' sides. But among writers of earlier times, Shakespeare, Pope, Blake, Keats and Dickens are only some of those who needed translations (in Pope's case translators). The fatuity of compulsory languages at school, regardless of pupils' ability, is obvious from Victorian fiction.[10] Mary Renault might have commented on 'educated *men*'. Most of us now profit from the excellent annotated translations in Penguin classics as well as from the Loeb. Far too many people visit classical sites. There is still a literary influence from the classics (Yeats, Eliot, Joyce, Graves, Golding, Iris Murdoch). This is only a strand in modern

English culture, but although it was stronger in the past it has always been only a strand; the recent decline in ancient learning is not a 'second death'. Lewis's 'un-christening of Europe' seems based on a narrow view of European Christendom. Professedly Christian writers in Britain in the second rank, after Eliot, Waugh, Greene and Auden, would make a long list. Piers Paul Read's *Monk Dawson* (1969) and David Lodge's *How Far Can You Go?* (1981) achieve a balanced view of contemporary Catholicism which was beyond the reach of 'Old Western' writers. It would be hard to maintain that an historical novelist depicting an age of faith goes beyond the limits of experience to which a contemporary writer can appeal. Although Lewis lumps together the Pagan and the Christian consciousness in contrast to ours, many agnostic writers in antiquity (Lucian, for example) were familiar with a state of declining traditional religion, combined with rife superstition and mercenary oriental cults, which is not unlike ours, except that Christianity carries more weight now than Paganism in the second century AD. Anyone who has lived in Africa is likely to think Lewis excessively Oxford-and-Cambridge-tied in his view of contemporary civilisation – as are most intellectual comentators in Europe and America who write about 'our present plight'. They are also likely to think him wrong about a basic change in the nature of government. Almost every form of government known to the Greeks exists today – the chief exception being city-state democracy. The methods of oppression are only more efficient than when Dionysios of Syracuse listened to his 'Ear'.

Mary Renault's novels are for readers who are relatively unlikely to have stereotyped images of the ancient world derived from schoolmasters, less likely to assume that Demosthenes was right and Philip wrong, or that Greek religion was divided between primitive animal-sacrifice and the almost-Christian insights of Plato, more prepared to consider Greek sexual mores, and to share the philosophers' ideal (not practice) of questioning everything. This is a time in which Protestant and Catholic elements in a novelist's readership are able to consider the history of the other persuasion, and religious belief before Christianity, without requiring an admixture of polemic. Weakened commitment need not mean indifference or estrangement in political matters either. Nor do we see these advantages as 'progress'. Historical novelists are not inclined to flatter us on our detachment-with-sympathy, as a superior stance to the yearnings and rivalries of Renault's Athens or Burgess's Elizabethan London.

Burgess and Nye can expect from their readers a knowledge of and a personal involvement in earlier English literature. It was quirky if not malicious of Lewis to tell his audience that to read Medieval and Renaissance texts they must 'suspend most of the responses and unlearn most of the habits you have acquired in reading modern literature' since they must read as foreigners what he read as a native. But who learns to read from Pound, Eliot, Joyce, Proust or Hermann Broch? Our earliest experience of literature comes from nursery rhymes and Victorian jingles, hymns, the Authorised Version, and bits of Bunyan, *Gulliver's Travels* and *Robinson Crusoe*, besides *Treasure Island* and modern children's writers whose imaginations were formed from 'Old Western' literature. One reads Shakespeare at an earlier age than Brecht, Elizabethan lyrics years before Pound, Jane Austen before Virginia Woolf. Most modern literature is meaningless without early reading of 'Old Western'. Neither Lewis nor Tolkien found young readers of the 1960s and 1970s estranged in sympathy or instinct from the products of their rather old-fashioned imaginations. Lewis knew this, although for the sake of his argument he pretended to forget it. But critics who say that after the Modernist movement all novelists should write to disturb our normal experience of the world rather than exploit and improve it, forget that many of the earlier subjects of Auerbach's *Mimesis* (Homer, Shakespeare, Cervantes) are deeper in most readers than the species of realism he treats in his last chapter. Enjoyment of parody in Burgess and Nye is not meant to be at the expense of older literature, nor is it 'historicist' in the sense of isolating a period. Nye's point in *Falstaff* is that Falstaff is not contained by the Elizabethan world-picture. The character can speak to us in our idioms without seriously falsifying the spirit in which his author wrote.

Although Farrell went no further back into the British Empire than 1857, his trilogy and the 'nineteenth-century' novels by Fowles and Golding take advantage of the continuity which unites the nineteenth and twentieth centuries as a single 'modern' period. Every decade is distinct and conscious of the rapidly changing times, brought on by Napoleon or the cutting of the railways, the Great Exhibition or the Education Act, Darwin or Freud, the Somme or Hiroshima. But most present trends and fashionable ideas originated in the nineteenth century. Matthew Vaughan's first novel *Chalky* (1975) is the story of a boy from a Victorian orphanage who becomes an army officer and is socially unacceptable among the more snobbish officers and gentleman; the same theme, given a 1920s or 1960s setting, would need different tuning but its implications and connotations would be much the same. George Macdonald Fraser's tales in the *Flashman* series create much of their comedy from features of Victorian social life which are unlike ours in emphasis but not in kind.[11] The novels of Anthony Powell which span the century (and the author's lifetime) are studies, among other things, of how strands of nineteenth-century life persist and interweave with more recent social phenomena. Powell's work shows that history is still evolving and that we are not yet in a 'post-culture'.

Perhaps the best evidence for what we and our literature share with the past comes from the 'apocalyptic' fiction which contemplates a near-future in which the world loses touch with history and becomes enslaved to it, returning to barbarism. Anthony Burgess's lightly comic *The End of the World News* (1982) depicts such an outcome. Its final pages describing the departure of an Ark-like spaceship when the planet is to be destroyed are powerful because they evoke the interconnection of culture with the physical environment. Nothing from history can be taken on the journey into space because, away from the planet, it will all become meaningless. That perspective unites us with Golding's Neanderthals.

If the prospect of a calamitous near-future concentrates the mind (and makes the past more precious), it may also bring to mind the relative brevity of recorded history. The discovery of geological time in the nineteenth century was unsettling to the Victorians, but it gives us a perspective which can be comforting. It makes the ancient Greeks seem close, although to 'Old Western Man' they were at the other end of time. Iris Murdoch's *The Fire and the Sun*, written twenty-five years after Lewis gave his lecture, and by a younger writer less affected by the impact of Modernism which shows in Lewis, is a lively argument with Plato. (Iris Murdoch, who shows some affection for her adversary, notes that he made the earliest and the best declaration of intellectual equality between the sexes.) In the course of it she says that 'of course art is huge and European philosophy strangely small, so that Whitehead scarcely exaggerates in calling it all footnotes to Plato'. Her liberal humanist argument for art and especially literature as an open forum, in which 'everything' can be freely debated, has its roots deep in 'Old Western' culture and shows itself pleasantly familiar (in both senses) with one of the originators of the culture. Iris Murdoch's fiction includes one (marginally) historical novel, *The Red and The Green* (1965). Her novels and criticism constitute a refutation of Lewis's great divide, and Plumb's 'death of the past'. They assume a reader who has read Plato (if not in Greek), who understands (perhaps without sharing) religious belief, who enjoys the contemporary and the traditional notes in her work.

Such readers exist, and not only in Iris Murdoch's two countries. They may be fewer than novelists would like, but the great numbers of writers of popular historical adventures and romances and the large sales of some such books of little literary merit show that there still is a wider readership to be won. Renault, Burgess, Farrell and Golding have encroached on it, without succumbing to the rival temptations to treat the past as though it were the present in different costume, or to treat it as though it were completely unlike what we know. Talking about historical fiction in relation to Scott's influence, A. O. J. Cockshut said that the first leads to tushery and the second to the Gothic.[12] It has been so since Scott's time, in popular fiction where there is little attempt at a perspective. At a higher level of writing, the denial of perspective which follows from 'the death of the past', 'all history is contemporary history', 'history has no *mythic* authority', leads either to fantasy or to propaganda, or to a blend of them such as John Berger's *G*.[13] Abler novelists have resisted these temptations too.

Mary Renault's bold assurances about the genre are refreshing after reading Sheldon Rothblatt on *The French Lieutenant's Woman* or Frank Kermode on *The Crying of Lot 49*. The true historical novelist is to dispel fantasy and resist propaganda. It is the resolve in her novels which impresses. W. W. Tarn, the historian, is equally resolved but he argues out of historical existence a character on whom Mary Renault builds the whole of one novel and parts of another. Renault and Tarn share a sense that it matters whether or not Bagoas existed. We may think that their different conceptions of what he might have been like reveal a greater maturity of vision in the later writer. We may think that the question does not affect the novel's quality. Bagoas makes an ideal observer even if he is moved entirely from the history into the fiction in the reader's mind. But it matters that the novel is arguing for the evidence that he existed, by creating a character who is compatible with the history. It reopens the Bagoas question and makes a human character out of a mental label – a 'spayed catamite'. The history and the fiction cannot be judged apart, and this sort of writing will never satisfy purists. In this case, a dubious fragment of history provided the character and the realisation of the character made the history a shade less dubious.

Anthony Burgess makes no real claim for his candidate for dark mistress. Her role in *Nothing Like the Sun* is what the book says, the ingenious whimsy of a lecturer off duty. Reading of Bagoas or Lucy Negro prompts thoughts about how such a person would have seen Alexander or Shakespeare and historical imagination may work on our thoughts in earnest or game. If it is to be historical imagination, the game must be played fairly and Burgess is as true as he can be to what we know about Shakespeare, except in matters where we know nothing at all. Given Shakespeare, the essential task is a degree of truth to the language restored to the life of Shakespeare's time, as well as we can imagine it. Burgess is apparently moving closer to what Barthes would want, turning history into fiction, making a new 'construct' out of Shakespeare and showing that it is invention. 'The real is never any more than a meaning', wrote Barthes, 'which can be revoked when history requires it and demands a thorough subversion of the very foundations of civilised society'.[14] But Burgess would say that the real is what enables him to appreciate Shakespeare, and that the reality Shakespeare knew comes, imperfectly, through his language; that to attribute meanings where we know nothing need not disturb the little we have of the real life.

Burgess and Mary Renault recognise that although there is no history without imagination to give it life, and so in a sense no history without fiction, the freedom the novelist brings to creating the past is subject to the authority of history to preserve it. They also believe that fiction defers to the truth about human life which we share with Shakespeare – or with Arrian. They are as 'Old Western' as C. S. Lewis in finding open access to the past. It is therefore possible for them to achieve an accommodation of past to present, to create an Alexander or a Shakespeare to interest us without allowing our interest to 'revoke' the meanings they gave their lives. That is the common interest of their very different styles of fiction. I have argued that the interest is present, rather weirdly, in the Nye of *Falstaff* where the games the book plays have a meaning because the novelist persuades us of reality behind them. The interest depends on trust in the imagination, which John Fowles worries about so unhelpfully in *The French Lieutenant's Woman*, and which Golding exploits creatively in *Rites of Passage*. If that trust were to fail, the past might recede from serious interest.

It should have been possible to conclude with the bright prospect of another Farrell novel, quizzically contemplating some new imperial catastrophe.

> Who knows what magnificence he might have given us? For, marvellous as the 'Empire Trilogy' is, it was only the beginning of something. One sensed that his artistic ambitions were large, although he himself would have repudiated the idea. . . . There is nothing meretricious or merely topical about Farrell's work; it has the detachment and repose of great art.[15]

Derek Mahon's was one of many newspaper tributes which recorded 'a blow to literature'. Farrell's advent, with *Troubles*, in 1970 was unlooked for – a major talent devoted to historical fiction. Benny Green's article when Farrell died seems almost apologetic about the fact that the novels are, after all, historical.[16] But there has been a strong current of imaginative work in the last thirty years, and the old embarrassment about the hybrid genre may well be provoked again.

Notes and References

1 INTRODUCTION

1. Avrom Fleishman, *The English Historical Novel: Walter Scott to Virgina Woolf* (Baltimore: Johns Hopkins University Press, 1971) p. 255.
2. Ibid., p. 256.
3. J. R. Seeley, *The Expansion of England* (London: Macmillan, 1883) p. 3.
4. W. M. Thackeray, *Henry Esmond, The English Humourists, The Four Georges*, The Oxford Thackeray, XIII (Oxford University Press, 1908) 545.
5. Andrew Sanders, *The Victorian Historical Novel 1840–1880* (London: Macmillan, 1978) p. 30.
6. David Brown, *Walter Scott and the Historical Imagination* (London: Routledge & Kegan Paul, 1979) p. 209.
7. James Anderson, *Sir Walter Scott and History* (Edinburgh: Edina Press, 1981) p. 108.
8. J. H. Raleigh, *Time, Place and Idea: Essays on the Novel* (Southern Illinois University Press, 1968) p. 121.
9. Robert Lee Wolff, 'Present Uses for the Past', *Times Literary Supplement*, 13 December 1974, p. 1404.
10. Flaubert, *Correspondence. Supplément*, ed. R. Dumesnil, J. Pommier and C. Digeon (4 vols. Paris, 1954). Quoted in Anne Green, *Flaubert and the Historical Novel: 'Salammbó' reassessed* (Cambridge: Cambridge University Press, 1982) p. 16.
11. *Times Literary Supplement*, 31 March 1972, p. 352.
    The article, on Alfred Duggan, is reprinted in *TLS: Essays and Reviews*, 11 (1973) pp. 179–83.
12. Mary Renault, *The Nature of Alexander* (Harmondsworth: Penguin, 1983) p. 17.
13. Sir Richard Southern, 'The Sense of the Past', *Proceedings of the Royal Historical Society*, Fifth Series, 23 (1973) 242–63.
14. A. J. P. Taylor, *A Personal History* (London: Hamish Hamilton, 1983) p. 25.
15. Peter Green, 'Aspects of the Historical Novel', *Essays by Divers Hands*, Proceedings of The Royal Society of Literature, New Series, 21 (1962) 54.
16. Fleishman, *The English Historical Novel*, p. 212. Refers to M. D. Zabel's Introduction to Joseph Conrad: *Tales of Heroes and History* (New York 1960) p. xii.
17. Fleishman, *The English Historical Novel*, pp. 252–3.
18. Ibid., p. 255.
19. Ibid., p. 255.

20. Peter Green, 'Aspects of the Historical Novel', p. 36.
21. The titles which seem to be standing the test of time are given in the bibliography.
22. Fleishman, *The English Historical Novel*, p. 256.
23. See H. M. F. Prescott, *The Man on a Donkey* (London: Eyre & Spottiswoode, 1952).
24. See Geoffrey Aggeler, *Anthony Burgess: The Artist as Novelist* (University of Alabama Press, 1979) p. 99.
25. Frank Kermode, *The Genesis of Secrecy* (Cambridge, Mass: Harvard University Press, 1979) pp. 107–8.
26. Ibid., pp. 108–9.
27. Roland Barthes, 'Discourse of History', translated by Stephen Bann, in *Comparative Criticism: A Year Book*, 3 (Cambridge: Cambridge University Press, 1981) pp. 7–18.
28. Ibid., p. 6.
29. Ibid., p. 18.
30. See Jonathan Culler, *Saussure* (London: Fontana, 1976).
31. See Kermode, *The Genesis of Secrecy*, p. 160 n. 26.
32. *Lire*, April 1979, p. 36.
33. Frank Kermode, 'The Burgess Emperor', *Guardian*, 5 October 1974, p. 19.
34. Oscar Handlin, *Truth in History* (Cambridge, Mass: Harvard University Press, 1979) p. 405.
35. Ibid., p. 409.
36. He gave the Charles Eliot Norton lectures at Harvard in the academic year 1977–8.
37. Thomas McCormack (ed.), *Afterwords: Novelists on their Novels* (London: Harper & Row, 1969) pp. 84–6. Quoted in Fleishman, *The English Historical Novel*, p. xii.
38. *Encounter*, letter by Mary Renault, April 1969, p. 92.
39. James Vinson and D. L. Kirkpatrick (eds), *Contemporary Novelists*, 3rd edn (London: Macmillan, 1982) p. 556.
40. David Lodge, *Guardian*, 16 August 1979, p. 9. 'Some modern writers complicate the simple pleasures of recognition by stylistic device, foregrounding the texuality of their texts.' 'This', he adds, 'is not always an unqualified blessing.'
41. See Mikhail Bakhtin, *Problems of Dostoevsky's Poetics*, translated by R. W. Rotsel (Ann Arbor: Ardis, 1973). Much of Bakhtin's book is a discussion of this tradition, which he calls 'Menippean'.
42. J. H. Plumb, *The Death of the Past* (London: Macmillan, 1969) p. 145.
43. R. G. Collingwood, *The Idea of History* (Oxford: Clarendon Press, 1946) p. 202.
44. Aggeler, *Anthony Burgess*, pp. 98–9.
45. See Robert Scholes, *The Fabulators* (Oxford University Press, 1967).
46. David Lodge, *The Novelist at the Crossroads* (London: Routledge & Kegan Paul, 1971) p. 46.
47. Timothy Mo, 'Magpie Man', *New Statesman*, 15 September 1978, p. 337.
48. Norman F. Dixon, *On the Psychology of Military Incompetence* (London: Jonathan Cape, 1976) p. 130.

49. If Burgess's *Man of Nazareth* (Magnum, 1979), a shameless money-maker, is counted as an historical novel.
50. Bernard Bergonzi, *The Situation of the Novel*, 2nd edn (London: Macmillan, 1979) p. 228.
51. In the opening lines of the verse epilogue to *Napoleon Symphony* (London: Jonathan Cape, 1974) p. 348.

2 MARY RENAULT: THE EARLIER NOVELS

1. A good example of how well materials are absorbed occurs in Chapter 1 of *Fire from Heaven* where Philip tells the child Alexander the version of the story of how their ancestor Alexander I dealt with Persian envoys which is told in Herodotus, v, 17–21.
2. Ricks, *New York Times Book Review*, 17 January 1982, p. 7.
3. Fleishman, *The English Historical Novel*, p. 256.
4. Diodorus Siculus, *History*, xv.
5. 'Author's Note' to *The King Must Die*.
6. John D. S. Pendlebury, *The Archaeology of Crete* (London: Methuen, 1939) pp. 230–1.
7. See Leonard Cottrell, *The Bull of Minos* (Evans Brothers, 1953, 1971) plates 27 and 29.
8. *Times Literary Supplement*, 16 March 1962, p. 181.
9. John Fowles, 'Notes on an Unfinished Novel', in *The Novel Today*, edited by Malcolm Bradbury (London: Fontana, 1977) p. 138.
10. See W. Iser, *The Implied Reader* (Baltimore: Johns Hopkins University Press, 1974) and John Preston, *The Created Self: The Reader's Role in Eighteenth-Century Fiction* (London: Heinemann, 1970).
11. Peter Wolfe, *Mary Renault* (New York: Twayne, 1969), comments on use of first person which 'creates a mood of confidential intimacy and historical urgency.' (ch. 4).
12. Naomi Mitchison, *Black Sparta: Greek Tales* (London: Jonathan Cape, 1928) p. 25.
13. *Times Literary Supplement*, 6 June 1929, p. 452. The review was anonymous.
14. *Sunday Times*, 7 September 1958, p. 6.
15. *Times Literary Supplement*, 19 September 1958, p. 528. Anonymous.
16. Auberon Waugh, 'The Colonel's Mede is Miss Renault's Persian', *Spectator*, 6 January 1973, p. 13.
17. See Wole Soyinka *Myth, Literature and the African World* (Cambridge: Cambridge University Press, 1973) *passim*.
18. Peter Green, 'Tough Act to Follow', *New York Review of Books*, 18 March 1982, pp. 29, 35.
19. See Leonard Cottrell, *The Bull of Minos*, p. 158.
20. Peter Wolfe, *Mary Renault*, p. 140.
21. Sarraute, *'Quelle histoire inventée pourrait rivaliser avec les récits des camps de concentration?' L'Ere du soupcon* (1964) p. 82.
22. Iris Murdoch's *The Fire and the Sun: Why Plato Banished the Artists* (Oxford: Oxford University Press, 1977) is based on the Romanes lecture for 1976.

23. Ibid., p. 20.
24. Ibid., p. 13.
25. Ibid., p. 13.
26. Ibid., p. 21.

3   MARY RENAULT'S *FIRE FROM HEAVEN, THE PERSIAN BOY* AND *FUNERAL GAMES*

  1. W. W. Tarn, *Alexander the Great*, I (1948) p. 1.
  2. Ibid., II, p. 399–449.
  3. Mary Renault, *The Nature of Alexander* (Harmondsworth: Penguin, 1983) pp. 17–18.
  4. Tarn, *Alexander the Great*, I, p. 142.
  5. Edward W. Said, *Orientalism* (London: Routledge & Kegan Paul, 1979) *passim*.
  6. See Tarn, *Alexander the Great*, II, p. 399–449, for a discussion of this question.
  7. Ibid., I, p. 126.
  8. 'Author's Note' to *The Persian Boy*.
  9. Ibid.
10. 'Boucephalus', usually.
11. *Times Literary Supplement*, 11 December 1970, p. 143.
12. *The Nature of Alexander*, p. 26.
13. Ibid., p. 24.
14. Tarn, *Alexander the Great*, I, 1.
15. See R. D. Milns's *Alexander the Great* (London: Hale, 1968), for example. He claims to give a 'balanced' view but is consistently hostile to Arrian.
16. *The Nature of Alexander*, p. 31.
17. See George Cary, *The Medieval Alexander*, edited by D. J. A. Ross (Cambridge: Cambridge University Press, 1956).
18. Schachermeyer's *Alexander der Grosse: Ingenium und Macht* (Wien: 1949) is said to have been influenced in its conception by recent German history. I have not read Schachermeyer.
19. *The Nature of Alexander* offers a discussion, and some second thoughts.
20. According to Curtius, Alexander kissed Bagoas before the troops. Tarn disbelieves it. See the next reference.
21. Tarn, *Alexander the Great*, II, pp. 319–26.
22. 'The lovely Thais by his side
    Sat like a blooming Eastern bride.'
    Dryden, *Alexander's Feast*, 9.
    'None but the brave deserve the fair.'
    Ibid., 15.
23. Dover attributes hostile modern opinion to the Christian prohibition.
24. *The Nature of Alexander*, p. 17.
25. Dover, *Greek Homosexuality* (London: Duckworth, 1978) p. 203.
26. Oswyn Murray, *Times Literary Supplement*, 1 January 1982, p. 12, calls the novel 'a series of vignettes'. Peter Green, *New York Review of Books*, 18 March 1982, pp. 29, 35, thinks that it lacks a dominant central character, in the absence of Alexander.

4 ANTHONY BURGESS; *NOTHING LIKE THE SUN* AND *NAPOLEON SYMPHONY*

1. Burgess was an army lecturer in Gibraltar in 1943; he taught at Banbury Grammar School for four years after the war and later at a public school in Malaya. See Geoffrey Aggeler, *Anthony Burgess: The Artist as Novelist*, pp. 7–9.
2. He was engaged in cipher-work during the war. See Aggeler, p. 7.
3. See *Here Comes Everybody: An Introduction to James Joyce for the Ordinary Reader* (London: Longman, 1965), *English Literature: A Survey for Students*, as John Burgess Wilson (1958), and *Shakespeare* (London: Jonathan Cape, 1970).
4. *Fatimah* or *Fatmah* (destiny) in Arabic written without vowels.
5. Schoenbaum actually wrote, in *Shakespeare's Lives* (Oxford: Oxford University Press, 1970): '*Nothing Like the Sun* is the only novel about Shakespeare acceptable on its own terms as a novel' (p. 766).
6. E. K. Chambers, *William Shakespeare: A Study of Facts and Problems* (Oxford: Clarendon Press, 1930) 1, 26.
7. Schoenbaum, *Shakespeare's Lives*, p. 768.
8. See C. J. Sisson, *The Mythical Sorrows of Shakespeare* (Oxford: Oxford University Press, 1934).
9. Ivor Brown, *Shakespeare* (London: Collins, 1949) pp. 164–5.
10. See Schoenbaum, *Shakespeare's Lives*, p. 651.
11. E. K. Chambers, *Carmina Argentea* (Oxford: Oxford University Press, 1918) p. 25.
12. Reviewing *Napoleon Symphony*, *New York Review of Books*, 19 August 1974, pp. 32–3, John Bayley says that his Napoleon and Shakespeare are versions of Enderby.
13. Francis Meres, *Palladis Tamia: Wit's Treasury* (1598).
14. E. K. Chambers, *William Shakespeare*, II, 254.
15. See Schoenbaum, *Shakespeare's Lives*, pp. 687–8.
16. 'Fair is as fair as fair itself allows,
    And hiding in the dark is not less fair.
    The married blackness of my mistress' brows
    Is thus fair's home . . .' (p. 17)
17. Anthony Burgess, *This Man and Music* (London: Hutchinson, 1982) p. 191.
18. 'Jakes Peer or Jacques Père', *Times Literary Supplement*, 23 April 1964, p. 329. Anonymous.
19. '. . . in his own conceit the only Shake-scene in a country', *Groats-worth of Witte* (1592).
20. Peter Buitenhuis, 'A Lusty Man was Will', *New York Times Book Review*, 13 September 1964, pp. 5, 26.
21. Warren Miller, 'Enter Will: Dressed in Prose', *Nation*, 5 October 1964, pp. 196–7.
22. *OED* gives a citing for 1576: an obscure hunting term apparently referring to a wound in the flank of a deer.
23. *Don Tarquinio* (1905), which was reissued (by Chatto) in 1969, is remarkable for its Italianised English.

24. Graham Fawcett, 'Symphonic Variations', *Books and Bookmen*, 20 January 1975, p. 49; Peter Ackroyd, *'Cacophony'*, *Spectator*, 28 September 1974, p. 405. The others are given below. Page references to *Napoleon Symphony* are to the Cape (1974) edition.
25. 'Most art is a failure, but art that does not risk failure is not worth attempting.' Burgess, *This Man and Music*, p. 191.
26. Kermode, *Guardian*, 5 October 1974, p. 19.
27. 'Prometheus Re-bound', *Times Literary Supplement*, 27 September 1974, p. 1033. Anonymous.
28. Roger Sale, *Hudson Review*, 27, 1974–75, pp. 623–35.
29. Jonathan Raban, 'What Shall We Do About Anthony Burgess?', *Encounter*, 43, November 1974, pp. 83–8.
30. Burgess, *This Man and Music*, p. 188.
31. Aggeler, *Anthony Burgess*, pp. 221–31.
32. John Bayley's review concedes, despite his stricture on almost all aspects of Burgess's fiction, his inability to be pretentious, even on subjects such as this where it might have seemed impossible not to be. See note 12.
33. Raban, 'What Shall We Do About Anthony Burgess?', p. 88.
34. See John Gore, *Creevey* (London: John Murray, 1948) p. 112.
35. See note 26.
36. See *New Cambridge Modern History*, IX, 308. Felix Markham writes here that there is 'no reason to doubt the statement of La Revellière' (a Director) that the appointment was on strictly military grounds.
37. See Vincent Cronin, *Napoleon* (Harmondsworth: Penguin, 1971) p. 131.
38. Cronin, p. 271, 'Napoleon found that his friendship with men often began with physical attraction, and that this took a curious form'; and p. 303, 'Were Alexander a woman I think I should fall passionately in love with him'.
39. Louis Marchand, *Mémoires* (Paris: Plon, 1952–55).
40. See note 12.
41. John A. Sutherland, *Fiction and the Fiction Industry* (London: Athlone Press, 1978).
42. David Thomson, *Europe Since Napoleon* (Harmondsworth: Penguin, 1966) pp. 76–8.
43. Morris, *Nation*, 3 August 1974, p. 87.
44. *Anthony Burgess: The Artist as Novelist*, (University of Alabama Press, 1979).
45. Alfred Knopf, *The Clockwork Testament: or, Enderby's End* (New York: 1974) p. 78.

5 ROBERT NYE; *FALSTAFF*

1. See David Hughes, 'Guts', *New Statesman*, 10 September 1976, p. 345.
2. 'Very readable and heartening'. Publisher's advertisement to the Sphere edition, 1976.
3. 'Falstaff: being the *Acta domini Johannis Fastolfe*, or *Life and Valliant Deeds of Sir John Faustoff*, or *The Hundred Days War*, as told by Sir John Fastolf, K. G., to his secretaries William Worcester, Stephen Scrope, Fr Brackley,

Christopher Hanson, Luke Nanton, John Bussard, and Peter Bassett; now first transcribed, arranged, and edited in modern spelling by Robert Nye' is the full heading on the title page (London: Hamish Hamilton, 1976).

4. All quotations from Shakespeare are from the 'Arden' edition.
5. See 'The Arden Shakespeare', Henry IV, Part 2, edited by A. R. Humphreys, pp. liv–lvii.
6. See E. F. Jacob, *The Fifteenth Century* (Oxford: Clarendon Press, 1961) p. 342; and M. H. Keen, *England in the Later Middle Ages: A Political History* (London: Methuen, 1973) p. 22, 181.
7. See Keen, *England in the Later Middle Ages*, p. 392.
8. Maurice Morgann (ed. W. A. Gill, Froude, 1912) *An Essay on the Dramatic Character of Sir John Falstaff* (1777).
9. E. K. Chambers, *Shakespeare: A Survey* (London: Sidgwick & Jackson, [1925], 1964) p. 96.
10. Peter Conrad, 'The Less Deceived', *Spectator*, 4 September 1976, p. 16.
11. J. I. M. Stewart, 'Plump Jack Enlarged', *Times Literary Supplement*, 3 September 1976, p. 1069.
12. Roland Barthes, *S/Z* (Paris: Editions du Seuil, 1970); translated by Richard Miller (London: Jonathan Cape, 1975). See too Philip Thody, *Roland Barthes: A Conservative Estimate* (London: Macmillan, 1977).
13. J. Dover Wilson, *The Fortunes of Falstaff* (Cambridge, Cambridge University Press, 1943) p. 35.
14. See Keen, p. 335.
15. J. Huizinga, *The Waning of the Middle Ages*, translated by F. Hopman (Harmondsworth: Penguin, 1965) p. 105.
16. Ibid., p. 106.
17. Ibid., p. 108.
18. Ibid., p. 110.
19. Ibid., p. 113.
20. Ibid., pp. 113–15.
21. 'I could prayse Heywood now; or tell how long/Falstaff from cracking nuts hath kept the throng.' Sir Thomas Palmer, in the 1647 Folio of Beaumont and Fletcher.

6   J. G. FARRELL: EMPIRE TRILOGY

1. Margaret Drabble, 'Things Fall Apart', in J. G. Farrell, *The Hill Station*, edited by John Spurling (London: Fontana, 1982) pp. 178–84.
2. See *The Hill Station*, p. 230.
3. James Vinson and D. L. Kirkpatrick (eds), *Contemporary Novelists*, 3rd edn (London: Macmillan, 1982) p. 728.
4. John Spurling, 'As Does the Bishop', in *The Hill Station*, pp. 155–77.
5. Lamartine was briefly a soldier in Italy, 1814–15.
6. *The Hill Station*, p. 189.
7. Ibid.
8. See Malcolm Dean, 'A Personal Memoir', in *The Hill Station*, p. 202.

9. *The Hill Station*, p. 191.
10. 'Ireland Agonistes' – a critical study by Elizabeth Bowen in *Europa*, I (London) 1971, quoted in *The Hill Station*, p. x.
11. See F. S. L. Lyons, *Culture and Anarchy in Ireland 1890–1939* (Oxford: Oxford University Press, 1979) pp. 106–9.
12. Bernard Bergonzi, *The Situation of the Novel*, 2nd edn (London: Macmillan, 1979) p. 231.
13. See F. S. L. Lyons, *Ireland Since the Famine* (London: Fontana, 1973) pp. 419–20.
14. *The Hill Station*, p. 163.
15. James Fenton, 'Victims', *New Statesman*, 9 October 1970, p. 464. This could feature in an anthology of reviews whose writers had not read the novels reviewed.
16. Bergonzi, *The Situation of the Novel*, p. 232.
17. See Lyons, *Ireland Since the Famine*, pp. 273–86.
18. See also Charles Townshend, *The British Campaign in Ireland 1919–21* (Oxford: Oxford University Press, 1978).
19. Herbert Butterfield, *The Whig Interpretation of History* (Cambridge: Cambridge University Press, 1931) p. 73.
20. Farrell acknowledges sources from Lucknow and Muttra.
21. See J. A. B. Palmer, *The Mutiny Outbreak at Meerut in 1857* (Cambridge: Cambridge University Press, 1966) p. 29.
22. See James Morris, *Heaven's Command* (London: Faber & Faber, 1973) pp. 230–42.
23. See Palmer, *Mutiny Outbreak*, p. 137.
24. Ibid., pp. 52–7.
25. Morris, *Heaven's Command*, p. 230.
26. Palmer, *Mutiny Outbreak*, pp. 23, 28.
27. Ibid., p. 165, n. 21.
28. Mark Thornhill, Collector of Muttra, was such a man.
29. See Palmer, *Mutiny Outbreak*, pp. 129–37.
30. Ibid., pp. 120, 124, 128, 136.
31. Percival Spear, *India* (University of Michigan Press, 1961) p. 270; quoted in Christopher Hibbert, *The Great Mutiny* (London: Allen Lane, 1978) p. 392.
32. Hibbert, *The Great Mutiny*, p. 393.
33. *Memorials of the Life and Letters of General Sir Herbert Edwardes*, 'by his Wife', 2 vols (1886); quoted in Hibbert, *The Great Mutiny*, p. 389.
34. John Fowles, *The French Lieutenant's Woman* (London: Jonathan Cape, 1969), Note to Chapter 19.
35. J. G. Farrell 'Indian Diary', *The Hill Station*, p. 235.
36. Ibid., p. 234.
37. John Spurling, *The Hill Station*, p. 159.
38. Morris, *Heaven's Command*, p. 232.
39. See J. M. Pluvier, *South-East Asia from Colonialism to Independence* (Kuala Lumpur: Oxford University Press, 1974) p. 178.
40. Pluvier, *South-East Asia*, p. 179.
41. *The Hill Station*, p. 166.
42. *The Hill Station*, p. 176.

7 JOHN FOWLES'S *THE FRENCH LIEUTENANT'S WOMAN* AND WILLIAM GOLDING'S *RITES OF PASSAGE*

1. J. W. Burrow, *A Liberal Descent: Victorian Historians and the English Past* (Cambridge: Cambridge University Press, 1981) pp. 298–301.
2. Burrow, *A Liberal Descent*, p. 299.
3. Bernard Bergonzi, *The Situation of the Novel*, 2nd edn (London: Macmillan, 1979) p. 225.
4. Michel Butor, 'The Novel as Research', *Inventory: Essays* (London: Jonathan Cape, 1970).
5. John Fowles, 'Notes on an Unfinished Novel', in *The Novel Now*, edited by Malcolm Bradbury (London: Fontana, 1977) p. 136.
6. Christopher Ricks, 'The Unignorable Real', *New York Review of Books*, 14 March 1970, p. 22.
7. Sheldon Rothblatt, *'The French Lieutenant's Woman'*, *Victorian Studies*, March 1972, p. 348.
8. Ibid., p. 349.
9. Ibid., p. 348.
10. Fowles, (ed. Bradbury), *The Novel Now*, p. 140.
11. Rothblatt, *'The French Lieutenant's Woman'*, *Victorian Studies*, p. 348.
12. John Bayley, 'Technologists of the Text', *Times Literary Supplement*, 1 January 1982, pp. 3–4; 'The Pursuit of Signs', a letter to the editor, 5 February 1982, p. 138.
13. *Guardian*, 8 October 1983, p. 17.
14. *Observer*, 9 October 1983, p. 7.
15. There seems to be general agreement about this. See 'Origins of the Species', *Times Literary Supplement*, 5 November 1971, p. 1381.
16. See *Times Literary Supplement*, 16 April 1964, p. 310.
17. *Guardian*, 8 October 1983, p. 17.

8 CONCLUSION

1. Preface to the second Penguin edition of *Nothing Like the Sun* (1982); Vinson and Kirkpatrick, *Contemporary Novelists*, 3rd edn (London: Macmillan, 1982) p. 128.
2. Frank Kermode, *The Genesis of Secrecy*, (Cambridge, Mass: Harvard University Press, 1979) p. 121.
3. See note 16 to Chapter 1.
4. C. S. Lewis, *'De descriptione temporum'*, in *Twentieth Century Literary Criticism: A Reader*, edited by David Lodge (London: Longman, 1972) pp. 443–53.
5. Ibid., p. 451.
6. Ibid., p. 448.
7. Ibid., p. 445.
8. Ibid., p. 445.
9. Ibid., p. 448.
10. In Thomas Hughes's *Tom Brown's Schooldays* (1857), and in many scenes in Thackeray.

11. George Macdonald Fraser, *Flashman* (London: Barrie & Jenkins, 1969),
    was the first.
12. A. O. J. Cockshut, *The Achievement of Walter Scott* (London: Collins, 1969)
    p. 91.
13. John Berger, *G* (London: Weidenfeld and Nicolson, 1972). There is an
    account of this 'tersely titled' novel, in Bergonzi, *The Situation of the Novel*,
    pp. 220–2.
14. Barthes, 'The Discourse of History', p. 18. See Chapter 1, note 27.
15. Derek Mahon, 'J. G. Farrell 1935–1979', *New Statesman*, 31 August 1979,
    p. 313.
16. Benny Green, 'J. G. Farrell', *Spectator*, 25 August 1979, p. 20.

Bibliography

The place of publication is London unless otherwise stated.

1. HISTORICAL NOVELS

This list includes novels since 1900 which are mentioned in the text and the more durable-seeming works by other authors mentioned.

Arden, John, *Silence Among the Weapons* (Methuen, 1982): Sulla.

Banville, John, *Doctor Copernicus* (Secker & Warburg, 1976).

——————, *Kepler* (Secker & Warburg, 1981).

Berger, John, *G* (Weidenfeld & Nicolson, 1972).

Brophy, John, *Gentleman of Stratford* (Collins, 1939).

'Bryher' (Annie W. Ellerman), *Roman Wall* (Collins, 1955).

——————, *Player's Boy* (Collins, 1957): Jacobean theatre.

——————, *The Gate to the Sea* (Collins, 1959): 7th century BC

Buchan, John, *The Path of the King* (Hodder & Stoughton, 1921).

——————, *The Blanket of the Dark* (Hodder & Stoughton, 1931).

Burgess, Anthony, (John Anthony Burgess Wilson), *Nothing like the Sun: A Story of Shakespeare's Love-Life* (Heinemann, 1964).

——————, *Napoleon Symphony* (Jonathan Cape, 1974).

——————, *Man of Nazareth* (Magnum, 1980).

Conrad, Joseph, *The Inheritors*, with Ford Madox Hueffer [later Ford Madox Ford] (Heinemann, 1901).

——————, *The Arrow of Gold* (T. Fisher Unwin, 1919).

——————, *The Rover* (T. Fisher Unwin, 1923).

——————, *Suspense: A Napoleonic Novel* (J. M. Dent, 1925), unfinished.

Duggan, Alfred, *The Lady for Ransom* (Peter Davies, 1953): twelfth century.

——————, *Leopards and Lilies* (Faber, 1954): King John and Henry III.

——————, *Winter Quarters* (Faber, 1956): Crassus.

Eco, Umberto, *The Name of the Rose*, translated by William Weaver (New York: Secker & Warburg, 1983). First published in Italian in 1980.

Farrell, James Gordon, *Troubles* (Weidenfeld & Nicolson, 1970).

——————, *The Siege of Krishnapur* (Weidenfeld & Nicolson, 1973).

——————, *The Singapore Grip* (Weidenfeld & Nicolson, 1978).

——————, *The Hill Station: An Unfinished Novel and an Indian Diary*, ed. by John Spurling (Weidenfeld & Nicolson, 1981), posthumous.

Forester, C. S., *The Happy Return* (Michael Joseph, 1937): the best Hornblower story.

Fowles, John, *The French Lieutenant's Woman* (Jonathan Cape, 1969).

Fraser, George Macdonald, *Flashman* (Barrie & Jenkins, 1969): the first of a
　series.
Garfield, Leon, *The House of Cards* (Bodley Head, 1982): nineteenth century.
　Garfield is also a distinguished author of historical novels for children.
Golding, William, *The Inheritors* (Faber, 1956).
————, *The Spire* (Faber, 1964).
————, *The Scorpion God* (Faber, 1971).
————, *Rites of Passage* (Faber, 1980).
Graves, Robert, *I, Claudius* (Arthur Barker, 1934).
————, *Claudius the God* (Arthur Barker, 1934).
————, *Count Belisarius* (Cassell, 1938).
————, *Proceed, Sergeant Lamb* (Methuen, 1941).
————, *Wife to Mr Milton* (Cassell, 1943).
Green, Peter, *Achilles his Armour* (John Murray, 1955): the Peloponnesian
　War.
————, *The Sword of Pleasure* (John Murray, 1957): Sulla.
Irwin, Margaret, *Gay Galliard* (Chatto & Windus, 1941).
Kipling, Rudyard, *Puck of Pook's Hill* (Macmillan, 1906).
————, *Rewards and Fairies* (Macmillan, 1910).
Koestler, Arthur, *The Gladiators* (Jonathan Cape, 1939).
Lucie-Smith, Edward, *The Dark Pageant: A Novel about Gilles de Rais* (Blond &
　Briggs, 1977).
Malouf, David, *An Imaginary Life* (Chatto & Windus, 1978): a novel by the
　Australian poet. The narrator is Ovid.
Mitchison, Naomi, *The Conquered* (Jonathan Cape, 1923).
————, *Black Sparta: Greek Tales* (Jonathan Cape, 1928).
————, *The Corn King and the Spring Queen* (Jonathan Cape, 1931): stories
　and poems.
Murdoch, Iris, *The Red and the Green* (Chatto & Windus, 1965).
Nye, Robert, *Falstaff* (Hamish Hamilton, 1976).
————, *Merlin* (Hamish Hamilton, 1978).
————, *Faust* (Hamish Hamilton, 1981).
————, *The Voyage of the Destiny* (Hamish Hamilton, 1982): Walter
　Raleigh.
Prescott, H. F. M., *Son of Dust* (Constable, 1932; Eyre & Spottiswoode, 1958):
　eleventh century Normandy.
————, *The Man on a Donkey* (Eyre & Spottiswoode, 1952): sixteenth
　century.
Renault, Mary (Eileen Mary Challans), *The Last of the Wine* (John Murray,
　1956).
————, *The King Must Die* (John Murray, 1958).
————, *The Bull from the Sea* (John Murray, 1962).
————, *The Mask of Apollo* (John Murray, 1966).
————, *Fire from Heaven* (John Murray, 1970).
————, *The Persian Boy* (John Murray, 1972).
————, *The Praise Singer* (John Murray, 1979).
————, *Funeral Games* (John Murray, 1981).
Vaughan, Matthew, *Chalky* (Secker & Warburg, 1975): Victorian.
Warner, Rex, *The Young Caesar* (Collins, 1950).

Warner, Rex, *Imperial Caesar* (Collins, 1960).
————, *Pericles the Athenian* (Collins, 1963).
Woolf, Virginia, *Orlando: A Biography* (Chatto & Windus, 1928).
————, *Between the Acts* (Hogarth Press, 1941).

2. CRITICAL BOOKS

Aggeler, Geoffrey, *Anthony Burgess: The Artist as Novelist* (Alabama: University of Alabama Press, 1979).
Alexander, Peter (ed.), *Studies in Shakespeare: British Academy Lectures* (British Academy, 1964). Includes C. J. Sisson's 1934 lecture, 'The Mythical Sorrows of Shakespeare'.
Anderson James, *Sir Walter Scott and History* (Edinburgh: Edina, 1981).
Auerbach, Erich, *Mimesis*, translated by W. Trask (Princeton: Princeton University Press, 1953).
Barthes, Roland, *S/Z* (Paris: Editions du Seuil, 1970); translated by Richard Miller (Jonathan Cape, 1976).
Bergonzi, Bernard, *The Situation of the Novel* (London: Macmillan, 1970, 1979).
Bradbury, Malcolm (ed.), *The Novel Today: Contemporary Writers on Modern Fiction* (Fontana, 1977).
Brown, David, *Walter Scott and the Historical Imagination* (Routledge & Kegan Paul, 1979).
Burgess, Anthony, *The Novel Now: A Student's Guide to Contemporary Fiction* (Faber, 1967).
————, *Shakespeare* (Harmondsworth: Penguin, 1970).
————, *This Man and Music* (Hutchinson, 1982): musical and literary autobiography.
Butor, Michel, *Inventory: Essays* (Jonathan Cape, 1970).
Butterfield, Herbert, *The Historical Novel: An Essay* (Cambridge: Cambridge University Press, 1924).
Cam, Helen, *Historical Novels*, The Historical Association General Series, 48 (1961). A 27-page pamphlet.
Chambers, E. K., *Shakespeare: A Survey* (Sidgwick & Jackson, 1925).
————, *William Shakespeare: A Study of Facts and Problems* (Oxford: Clarendon Press, 1930).
Cockshut, A. O. J., *The Achievement of Walter Scott* (Collins, 1969).
Culler, Jonathan, *Saussure* (Fontana, 1976).
Fleishman, Avrom, *The English Historical Novel: Walter Scott to Virginia Woolf* (Baltimore and London: Johns Hopkins University Press, 1971).
Green, Anne, *Flaubert and the Historical Novel: Salammbó Reassessed* (Cambridge: Cambridge University Press, 1982).
Grierson, H. J. C., (ed.), *Sir Walter Scott Today* (Constable, 1932). Includes Hugh Walpole's essay 'The Historical Novel since Sir Walter Scott'.
Iser, Wolfgang, *The Implied Reader* (Baltimore: Johns Hopkins University Press, 1974).
Kermode, Frank, *The Genesis of Secrecy* (Cambridge, Mass.: Harvard University Press, 1979).

Kinkead-Weekes, Mark, and Ian Gregor, *William Golding: A Critical Study* (Faber, 1967).

Lascelles, Mary, *The Storyteller Retrieves the Past* (Oxford: Oxford University Press, 1980).

Lodge, David, *The Novelist at the Crossroads* (Routledge & Kegan Paul, 1971).

Lukacs, Georg, *The Historical Novel,* translated by H. and S. Mitchell (Merlin Press, 1962).

McCormack, T., (ed.), *Afterwords: Novelists on their Novels* (Harper & Row, 1969): includes Mary Renault on *The King Must Die.*

Murdoch, Iris, *The Fire and the Sun: Why Plato Banished the Artists* (Oxford: Oxford University Press, 1977).

Preston, John, *The Created Self: The Reader's Role in Eighteenth Century Fiction* (Heinemann, 1970).

Rabinovitz, Rubin, *The Reaction Against Experiment in the English Novel 1950-1960* (New York: Columbia University Press, 1967).

Raleigh, J. H., *Time, Place and Idea: Essays on the Novel,* (London and Amsterdam: Southern Illinois University Press, 1968).

Robson, W. W., *Modern English Literature* (Oxford: Oxford University Press, 1970).

Sanders, Andrew, *The Victorian Historical Novel* (Macmillan, 1978).

Schoenbaum, S., *Shakespeare's Lives* (Oxford: Clarendon Press, 1970).

Scholes, Robert, *The Fabulators* (New York: Oxford University Press, 1967).

Sheppard, Alfred T., *The Art and Practice of Historical Fiction* (Humphry Toulmin, 1930).

Soyinka, Wole, *Myth, Literature and the African World* (Cambridge: Cambridge University Press, 1973).

Thody, Philip, *Roland Barthes: A Conservative Estimate* (Macmillan, 1977).

Wilson, John Dover, *The Fortunes of Falstaff* (Cambridge: Cambridge University Press, 1943).

Wolfe, Peter, *Mary Renault,* Twayne's English Authors (New York: Twayne, 1969).

3. BOOKS ON HISTORY AND THEORY OF HISTORY

Arrian, *The Campaigns of Alexander,* trans. by Aubrey de Selincourt, ed. by J. R. Hamilton (Harmondsworth: Penguin, 1971).

Burrow, J. W., *A Liberal Descent: Victorian Historians and the English Past* (Cambridge: Cambridge University Press, 1981).

Cary, George, *The Medieval Alexander,* edited by D. J. A. Ross (Cambridge: Cambridge University Press, 1956).

Collingwood, R. G., *The Idea of History* (Oxford: Clarendon Press, 1946).

Cottrell, Leonard, *The Bull of Minos* (Evans Brothers, 1953, 1971): illustrated.

Cronin, Vincent, *Napoleon* (Collins, 1971).

Curtis, L. P., *The Historian's Workshop* (New York: Alfred A. Knopf, 1970).

Dixon, Norman F., *On the Psychology of Military Incompetence* (Jonathan Cape, 1976).

Dover, John, *Greek Homosexuality* (Duckworth, 1978).

Edwardes, Herbert, *Memorials of the Life and Letters of General Sir Herbert Edwardes*, ed. by Lady Herbert, 2 vols (Kegan Paul, 1886).

Gore, John, *Creevey* (John Murray, 1948).

Green, Peter, *Alexander the Great* (Weidenfeld & Nicolson, 1970): illustrated.

Hammond, N. G. L., *Alexander the Great* (London: Chatto & Windus, 1981).

Handlin, Oscar, *Truth in History* (Cambridge, Mass.: Harvard University Press, 1979).

Herodotus, *The Histories*, trans. by Aubrey de Selincourt (Harmondsworth: Penguin, 1971).

Hibbert, Christopher, *The Great Mutiny* (Allen Lane, 1978).

Huizinga, J., *The Waning of the Middle Ages*, trans. by F. Hopman (Harmondsworth: Penguin, 1955, 1965).

Jacob, E. F., *The Fifteenth Century* (Oxford: Clarendon Press, 1961).

Keen, M. H., *England in the Later Middle Ages: A Political History* (Methuen, 1973).

Lyons, F. S. L., *Ireland Since the Famine* (London: Weidenfeld & Nicolson, 1971).

———————, *Culture and Anarchy in Ireland 1890–1939* (Oxford: Clarendon Press, 1979).

Marchand, Louis, *Mémoires* (Paris: Plon, 1952–55).

Milns, R. D., *Alexander the Great* (Hale, 1968).

Morris, James, *Heaven's Command: An Imperial Progress* (Faber, 1973).

Palmer, J. A. B., *The Mutiny Outbreak at Meerut in 1857* (Cambridge: Cambridge University Press, 1966).

Pendlebury, John D. S., *The Archaeology of Crete* (Methuen, 1939).

Plumb, J. H., *The Death of the Past* (Macmillan, 1969).

Plutarch, *The Age of Alexander*, trans. by Ian Scott-Kilvert (Harmondsworth: Penguin, 1973).

Pluvier, J. M., *South-East Asia from Colonialism to Independence* (Kuala Lampur: Oxford University Press, 1974).

Poggioli, Renato, *The Theory of the Avant Garde*, (Cambridge, Mass.: The Belknap Press of Harvard University Press, 1968).

Raglan, Lord (Fitzroy Raglan Somerset), *The Hero: A Study in Tradition, Myth and Drama* (Methuen, 1936).

Renault, Mary, *The Nature of Alexander* (Harmondsworth: Penguin, 1975, 1983). The 1975 edition is well illustrated.

Said, Edward W., *Orientalism* (Routledge & Kegan Paul, 1979).

Seeley, J. R., *The Expansion of England* (Macmillan, 1883).

Spear, Percival, *India* (Ann Arbor: University of Michigan Press, 1961).

Tarn, W. W., *Alexander the Great*, 2 vols (Cambridge: Cambridge University Press, 1948).

Thomson, David, *Europe Since Napoleon* (1957; Harmondsworth: Penguin, 1966).

Thucydides, *The Peloponnesian War*, trans. by Rex Warner (Harmondsworth: Penguin, 1954).

Townshend, Charles, *The British Campaign in Ireland 1919–1921* (Oxford: Oxford University Press, 1978).

4. ARTICLES, ESSAYS AND LECTURES

Barthes, Roland, 'The Discourse of History', trans. by Stephen Bann, *Comparative Criticism: A Year Book*, 3 (Cambridge: Cambridge University Press, 1981) 7–20.
Bayley, John, 'Technologists of the Text', *Times Literary Supplement*, 1 January 1982, p. 3.
Burns, C. Landon Jr., 'Men are only Men: the Novels of Mary Renault', *Critique*, VI, 3 (Minneapolis, 1964) 102–21.
Cam, Helen, 'Historical Novels: Fact or Fiction', *Listener*, 30 May 1963, pp. 914–15.
Green, Peter, 'Aspects of the Historical Novel', *Essays by Divers Hands*, Proceedings of the Royal Society of Literature, New Series, 21 (1962) 35–60.
Lewis, C. S., *'De descriptione temporum'*, in *20th Century Literary Criticism: A Reader*, ed. by David Lodge (Longman, 1962) pp. 443–53.
Rothblatt, Sheldon: *'The French Lieutenant's Woman'*, *Victorian Studies*, 15 (March 1972) 348–56
Southern, Sir Richard W. 'The Sense of the Past', *Proceedings of the Royal Historical Society*, 5th series, 23 (1973) 242–63
Wolff, Robert Lee, 'Present Uses for the Past', *Times Literary Supplement*, 13 December 1974, p. 1404

5. NOVEL REVIEWS

Anthony Burgess, *Nothing Like the Sun*

Buitenhuis, Peter, ' A Lusty Man Was Will', *New York Times Book Review*, 13 September 1964, pp. 5, 26
Enright, D. J., 'Mr W.S.', *New Statesman*, 24 April 1964, pp. 642–4
Miller, Warren, 'Enter Will: Dressed in Prose', *Nation*, 5 October 1964, pp. 196–7
'Jakes Peer or Jacques Père', *Times Literary Supplement*, 23 April 1964, p. 329 (anonymous).

Anthony Burgess, *Napoleon Symphony*

Bayley, John, 'From the Ridiculous to the Ridiculous', *New York Review of Books*, 19 August 1974, pp. 32–3
Kermode, Frank, 'The Burgess Emperor', *Guardian Weekly*, 5 October 1974, p. 19.
Morris, R. K., *Nation*, 3 August 1974, p. 87
Raban, Jonathan, 'What Shall We Do About Anthony Burgess?' *Encounter*, 43 (November 1974) 83–8

Sale, Roger, 'Fooling Around and Serious Business'. *Hudson Review*, 27 (Winter 1974–5) 623–35
'Prometheus Re-bound', *Times Literary Supplement*, 27 September 1974, p. 1033 (anonymous).

J. G. Farrell, *Troubles*

Bowen, Elizabeth, 'Ireland Agonistes', *Europa* 1 (London) 1971.
Fenton, James, 'Victims', *New Statesman*, 9 October 1970, p. 464.
'End of a Dream', *Times Literary Supplement*, 22 January 1971, p. 85 (anonymous).

J. G. Farrell, *The Siege of Krishnapur*

Cunningham, Valentine, 'Good Pig', *Listener*, 30 August 1973, p. 288.
Spurling, John, 'Sahibs at Bay', *New Statesman*, 21 September 1973, p. 394.

J. G. Farrell, *The Singapore Grip*

Mo, Timothy, 'Magpie Man', *New Statesman*, 15 September 1978, p. 337.
Symons, Julian, 'Heading for a Fall', *Times Literary Supplement*, 6 October 1978, p. 1110.
Green, Benny, 'J. G. Farrell', *Spectator*, 25 August 1979, p. 20.
Mahon, Derek, 'J. G. Farrell 1935–1979', *New Statesman*, 31 August 1979, p. 313.

William Golding, *The Spire*

'The Cost of a Vision', *Times Literary Supplement*, 16 April 1964, p. 310 (anonymous).

William Golding, *The Scorpion God*

'Origins of the Species', *Times Literary Supplement*, 5 November 1971, p. 1381 (anonymous).

William Golding, *Rites of Passage*

T. J. Binyon, 'Speaking the Tarry Language', *Times Literary Supplement*, 17 October 1980, p. 1161.

Robert Nye, *Falstaff*

Conrad, Peter, 'The Less Deceived', *Spectator*, 4 September 1976, p. 16.
Hughes, David, 'Guts', *New Statesman*, 10 September 1976, pp. 345.
Stewart, J. I. M., 'Plump Jack Enlarged', *Times Literary Supplement*, 3 September 1976, p. 1069

Mary Renault, *The King Must Die*

Mortimer, Raymond, *Sunday Times*, 7 September 1958, p. 6.
'Theseus and the Hellenes', *Times Literary Supplement*, 19 September 1958, p. 528 (anonymous).

Mary Renault, *The Bull from the Sea*

Times Literary Supplement, 16 March 1962, p. 181 (anonymous).

Mary Renault, *The Mask of Apollo*

'Purely Platonic', *Times Literary Supplement*, 15 December 1966, p. 1165 (anonymous).

Mary Renault, *Fire from Heaven*

'The Conqueror as a Boy', *Times Literary Supplement*, 11 December 1970, p. 1437 (anonymous).

Mary Renault, *The Persian Boy*

Waugh, Auberon, 'The Colonel's Mede is Miss Renault's Persian', *Spectator*, 6 January 1973, p. 13.

Mary Renault, *Funeral Games*

Green, Peter, 'Tough Act to Follow', *New York Review of Books*, 18 March 1982, pp. 29, 35.
Murray, Oswyn, 'Death of the Hero', *Times Literary Supplement*, 1 January 1982, p. 12.
Ricks, Christopher, *New York Times Book Review* 17 January 1982, p. 7.

Index